This is the Mac. It's supposed to be fun!

all the stuff beginners need to know, drawn from the most popular Mac book ever

Arthur Naiman, John Kadyk
and a cast of thousands

A *Goldstein & Blair* book from
Peachpit Press

This book is dedicated to the people of East Timor
whose eighteen-year struggle for independence
has been virtually ignored by the media
despite the murder of perhaps
a quarter of the population

For information on East Timor, call 914 428 7299 (NY),
415 387 2822 (SF) or 604 264 9973 (BC).

Additional copies of *This is the Mac. It's* supposed *to be fun!* are available from Peachpit Press, 2414 Sixth St, Berkeley CA 94710, 800 283 9444, 510 548 4393. Single copies cost $15 + $4 for shipping and tax (if any) to US addresses. (For information on other products, and shipping rates to addresses outside the US, see the order pages at the back of the book.)

We offer quantity discounts to computer stores, other retailers and wholesalers (except bookstores and book wholesalers), user groups, businesses, schools and individuals. Distribution to the book trade is through Publishers Group West, Box 8843, Emeryville CA 94662, 800 788 3123 or 510 658 3453.

Printed in the United States of America   First printing—August 1993

Library of Congress Cataloging-in-Publication Data

The is the Mac : it's supposed to be fun! / Arthur Naiman, John Kadyk.
     p. cm.
   Includes index.
   ISBN 1-56609-082-2 : $32.00
   1. Macintosh (Computer)   I. Kadyk, John, 1961– II. Title.
QA76.8.M3N38   1993
004.165—dc20   93-11372
                                                 CIP

Credits

Project coordination and supervision—Arthur Naiman   *Book concept*—Ted Nace

Compilation, editing, updating and logistics—John Kadyk

Proofreading— Susan McCallister, John Kadyk, Karen Faria

Index—Ty Koontz (415 924 6308)

Inside design—Arthur Naiman, Byron Brown

Page layout—Byron Brown (510 527 6374), Arthur Naiman, Karen Faria, Lisa Munro

Cover design—Visual Strategies, San Francisco (415 296 9702)

Incidental illustrations—Visual Delights (from SunShine, 512 453 2334)

Icons—Thomas Friesch, Joel Friesch, Arthur Naiman, WetPaint, Steve Shelden, Esther Travis, Byron Brown

Main fonts used—Bookman, Optima, Zapf Dingbats (Adobe); PIXymbols Command, S2113, A2020, Icons & Icons Two (Page Studio Graphics); Manhattan (Dubl Click); *Ten Commandments:* Gregorian (Casady & Greene) and Zapf Chancery (Adobe).

Printing—Consolidated Printers, Berkeley, California (510 843 8524)

Trademark notice

Because one purpose of this book is to describe and comment on various hardware and software products, many such products are identified by their tradenames. In most—if not all—cases, these designations are claimed as legally protected trademarks by the companies that make the products.

It is not our intent to use any of these names generically, and the reader is cautioned to investigate a claimed trademark before using it for any purpose except to refer to the product to which it is attached. In particular: *Apple* and *Macintosh* are registered trademarks of Apple Computer, Inc. *The Macintosh Bible* is a trademark of Goldstein & Blair, licensed to Peachpit Press, Inc., neither of which is affiliated with Apple Computer, Inc.

Disclaimer

We've got to make a disclaimer that common sense requires: Although we've tried to check all the tips, tricks and shortcuts described in this book to make sure they work as described, we can't guarantee that they do. Don't try anything except on a backup file. Satisfy yourself that the technique you're trying works before using it on your valuable files.

We can't be—and aren't—responsible for any damage to, or loss of, your data or your equipment, or injury to yourself, that results directly or indirectly from your use of this book. We make no warranty, express or implied, about the contents of this book, its merchantability or its fitness for any particular purpose. The exclusion of implied warranties is not permitted by some states. The above exclusion may not apply to you. This warranty provides you specific legal rights. There may be other rights that you may have which vary from state to state.

Contents

Introduction (AN)

For several years now, a bunch of Macintosh enthusiasts have been putting together a book called the *Macintosh Bible.* Its clarity and humor have made it far-and-away the best-selling Mac book ever (coming up on a million copies in print) but its 1250-page heft and $32 price scare away many Mac beginners.

That's understandable—you just want to learn how to use the computer, not become an expert on it. That's why we created this book.

A supremely talented editor named John Kadyk strode off into the lush rainforest of tips, tricks, shortcuts and product evaluations that make up the *Macintosh Bible,* machete in hand. He selected only the freshest, tenderest, most digestible entries—those that beginning Mac users will find the most nutritious. Then he spent many moons editing, reorganizing, updating, rewriting, simplifying and adding to them. Finally, he emerged with this superb little book in his trembling, malarial hand.

If this isn't the most useful, most readable and most enjoyable beginning Mac book ever published, we'll eat our hats (and after John's sojourn in the rainforest, that's saying something—he has to keep his hat on a leash to stop it from wandering off).

'Tis the gift to be simple, and we've made this book as clear and easy to follow as possible. We've tried to always define terms when they're introduced, and to present ideas in a logical order. But that doesn't mean the book is stiff and dull—far from it (as you'll see).

One way we liven things up is with *icons*—little cartoons that appear in the text to guide you to information you're interested in. There are ten of them:

shortcut

This beautiful icon points you to information that can help speed your work.

very good feature

We're critical enough when that's what's called for, so we also like to give credit where credit is due.

very bad feature

These two icons are a subtle plug for left-handers.

bug

Bugs are unintentional, unanticipated occurrences—as opposed to misguided but intentional design flaws, which get the previous icon.

bargain

Good is good, but good and cheap is even better.

very hot tip

All our tips are hot, but these tips are *really* hot.

important warning

You won't die (usually) if you ignore this icon, but you'll be a lot happier if you don't.

things to come

Nobody can predict the future, but we try. Since we're not afraid to be wrong (we could hardly afford to be), it's not a problem.

gossip/ trivia

This icon is for stuff that's more interesting than useful. Look for it when you need a break.

rant

Sometimes calm, reasoned discourse simply isn't enough.

(Now that we've introduced the icons, we'll begin using them.)

This book is organized into four parts: The ABCs of the Mac, Hardware, Software and Reference. The ***table of contents*** (on pages 4–5) shows you what chapters are in each part, as well as what topics are covered in each chapter. (The title page of each chapter also lists the topics that are in it.)

We've also provided a *real **index***, not one of those fake ones that's just there so the publisher can say the book is indexed. It's not merely possible to find what you're looking for in our index—it's virtually impossible *not* to.

very good feature

As mentioned above, we always try to define terms the first time we use them, but it's sometimes hard to do that (in this introduction and in Chapter 1, for example). So if you see a term you don't know, look it up in the ***glossary*** at the back of the book.

The glossary and index free you from having to read the book from front to back, but it's probably a good idea to do that anyway. If you're new to the Mac, you should, at the very least, begin by reading Chapter 2, *Learning the Mac*.

very hot tip

We use **keycap symbols** (⌘W) throughout the book to make it easier for you to locate keyboard shortcuts for commands. On early Macs, the **command key** looked like this: ⌘ ; on your keyboard, it still may. But on the keyboards Apple is currently selling, it looks like this: ⌘. Since most of you are probably using the current keyboards, ⌘ is the symbol we use.

shortcut

Some third-party keyboards simply label the command key with the word *command* and don't even put the ⌘ or ⌘ symbols on it. *O tempora! O mores!* (Who says computer books can't be literate?) In any case, whatever's printed on your command key, just hit it when you see ⌘ and everything will work out fine.

We show the characters in keyboard command shortcuts as capital letters (A B C), which is how the keys are labeled on the keyboard. But you don't actually need to press the Shift key—unless we specifically indicate that you should.

Sometimes we show a key with both the shifted and unshifted characters on it, like this: 0. We do that to make sure you know we're referring to—say—the zero key on the keyboard (as in this case) and not the letter O or the zero key on the numerical keypad.

We've tried to make this book as visually interesting as possible. For example, when a substantial amount of blank space cropped up, we've filled it in with an illustration from our favorite collection of Macintosh clip art, Visual Delights. (Computer **clip art** lets you paste pictures into your documents electronically. For information on other clip art collections, see pp. 796–802 of the *Macintosh Bible, Fourth Edition.*)

These **incidental illustrations** seldom have anything to do with the text they're next to, but when there was an opportunity to make a whimsical connection, we sometimes seized it. Of course there are also many *nonincidental* illustrations in the book, and they have a lot to do with the text. For dozens of examples of them, see Chapter 2.

Drop caps (big letters at the start of paragraphs, like the *D* at the start of this one) are another kind of graphic element we use for visual interest. Although we try to place drop caps at the beginning of new discussions whenever possible (as in the next paragraph), they're basically just there to keep your eyes interested. Another form of visual massage we use is the **sidebar** (text in a box with a gray background).

So many people contributed information to this book that attaching their names and initials to the entries for which they're responsible would quickly become cumbersome. So we only do it when something is personal in tone and it would have seemed strange not to identify the author.

When that isn't the case and you want to know who wrote what, check out the equivalent entry in the *Macintosh Bible.* Meanwhile, here are the names of the people whose material made it into this book (along with their initials, if we've used them): Alan Winslow, Arthur Naiman (AN), Barnard Sherman, Brad Bunnin (BB), Bill Davies, Byron Brown, Chris Allen, Chris Ferino, C.J. Weigand, Clair Whitmer, Charles Rubin, Craig O'Donnell, Charles Seiter, David Blatner, Dale Coleman, David Hauer (DH), Erfert Fenton, Hal Lewis, John Kadyk (JK), Joe Matazzoni, Keith Stimely, Karen Faria, Lauren Antonoff, Larry Pina, Lofty Becker, Lyn Cordell, Mac Kenny, Michael Miley, Nancy Dunn (ND), Nicholas Lavroff, Paulann Thurmon, Peter Ryce, Paul Hoffman, Rich Wolfson, Randy Singer (RS), Sharon Aker, Scott Beamer, Stephen Howard, Skye Lininger, Susan McCallister, Steven Schwartz, Steve Lukrofka and Steve Michel.

In addition to the writers listed above, many other people contributed in many other ways to the *Macintosh Bible,* and therefore to this book as well ("a cast of thousands" isn't really much of an exaggeration). For their names, see the credit page and acknowledgements (pp. 5 and 24–26) in the *Macintosh Bible, Fourth Edition.*

If you like this book and want more of the same, pick up a copy of the *Macintosh Bible,* or use the form at the back of the book to order it directly from the publisher. As one reviewer put it, "if you own a Mac, you should own this book."

very
hot
tip

Meanwhile, we hope you find *This is the Mac. It's supposed to be fun!* both useful and enjoyable.

Part One

The ABCs of the Mac

The ten command- ments

I. This is the Mac. It's supposed to be fun.

For years, many businesspeople treated the Mac as a toy, while those of us who'd already had a bellyful of the deranged command structure of more primitive computers romped happily in the fields of Macintosh. Now the Mac has gotten some corporate acceptance and Windows has made the PC much more like the Mac. Both developments are basically good, but there's a risk that they'll engender a lifeless, "businesslike" homogenization of how personal computers relate to their users.

rant

The rigid dichotomy between work and fun—and the acceptance of that dichotomy as inevitable and necessary—is, to quote The Firesign Theatre's Dr. "Happy" Harry Cox, "Old Age thinking." More clearly than any other computer, the Mac demonstrates that aesthetics enhance, rather than detract from, efficient work.

So don't let them turn the Mac into an expensive version of the PC, or the PC into a clumsy, bloodless imitation of the Mac. Demand fun as your birthright!

II. Easy is hard.

There's a macho attitude among some computer jocks (although certainly not among the best of them) that the harder something is to deal with, the more advanced it is. Actually, of course, it's very hard to make things easy. The more work you put into something, the less work the person who uses it has to do.

So if you find yourself beating your head against a wall erected by someone's laziness (or greed), look around for a different wall that someone else took the trouble to put a door in. And if anybody mocks what you're using as a toy, just smile and say, "Easy is powerful. Hard is primitive."

III. It's not your fault you're confused.

Over the years, manuals have gotten better and programs are designed more sensibly than they used to be, but that's a little like saying how much nicer Himmler has been since his lobotomy. Often the problem is expertosis (the inability of experts in a given field to remember what it's like not to be an expert). Sometimes it's simple money-grubbing. In any case, the thing to remember is this:

If you're confused, it's not because you're stupid—it's because the people who designed that product, or wrote that manual, or rushed their employees so they couldn't do a good job, are stupid. Just make sure its them, not you, who pays for their stupidity.

very hot tip

IV. You can't do it all.

Some experienced Mac users can make you feel like a loser because you're not up on the new products and techniques they're always discovering. But it's really just that you have different interests. Theirs is exploring the Mac and yours—if you're like most people—is simply using it.

Each approach has its virtues and neither is inherently superior to the other. So feel free to restrict yourself to a small number of Mac programs that you master and use intensively. Remember: you can't do it all—nobody can—so don't feel guilty about not trying.

V. Make the Mac your own.

There's never been a computer you could, as Omar put it, "re-mould...nearer to the Heart's Desire." So give yourself time to customize your Mac. Find the software you like best. Spend hours rearranging the desktop or the files on your disks. The more the Mac feels like your own creation, the more efficient and enjoyable your work on it will be.

Think of the Mac as your home. You wouldn't try to move every different piece of furniture in the world into your home, just because you could. You have furniture you feel comfortable with, appliances you need and use, decorations and toys that amuse you. Treat your Mac the same way.

VI. A file saved is a file saved.

What shall it profit you if you create the greatest piece of work in the world only to lose it because you forgot to save it?

Despite how wonderfully easy it is to use, the Mac has as many traps and pitfalls as any other computer—maybe more. These don't have to be a problem, if you <u>save your work</u>! Of course it's a pain and interrupts the flow of your thoughts, but that's nothing compared to what it feels like to lose work.

important warning

People are always telling you to save, as if it mattered to <u>them</u>. It's too bad saving has acquired this taint of moralism. Saving your work isn't something you <u>should</u> do because some authority tells you to. The appeal here is pure pleasure principle—you'll be a lot happier if you get in the habit.

VII. Two, three, many backups.

Saving is only half the battle. Disks crash all the time. If you don't make regular backups, you may as well not save your work in the first place.

important warning

VIII. Combat the tragedy of the commons.

In English villages, the "commons," or "common," was a piece of land on which everyone could graze livestock. (That's what the Boston Common originally was.)

It's clearly in each villager's individual interest to graze as many head of—say—sheep on the commons as he or she can. And yet if all the villagers follow their own best interest, the commons gets grazed bare and all the sheep starve. This is called "the tragedy of the commons."

The solution, of course, is simple: limit the number of sheep each villager can graze (hopefully in some sort of equitable way). But that can be hard to enforce since, even when a quota exists, it's <u>still</u> in each villager's individual interest to graze as many sheep as possible on the commons. It requires some social and *environmental consciousness on the part of all the villagers, some long-range, unselfish thinking, to avoid the ecological catastrophe.*

Just the same thing is true on the Mac. It's no big deal if one person doesn't pay for a shareware program, but if a lot of people don't, good shareware stops getting written. It's no big deal if one person copies a commercial program and uses it for free, but if a lot of people do that, software developers have trouble making money and start cutting corners. In both cases, slowly but surely, the commons becomes a barren patch of dirt.

IX. Allow for Murphy's Law (since you can't avoid it).

Here's a piece of trivia few people know—the origin of Murphy's Law. In 1949, Captain Ed Murphy was an engineer working at Edwards Air Force Base in California. When a technician working in his lab miswired something, Murphy said, "If there's any way to do it wrong, he will." A co-worker of his, George E. Nichols, dubbed this Murphy's Law.

gossip/ trivia

Murphy's Law has evolved into, "If anything can go wrong, it will," but it's interesting to note that it originally referred to incompetence, not to some sort of impersonal malevolence on the part of the cosmos.

But here's the clincher—that anecdote itself is an example of Murphy's Law, as Duane Olesen of Houston explains:

"Your story about Captain Ed Murphy may be accurate, but it was not the first use of the expression. Way back in 1946...the term was already in use. As a matter of fact, we had a kid in my class [in the Navy] who had the misfortune to have the name Murphy. Whenever something went wrong, he was automatically blamed....

"Later, in 1948, when I started college, the Dean of Engineering asked a group of us freshmen if we had heard of Murphy's Law. Most us that had been in the service knew about it."

You know, maybe <u>any</u> explanation of the origins of Murphy's Law is bound to be wrong, just by the nature of what it's explaining. We could call this Murphy's Meta-Law.

In any case, things certainly do go wrong with distressing regularity. This happens less on the Mac than elsewhere, thanks to the care and dedication of its original designers. In fact, the Mac's ease of use can lull you into the dangerous delusion that Murphy's Law has been banished from its realm.

No sooner do you assume this than reality disabuses you of the notion— usually more abruptly than you'd like. It works sort of like the Greek concept of hubris: Pride—or, in this case, complaisance—goeth before a fall.

X. That goes double for Sturgeon's Law.

In the late '50s, Theodore Sturgeon (1918–85) wrote a book-review column for a magazine called Venture Science Fiction. It was there he first enunciated Sturgeon's Law. "It's well known," he wrote (I'm paraphrasing), "that 90% of all science-fiction writing is crap. But then, 90% of <u>everything</u> is crap."

When I first started writing about computers, I wasted a lot of time railing at some of the more wretched products popular back then, and at the brain-damaged ways they went about things. Today, you hardly ever hear their names. (In Bach's day, Hasse's music was more popular than Bach's. You remember Hasse, right?)

Natural selection is going on at a blinding pace in this field, so just find some good stuff, use it until something better comes along and forget about the rest.

very hot tip

The trick, of course, is <u>finding</u> the good stuff. That's one of the things this book is designed to help you do. So stop browsing and buy it already. (This is the famous Lost Eleventh Commandment.)

(continued on the next page)

The Mac is the most intuitive computer ever sold, but that's not saying much. There are still things about it that confuse beginning users, and Apple's Getting Started manuals, while better than most, tend to be too superficial. They also make you wade through a lot of stuff you already know—or that's obvious—to get to the useful information. This brief introduction should get you up and running a lot faster than they will.

We make a real effort to define terms the first time we use them, but haven't always been able to. We've had to assume you know some basic terms (like hardware, in the next paragraph), because defining every single one would have slowed us down too much. This book has an *excellent* glossary and index. Use them whenever you come across a word you don't know (or aren't completely sure about).

It's a good idea to go through this beginner's guide sitting at your Mac, so you can try things out. (We assume you've already set up your hardware according to the instructions that came with it, and have turned it on. If you're having trouble knowing what to connect where, see Appendix B.)

One more thing to be aware of: Apple is always updating and changing the Mac's basic **system software**. (System software is covered in Chapter 7; it includes the **Finder**, which is discussed below.) As of this writing, there are two versions in common use—System 7 (which comes with all new Macs) and System 6. The illustrations in this guide show how the Mac's screen looks when running System 7. If you're using System 6 (or an earlier version), what appears on your screen will look slightly different from the illustrations. Don't let that throw you—the basic principles are the same.

icons and the pointer

The Mac's way of communicating with people is typically referred to as the **graphical user interface** (for you fans of 19th-century diction). A better name (it's equally pompous, just to keep everyone happy) would be the *iconic user interface*, because it lets you control a computer by pointing at, moving and manipulating **icons** (little graphic symbols). See the top of the next page for some samples.

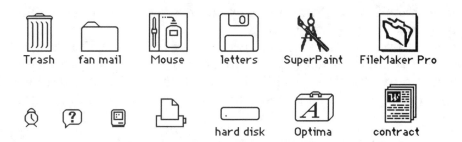

Trash   fan mail   Mouse   letters   SuperPaint   FileMaker Pro

hard disk   Optima   contract

As you can see, icons sometimes have names and sometimes don't. They can represent many things, including:

***C**omputer disks* (which store information; they're discussed in Chapter 4). Examples shown are the icons named *hard disk* and the one that looks like a floppy disk and is named *letters*.

***P**rograms* (groups of instructions that tell the computer what to do). The icons named *SuperPaint* and *FileMaker Pro* are examples.

***D**ocuments* (like paper documents, but created with a program on the computer and stored in its memory and on computer disks). An example is the icon named *contract* (you can tell from the icon itself that this document was created by a word processing program called Word, if you know what Word icons look like).

***F**olders* (which hold documents, programs, etc.). An example is the icon named *fan mail.*

While we're doing basic definitions, we should introduce the term *file*, which simply means any collection of information on a computer disk or in a computer's memory that's grouped together and called by one name. Documents are files, as are programs (sometimes programs occupy several related files).

What you point at icons *with* is an icon itself; it's called, with simple elegance, the ***pointer***. Actually, since the pointer can take many shapes, it's not one icon but a whole series of them. The most common pointer icon is a left-leaning arrow ( ). When you're dealing with text, the pointer takes the shape of an *I-beam* ( ). There are a whole slew of pointers for dealing with graphics, including , , , and .

In addition to pointing at icons, you also point at clear, simple, English words. This saves you from having to memorize a bunch of abbreviated commands, as you do on more primitive computers. (Since what you're doing in both cases is pointing, rather than typing commands, an even better name for how the Mac communicates with people would be the *pointing user interface*. But that sounds so...unimpressive. It would be like doctors calling *gastritis* a *stomachache*. How much money could they charge if they did *that?)*

Only one part of any pointer—called the *hot spot*—actually points. On the arrow pointer, the hot spot is the tip. If just the tip of the arrow is inside something, then you're pointing at it (as in the illustration to the right); if all the arrow *except* the tip is inside, then you're not pointing at it.

You typically control the pointer with a **mouse**—a small box with a ball on the bottom and a button on the top (other devices, like **trackballs**, are also used). When you roll the mouse around, the pointer moves in the same direction on the screen (although normally a greater distance). You get so used to the mouse after a while, it begins to feel as if you're moving the pointer directly with your hand.

Here's a chance to clear up a very common problem beginners run into (we vividly remember the frustration ourselves): Often the mouse runs into something on the desk, or gets to the edge of the desk; if the pointer still isn't where you want it to be, what do you do?

The solution is simplicity itself. The pointer only moves when the mouse is in contact with a surface, so all you need to do to move the pointer further is *pick the mouse up* and put it down where you have more room to roll it in the direction you want. Aha!

the desktop

A basic program that comes with the Mac (called the **Finder***)* creates a gray area that covers the screen. Since most of what you do on a Mac would be done on the top of a desk if you didn't have a computer, this gray area is called the **desktop**. (Everything that follows describes how things look on the desktop, unless otherwise indicated.)

The first icons you point at are arranged on the Mac's desktop—disks, programs, documents, folders, etc. There's even a wastebasket called **Trash**—except, of course, in the real world, the trash can is *next* to the desktop, not on top of it. (The Trash is a special kind of folder you put things into when you want to throw them away.) The illustration below shows you what a (very empty) desktop looks like:

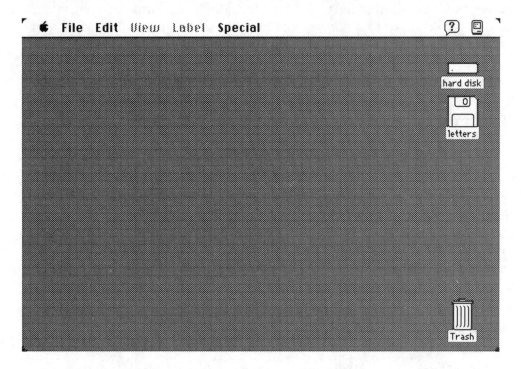

The icon in the upper right corner represents the hard disk this Macintosh is running off of. (It wasn't called **hard disk** when it was purchased, but you can change the names of most things on the Mac and make them whatever you want.) The icon below, named *letters,* represents a floppy disk that has been inserted into the Macintosh (if you're following along on your Mac, insert a floppy disk now). The floppy can also be given any name you like.

(You can think of the hard disk as a massive filing cabinet perched on your desktop. Floppy disks, which are portable and hold much less information, are more like briefcases full of files that you carry around with you.)

 menus

The only thing on the desktop that isn't composed of icons is the line of words across the top left. This is called the **menu bar** and the words on it are called **menu titles** ( isn't a word, of course, but most other menu titles are). If you put the pointer on a menu title and hold down the mouse button, a menu pops down over the desktop. Just as a menu at a restaurant is a list of things you can order, a menu on the Mac is a list of things you can order the computer to do. They're called **commands** or **menu items**.

(If you're holding the mouse button down to look at a menu, you may want to release it; your finger will need the rest while Arthur rants on about a matter of crucial linguistic importance. The fainthearted among you may want to skip the next couple of paragraphs altogether.)

A pple insists on calling these **pull-down menus**—presumably on the theory that, in real life, things pop *up* (like toast) but *pull* down (like window shades). Well, first of all, that isn't always the case; for example, those oxygen masks flight attendants demonstrate before a flight pop *down* from overhead if the air pressure in the cabin drops (at least you hope they do).

rant

But even if nothing in the real world ever popped down, that's *still* what the Mac's menus do. You don't grab the menu title and *pull* the menu down over the desktop; you *touch* the menu title with the pointer, press the mouse button and the menu *pops* down over the desktop (or *drops* down, if you prefer). The pointer stays up at the menu title, not down at the bottom of the menu, which is where it would have to be if you were pulling it.

I could go on about this important point for days, but it's probably easiest simply to say **menus** instead of **pop-down menus** and to save the adjectives for describing other sorts of specialized menus (we'll be talking about some later).

Anyway, the illustration at the top of the next page shows you what a menu looks like. This particular one is called the **Apple menu** (since so few people can pronounce ). The first item on the  menu always tells you about the software you're using. If you're in the Finder (that's where you'll be if you've just started up your Mac), choosing this command tells you what version of the system software you're using, who wrote it, how much space it takes up in the Mac's memory, etc. (it also tells you what model your Mac is). When you're in another program than the Finder, you get similar information about that program.

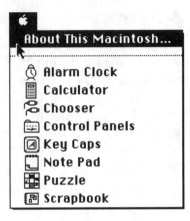

To select a command on a menu, slide the pointer down the menu, keeping the mouse button pressed down. As you pass each command, it **highlights**—that is, instead of appearing as black letters on a white background, it appears as white letters on a black background. When the command you want is highlighted (as *About This Macintosh...* is on the menu above), you just release the mouse button and the command executes.

If you slide the pointer down a menu and then decide not to choose any of its commands, you don't have to slide the pointer back to the top; just slide it off the side of the menu and let go of the mouse button (unless you've got special software installed that causes the menu to "tear off" from the menu bar and remain on the screen).

Other than *About This Macintosh...*, all the items on the menu above are programs that let you control what you see on the screen and how your Mac works, or handy little programs called **desk accessories** (also called *DA's)* that come with your Mac.

Desk accessories have a history. For the Mac's first several years, you could generally open only a single program at a time, but DA's were the exception—the menu was (almost) always available and you could run programs listed on it while you were working in other programs. For example, you could open the Calculator DA and add up some figures while you were in a word processing program.

However, in System 7 (and under *MultiFinder* in System 6), you *can* open more than one program at a time, and switch between them as you wish. Programs that have been designated DA's by their developers now differ only very slightly from other programs. They're designed to be installed on the menu, but you can put them anywhere. And you can add the name of practically any other program, document or folder to the menu yourself, to make them more easily accessible. (See the entry called *adding items to the menu* in Chapter 7 for more details.)

You can also remove any of the standard DA's from the menu (or anything else that's been put on it). A customized menu might look like this:

Shown below is the next menu on the menu bar—the File menu. As you can see, some of the commands are

File

New Folder	⌘N
Open	⌘O
Print	⌘P
Close Window	⌘W
Get Info	⌘I
Sharing...	
Duplicate	⌘D
Make Alias	
Put Away	⌘Y
Find...	⌘F
Find Again	⌘G
Page Setup...	
Print Desktop...	

dimmed (or grayed). This means you can't use them at the present time—if you slide the pointer past them, they won't highlight. For example, *Print* is dimmed because we haven't yet picked a document to print.

 About This Macintosh...

- 🕐 **Alarm Clock**
- 📁 **AppleLink 6.1 alias**
- 🧮 **Calculator**
- **Calendar 1.7**
- **Calendar File**
- 📁 **Capture 4.0.2 alias**
- **CEToolbox**
- **Chooser**
- **Control Panels**
- **DiskTop**
- **Fax Center**
- **INFODESK**
- **Key Caps**
- **Scrapbook**

Once you enter a program, you'll notice that some of its menus, and many of the commands on the menus, are different from the Finder's. For example, just about every program has a File menu, but you'll only find *New Folder* on the Finder's File menu and you'll only find *Save As...* on a program's File menu.

Sometimes a menu has so many commands on it that they run off the bottom of the screen. In that case, a downward-pointing triangle appears at the bottom of the part of the menu you can see (as on the menu shown at the top of the next page). Sliding the pointer past this triangle makes the additional menu items **scroll** up (roll past you as if on a scroll, like the end credits of a movie).

When the command you want scrolls into view, you just slide the pointer to it to select it (menu scrolling tends to really zip along, so you may wind up sliding the pointer back *up* the menu to catch the item you want).

Some items on menus are followed by a right-pointing triangle (as on the menu shown below). If you highlight one of these, a **submenu** pops out to the right of the tri-angle (unless there's no more room on the right, in which case it pops out on the left). Without letting go of the mouse button, you then slide the pointer onto and down the submenu to select the command you want.

(Or you can just drag directly to the com-mand, as long as you angle toward the submenu and don't simply move ver-tically down the main menu.)

Format	
Show Ruler	⌘R
Character...	⌘D
Paragraph...	⌘M
Section...	
Document...	
Cells...	
Position...	⌘⇧P
Styles...	
Define Styles...	⌘T
✓**Plain For Style**	⌘⇧_
✓**Plain Text**	⌘⇧Z
Bold	⌘⇧B
Italic	⌘⇧I
<u>**Underline**</u>	⌘⇧U
Strikethru	⌘⇧/
▼	

Text		
Style	▶	✓**Plain**
Justify	▶	**Bold**
Spacing	▶	*Italic*
		<u>**Underline**</u>
9 point		**Outline**
10		**Shadow**
✓**12**		

Checkmarks like the ones next to *12* and *Plain* on the menus above mean that the checked choices are currently in effect. For example, if you select *Bold* from the submenu and then reopen the menu, it will be checked, and whatever you typed next will appear in bold.

Menu items that take checkmarks are **toggles**—when they're off, choosing them turns them on, and when they're on, choosing them turns them off. There are also toggles that don't take check-marks; instead, their names change to indicate what happens when they're selected. The *Show balloons* command described in *The Help menu* section (near the end of this chapter) is an example.

🍎 *keyboard commands*

Some commands have **keyboard equivalents** listed next to them on the menu—like ⌘O next to the *Open...* command on the File menu shown on page 27. (On Apple's current keyboards, the command key contains an apple symbol as well as the cloverleaf symbol: ⌘, while older keyboards show just the cloverleaf. The command key performs the same functions in either case.)

⌘**O** next to the *Open...* command means that instead of moving the pointer up to the File menu, pressing the mouse button to make the menu pop down, going down the menu to the *Open...* command and then releasing the mouse button, you can simply hold down the ⌘ key and hit the ⓪ key and get the same result. (In the Finder, you can also hit ⌘Ⓝ to open a new folder, ⌘Ⓘ to get information on a disk, file or folder, ⌘Ⓕ to find something, etc.) The standard keyboard equivalents for the Mac's basic commands are:

File menu		*Edit menu*	
New	⌘Ⓝ	**Undo**	⌘Ⓩ
Open	⌘Ⓞ	**Cut**	⌘Ⓧ
Save	⌘Ⓢ	**Copy**	⌘Ⓒ
Print	⌘Ⓟ	**Paste**	⌘Ⓥ
Quit	⌘Ⓠ	**Select All**	⌘Ⓐ

As you can see, keyboard commands are often simply the ⌘ key plus the first letter of the command name. These ten keyboard commands are pretty universal, though a few programs use some of them for different things. The only ones that are really sacred are ⌘Ⓩ, ⌘Ⓧ, ⌘Ⓒ and ⌘Ⓥ.

Sometimes other ***modifier keys*** are used with ⌘ to extend the power of the keyboard, like ⇧Shift, Option and sometimes Control. When they're listed in menus, the following symbols are used:

⇧ (Shift)	⌥ (Option)	∧ (Control)

You'll sometimes find other symbols in menus. Here's a guide to some of them, with the symbol that appears in the menu on the left and the key it represents on the right:

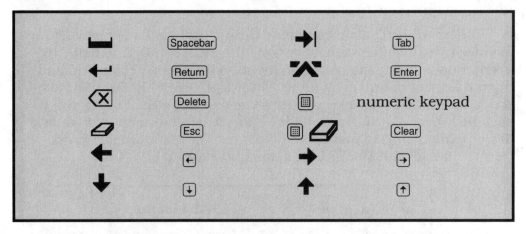

⎵	[Spacebar]	⇥|	[Tab]
⏎	[Return]	⋀	[Enter]
⌫	[Delete]	▦	numeric keypad
⌫	[Esc]	▦ ✐	[Clear]
←	[←]	→	[→]
↓	[↓]	↑	[↑]

The ▦ symbol is needed to indicate the numeric keypad—sometimes ⌘① and ⌘▦① (say) do different things. Since there's no symbol for the [Clear] key, which is on the keypad, it's referred to as—in effect—*keypad* [Esc].

⌘ *selecting, clicking and dragging*

Selecting is the single most important concept for understanding how Mac software works. The basic two principles are:

1. ***You always have to select something before you can do anything with it.*** (Apple calls this the "noun, then verb" or "hey, you—do this" approach. Another way to remember it is "select, then affect.")

2. ***Selecting, in and of itself, never alters anything.***

Trying to do something when nothing is selected, or with something different from what you think is selected, is the cause of 90% of the confusion people have when learning to use the Mac.

very hot tip

To select an icon, you **click** on it—that is, you put the pointer over it, then press and release the mouse button. The icon reverses—what was white becomes black and what was black becomes white (or, on a color monitor, the colors reverse)—to show it's selected:

Unselected   Selected

To move icons around the desktop, you have to select them. But after you put the pointer on an icon and press the mouse button, *hold it down* and move the mouse. A "ghost" of the icon sticks to the pointer until you release the mouse button, at which point the icon appears in the new location. This is called **dragging**:

When you click on an icon to select it, the previously selected icon automatically becomes deselected (turns from black to white). You can, however, select more than one icon at a time, by holding down the (Shift) key while clicking on them in turn. This is called **shift-clicking**.

Another way to select more than one icon at a time is to drag a **selection rectangle**, or **marquée** around them. To do that, start by imagining a rectangle that would enclose all the icons. Then point to one corner of that imaginary rectangle, hold the mouse button down, drag the pointer to the diagonally opposite corner, and release the mouse button (see the illustration at the top of the next page).

An icon will be selected if any part of the selection rectangle touches it. (In System 6, the selection rectangle has to touch the icon itself; just touching its name won't select it.)

1. Press in one corner.   *2. Drag to the opposite corner.*

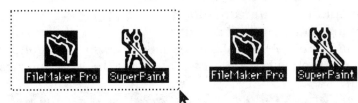

3. Release the mouse button.   *4. The items are selected.*

Up above we said you can change the name of just about any icon. You do it by clicking directly on the name (not on the picture part of the icon). An outline surrounds the name, allowing you to type in a new one:

If you just start typing when an icon is selected but without an outline around the name, another icon will get selected, instead of the name of the first icon being changed. That's because typing the first letter of an icon's name is a shortcut for clicking on it. (System 6 doesn't have this shortcut, so there's no distinction between selecting an icon and selecting its name. You can just click on an icon and start typing to change its name—you don't have to click on the name itself.)

In both system versions, you can edit icon names the way you edit text in a word processor (and here's as good a place as any to tell you about that). When you move the pointer over a selected icon name, it becomes an I-beam (⌶). Wherever you click the I-beam, a flashing bar called the ***insertion point*** appears, allowing you to start typing there, or to backspace over the characters behind it using the ⌈Delete⌉ key. If you drag the I-beam over a part of the name, you'll select it, and can then delete or type over that part.

You can use any character but the colon (:) in an icon name, including spaces, and it can be up to 31 characters long—or, in certain contexts, 27 characters long. (More primitive computers usually don't let you use spaces in the names of files, and require that the names be much shorter.)

Some Mac users favor techie names like *rec.rev4.exp.* Sure, it makes sense to use some abbreviations (*ltr* for *letter* is a good one), but why confuse yourself just so you can look high-tech? You've got 31 characters, punctuation, spaces—*use* them. Give your documents names like *Linda's 40th—it's all over now* and *BE/another psychotic break, eh?*, so you can immediately tell what they are, even years later. (There are times when you can only see the first 22 characters of a file name, so keep the essential part of the name within that limit. This happens in **dialog boxes,** which are described below.)

OK—now you're ready for another basic concept: ***Icons can (and often do) contain things.***

---

windows

To see what's in an icon, you *open* it—by pointing to it and clicking the mouse button twice in rapid succession. This is called **double-clicking**. (Be sure not to move the mouse between clicks or the Mac will interpret it as two separate clicks and not a double-click.)

You can also click once on the icon, go up to the File menu and choose the *Open...* command, but that's a whole lot more trouble than double-clicking. There's even a third possibility. If you look at the *Open...* command on the File menu above, you'll see that ⌘O follows it. So you can also click on an icon and hit ⌘O to open it. But why bother? Double-clicking is so much easier.

Double-click on the floppy disk icon called *letters* and it will open into a **window** like the one at the top of the next page. That window shows the contents of the disk (since the icon we opened was for a disk).

In order to do anything with—or to—a window, it has to be **active** (selected). When it is, you'll see six horizontal lines in the **title bar** (which runs across the top of the window with the title in the middle). A window is always active when it first opens (this is only logical, since you have to select its icon to open it). To select a different window—that is, to make a different window active—click anywhere in the other window.

When it overlaps other windows, the active window always appears on top of them, as shown in the illustration below:

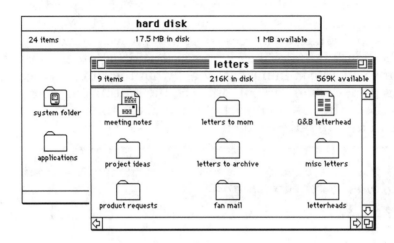

To close a window, you click in the little **close box** at the left end of the title bar (or choose the *Close* command from the File menu). The close box only appears in active windows, so a window must first be active before you can close it.

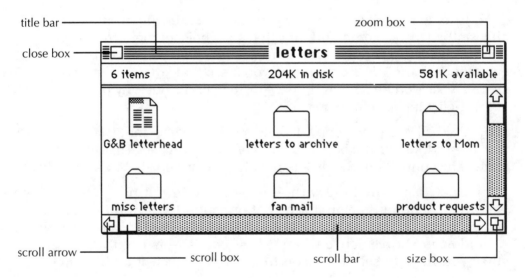

To move a window, you drag it by its *title bar*. To change its size, you drag the *size box*. The *zoom box* resizes the window to show all its contents and nothing more (if that's too big for your screen, it just expands to fill the screen); the next time you click the zoom box, the window goes back to its original size.

(In System 6, the zoom box works differently: in general, it expands windows to fill the screen, but in the Finder, it stops about an inch short of the right edge of the screen, so you can still see disk icons and the Trash. You can get this result in System 7 by holding down Option when you click the box.)

When the active window has gray *scroll bars* on its bottom and right sides, that generally means there are items in it that aren't showing (either that or you haven't left enough space around the items that are showing). When the scroll bars in an active window are blank, that means everything is already displayed in the window. Sometimes one scroll bar is gray and the other is white—it depends on where the missing information is located.

To bring missing information into view, you can use the *scroll box*, the *scroll arrows* or the gray area of the scroll bar itself. It's fairly tedious to explain in words exactly what each does (since they work in right-brained, Maclike ways), but if you experiment with them, it will quickly become obvious. (You may need to make your window smaller before you experiment so some of its contents are out of sight. To do that, point at the window's size box, hold the mouse button down and drag horizontally, vertically or diagonally.)

At first, the scroll controls may seem to work backwards. Click in an up arrow and things scroll down; click in a left arrow and things move to the right. Here's how to think of it:

> To see what's towards the bottom of the window, press the *down arrow*. To see what's towards the top of the window, press the *up arrow*. To see the items off to the right, press the *right arrow*. To see the items off to the left, press the *left arrow*.

It's as if a smaller window is sliding around on top of a larger one, as in the illustration below:

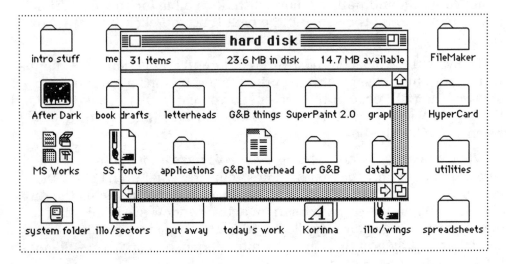

One final note on double-clicking to open windows: If an icon's window is already open before you double-click on the icon, all that will happen is that the window will become active (if it wasn't already). This is all that *should* happen, but sometimes beginners don't notice the change (expecting the dramatic zooming of a window opening) and think there's something wrong.

programs, documents and folders

Now let's talk about what the icons in a window *mean*. To do that, let's go back to our old friend, the hard disk icon, and double-click on it. That produces the window shown at the top of the next page.

Most of the icons in this window look like folders, and that's what they are. You use folders to organize your icons. Double-click on any folder icon and it will open into a window that contains more icons. You can put folders within folders to your heart's content—whatever you need to organize your work and make it easy to find.

Microsoft Word is a program (in this case, a word processor, which you use to enter and edit text). Double-click on its icon and the Word program is **launched** (copied from the disk into

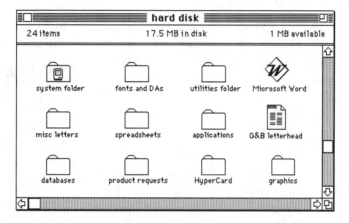

memory, so it will **run**; for more on this, see the entry called *memory, a.k.a. RAM* in Chapter 3). There are various kinds of programs:

Applications, which are devoted to relatively large, complicated tasks like word processing, graphics work, page layout, etc.;

Utilities, which perform support tasks, like searching for a specific file on a disk or counting all the words in a document, or relatively simple independent tasks, like Alarm Clock and Calculator on the 🍎 menu;

System software, which controls the basic operations of the computer (like the Finder).

But there's a tendency among Mac users—and especially Mac techies—to call all programs *applications*, regardless of their type.

Officially, even the Finder and the Alarm Clock are applications.

G&B letterhead is a document—in this case, a template for writing business letters that was created by the word processing application MacWrite. When you double-click on the G&B letterhead icon, it will first launch MacWrite (whether it's on the same disk or another disk attached to the Mac), then open itself so you can edit it, print it, etc. (More primitive machines won't automatically launch an application when you open a document created by it. You have to open the application first, then the document.)

🍎 *ways to view files*

It's mostly only in the Finder—in folder windows and on the desktop—that files are represented by icons; in most other places, they're identi-fied simply by their names. The View menu shown at the right lets you display things by name instead of by icon in the Finder as well. This comes in handy when the windows on your desktop begin to clutter up with icons (which won't take long).

```
┌─────────────────────┐
│ View                │
├─────────────────────┤
│   by Small Icon     │
│   by Icon           │
│ ✓ by Name           │
│   by Size           │
│   by Kind           │
│   by Label          │
│   by Date           │
│   by Version        │
│   by Comments       │
└─────────────────────┘
```

T here's a *Clean Up* command on the Special menu that will tidy up your icons, but **list views** give you more information, and you can organize things in several different ways, to help you find what you're looking for quickly. As you can see, in addition to viewing *by Icon* and *by Small Icon* (which is the same as *by Icon* except that the icons are smaller), you can also view files in a number of other ways:

☞ *by Name*—in alphabetical order

☞ *by Size*—from biggest to smallest, according to how much disk space they occupy

☞ *by Kind*—with all the documents of a particular sort (appli-cations, folders, Quark documents, Page-Maker documents, etc.) grouped together

☞ *by Label*—by cat-egories you've attached with the Label menu (for details, see Chapter 7)

☞ *by Date*—in order of when you last changed them, with the most recent one first

☞ *by Version*—with all the documents cre-ated by a certain ver-sion of a program grouped together

☞ *by Comments*—in alphabetical order according to comments that are attached to them

(You attach com-ments by selecting a file, choosing *Get Info* from the File menu and then typing notes in the box that appears. Under certain circumstances, the comments get erased.)

☞ *by Color*—according to the order of the colors in the Color menu (only available on color monitors, of course)

(Your View menu won't necessarily show all the above choices—the *by Label, by Version* and *by Comments* options appear only in System 7, the *by Color* option only in System 6. *By Version* and *by Comments* don't appear unless you've set them to.) Whatever view you've chosen is checked on the menu. Just below is an example of a window whose contents are viewed by name.

Once you're in a list view, you don't have to use the View menu to find out which you're in; the column heading that's underlined shows how the items are sorted. You can even change the sort order simply by clicking on a different column heading (this only works in System 7, though).

Name	Size	Kind	Label	Last Modified
Chapter 4 draft for Ned	141K	Nisus® 3.06 docu...	Project 1	Tue, May 12
eclipse pix note	5K	MacWrite II docum...	Personal	Mon, Aug 19
FileMaker Pro	779K	application program	—	Mon, May 20
FreeTerm 3.0	47K	application program	—	Fri, Aug 2, 1
ideas for Monday mtg	5K	Nisus® 3.06 docu...	Project 1	Sun, Apr 12
▷ letters, memos, etc	—	folder	—	Wed, May 20
▷ MacWrite II	—	folder	—	Wed, May 20
▷ MB4 stuff	—	folder	in progress	Wed, May 20
▷ Nisus	—	folder	—	Wed, May 20
practice space ad	5K	Nisus® 3.06 docu...	on hold	Mon, Feb 24
▷ System Folder	—	folder	—	Wed, May 20

In System 7, list views also allow you to look at a folder's contents without opening its window, using **outline views**. As you can see in the windows above and to the right, there's a triangle next to each folder's icon. When you click on one of them, it points downwards, and the folder's contents are displayed below it in outline form (see the *Nisus* folder in the illustrations).

hard disk

Name
Chapter 4 draft for Ned
eclipse pix note
FileMaker Pro
FreeTerm 3.0
ideas for Monday mtg
▷ letters, memos, etc
▷ MacWrite II
▷ MB4 stuff
▽ Nisus
▷   Envelope Stationeries
▷   Macros
Nisus Dictionary & Thes...
▷   Nisus Help Folder
Nisus Hyphenation
Nisus User Dictionary
Nisus® 3.06
Pleading Page Stationery
practice space ad
▷ System Folder

If there are folders among those contents, you can see *their* contents—still within the same window—by clicking their triangles. Click on a triangle again and the outline view collapses back into its folder.

❦ dialog boxes and alerts

Choosing a command with an ellipsis after it *(Open...,* for example, or *Print...)* opens a **dialog box** (it's called that because the Mac is telling you something and asking for a response). Here's an example of a Print dialog box (exactly how they look varies with the application you're in, the printer you're using, etc.):

```
┌─────────────────────────────────────────────────────────────┐
│ DeskWriter                              A.02.00    ╭───────╮  │
│                                                    │  OK   │  │
│ Copies:│1│      Pages:◉ All  ○ From:│   │ To:│   │ ╰───────╯  │
│                                                    ╭───────╮  │
│ Quality:      ◉ Best    ○ Faster                   │Cancel │  │
│                                                    ╰───────╯  │
│ □ Back to Front?                                   ╭───────╮  │
│                                                    │ Help  │  │
│                                                    ╰───────╯  │
└─────────────────────────────────────────────────────────────┘
```

One way you respond to a dialog box is by typing in a **text box**, like the three rectangles to the right of the words *Copies, From* and *To* in the dialog box above. You can move from one text box to the next by hitting ⌊Tab⌋. In this case you're asked for numbers, but sometimes you're asked for words.

T he other way to respond to a dialog box is by clicking on a **button**. There are three basic kinds:

Push buttons are rounded rectangles with commands inside them, like the three on the right of the dialog box above. When you "push" the button (click on it), the command inside the button is executed, just as if you'd selected a command from a menu. When a push button is framed by a thicker rectangle, like the *OK* button above, that means it's the **default** button—you can click on it simply by hitting the ⌊Return⌋ or ⌊Enter⌋ key.

Radio buttons are little circles with names next to them (like the circles to the left of *Best* and *Faster,* and *All* and *From,* in the Desk-Writer dialog box above). When you click on a radio button, it fills in (as with *Best* and *All).*

R adio buttons are called that because, like the presets on a car radio, they come in sets, and only one button in a set can be selected at a time (on the Mac, one radio button in each set *must* be selected at all times). In other words, when you click on one radio button, the radio button in the set that was previously selected is automatically deselected. So if you click on *Faster, Best* will automatically deselect, and if you click on *From, All* will automatically deselect.

Sometimes radio buttons activate text boxes. If you click on the *From* button (in the same illustration), you'll find yourself automatically in the text box to the right of it, with the program waiting for you to tell it what page you want to start from. It also works the other way around—if you click in that text box, the *All* button will automatically go blank and the *From* button will automatically fill in (since, if you're specifying a beginning page number, you obviously don't want to print all the pages).

Checkboxes are the third kind of button. They're little squares with names next to them (like the ones here). They're used for lists of options that *aren't* mutually exclusive. All the checkboxes in a set can be selected, or none (although sometimes at least one has to be selected). Clicking in a checkbox toggles it on and off (puts an *X* in it and blanks it again).

┌**Style**─────────
│ ⊠ **Bold**
│ ⊠ **Italic**
│ ☐ **Outline**
│ ☐ **Shadow**
│ ☐ **Strikethru**
│ ☐ **Small Caps**
│ ☐ **All Caps**
│ ☐ **Hidden**

Another common feature of dialog boxes is the **list box**. For example, if you choose the *Open...* command from the File menu while in a word processing program, you'll get a dialog box that looks something like the one below:

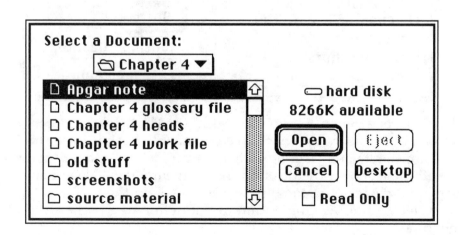

The list box is on the left; it displays the folders and documents that this program can open (it won't show documents that the program can't open). You can scroll through the list and open a document or folder by double-clicking on its name (or, if you're always looking for the hardest way to do something, by selecting it and then clicking the *Open* button on the right).

There are several ways to find the name you want in a list box—the two most basic are using the scroll bar and dragging down through the list itself.

Above a list box is the name of these items' location (a folder, disk or the desktop itself). The name is in a rectangle with a drop shadow, which indicates that it's actually a menu. (Menus like this that pop up out of dialog boxes instead of down from the menu bar are called **pop-up menus**; see the illustration below for an example.) While the list box shows what the *Chapter 4* folder contains, the pop-up menu shows what contains *it*—it's inside the *MB4 stuff* folder, which is on the hard disk called *hard disk,* which is on the desktop.

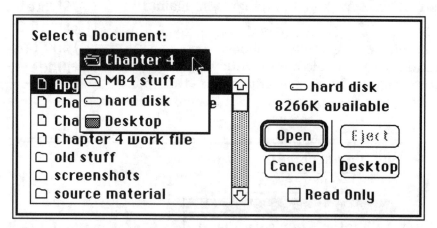

If you select *MB4 stuff* from the menu, the list below it will change to show all the folders and openable documents in that folder (the same happens if you select *hard disk*). If you select *Desktop,* you see a list of all the icons on the desktop that you can open—documents, folders, and disks your Mac has access to—as on the top of the next page. (Clicking the *Desktop* button to the right of the list box does the same thing.)

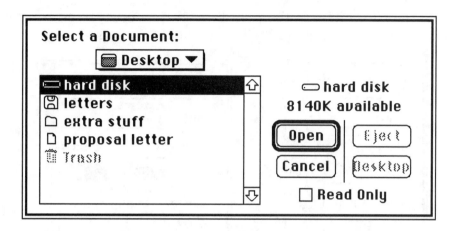

When you double-click on a different disk to select it from the list, its name appears next to the disk icon to the right of the list box. (In System 6, you can cycle through the available disks by clicking either on this icon or on a button labelled *Drive.)*

Here's a dialog box from PageMaker that contains eight checkboxes and five pop-up menus:

> **Type specifications**   (OK)
>
> Font: [Optima]   (Cancel)
>
> Size: [12 ▷] points   Leading: [Auto ▷] points
>
> Case: [Normal]   Position: [Normal]
>
> Type style:
> ⊠ Normal   ☐ Italic   ☐ Underline   ☐ Shadow
> ☐ Bold   ☐ Outline   ☐ Strikethru   ☐ Reverse

The *Font, Case* and *Position* pop-up menus work just like the one above the list box discussed in the last example (see the *Case* pop-up menu in the illustration to the right below). To access the *Size* and *Leading* menus, you click on the hollow, right-facing triangles:

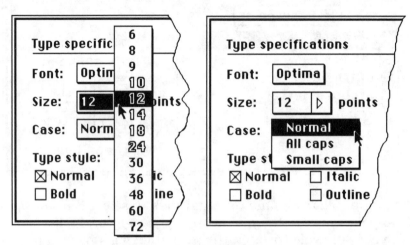

(The rectangles with triangles are really a combination of a pop-up menu and a text box, because you can either type text directly into the box or select it from the pop-up menu the arrow generates.)

If you make a lot of selections using a dialog box's menus, buttons, etc. and decide not to keep them, you can usually nullify all the changes you've made to all of them by clicking the *Cancel* button. Typing ⌘. will usually give you the same result.

An **alert box** (also called simply an *alert)* is similar to a dialog box, but without the dialog between you and the Mac. An alert either warns you or gives you some information, and often all you can do is acknowledge it by clicking on an *OK* button. Sometimes you can just do nothing and the alert will go away of its own accord, and sometimes there's a *Cancel* or *Stop* button that lets you stop whatever's going on, as in the alert box below:

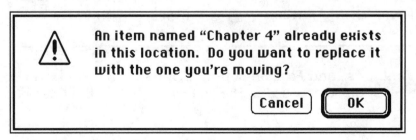

⌘ *saving, copying and throwing away*

After you've worked on a document for a little while, it's a good idea to save the changes you've made. **Saving** a document means copying it from the computer's memory to a disk (or other storage medium) where it will be preserved even after the computer is turned off.

To save the document you're working on without changing its name, select *Save* from the File menu of the program you're working in. If you've previously saved this document, or opened an existing document from the disk, the *Save* command substitutes the new version of the file for the original. For example, let's say a document called *G&B letterhead* needs a permanent change—a new area code. You don't want there to be a document lying around with the old area code on it, so after you make the change, you simply save the new document, thereby replacing the letterhead with the obsolete area code.

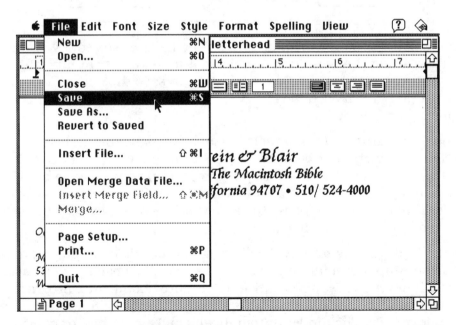

If you want to preserve both versions of the document on the disk, you can save the new one under a different name with the **Save As...** command. Let's say you want to create a new version of *G&B letterhead* that has fax information on it. You open the existing *G&B letterhead* document, add the words *fax to NAME at NUMBER / this page + 0 others,*

choose *Save As...* from the File menu, type the new name—*G&B letter-head with fax,* let's call it—in the text box, and click on the *Save* button:

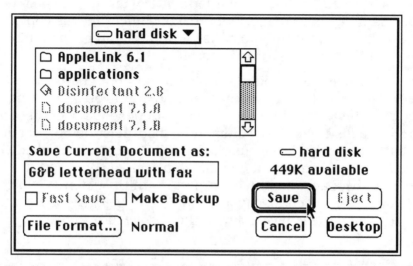

You can also change the place where the file gets stored, by using the list box and the pop-up menu above it to maneuver around the disk. And you can use the *Desktop* button to save the document onto a different disk. It's a good idea to keep backup copies of important files on more than one disk.

Apple's programmers had their reasons for using the desktop as a transfer point between disks, but it really isn't intuitive; in the real world, you don't have to put a report on your desk before you stow it in a different filing cabinet. Going to a different disk by way of the desktop is more like using the sidewalk when you leave your house to take a letter to the mailbox.

There's also a way to copy documents to other disks when you're out on the desktop, not in an application. It couldn't be easier—you just select whatever you want to copy (one or more documents, programs or folders) and drag it—or them—onto the other disk, as shown at the top of the next page. The Finder automatically makes a copy—or copies—of what you're dragging and places it on the target disk.

You can also copy the entire contents of a floppy disk onto a hard disk, by simply dragging its icon onto the hard disk icon. The contents of the floppy will be placed on the hard disk in a folder that's given

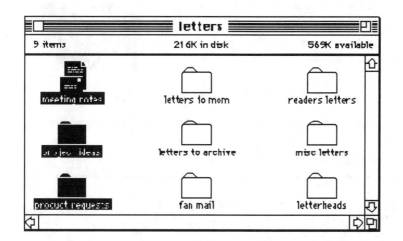

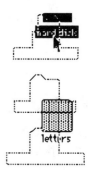

the floppy's name. If you drag the icon of one floppy disk on top of the icon of another floppy of the same size, the contents of the dragged disk will replace the contents of dragged-upon disk. (Of course, you'll get a warning dialog box before this happens—this *is* the Mac.)

You can drag things around on the same disk, but when you do that, the *original* moves, not a copy. To tell the Mac to make a copy and move that instead (even though you're putting it somewhere else on the *same* disk), hold down the Option key as you drag. If you just want to make a copy of something on the same disk *without* moving it, select it and hit ⌃⌘D.

You throw files out by dragging them to the Trash. Normally, things don't get thrown out immediately; they stay in the Trash in case you change your mind. If you do, just double-click on the Trash icon to open the Trash window and retrieve the file. (You can drag it out manually, or select it and choose *Put Away* from the File menu, which zips the item back to wherever it came from.)

To get rid of whatever's in the Trash, use the *Empty Trash* command in the Special menu. (In System 6, the Trash is also emptied automatically under certain conditions—for example, when you remove a floppy disk that contains a file you'd thrown away. But in System 7, the Trash only empties when you tell it to, or give your explicit consent in a dialog box.)

When there's something in the Trash, it bulges (as in the illustration on the right) to let you know it's not empty anymore. When it gets emptied, it goes back to its normal, straight-sided shape.

🍎 *Cut, Copy, Paste and the Clipboard*

One of the most elegant and useful tools on the Mac is the **Clipboard**—a temporary holding place for material that you *cut* or *copy* from one place so you can *paste* it in another. It's temporary for two reasons:

> ☞ *When you put something on the Clipboard, the Clipboard's current contents are replaced* (that is, it can only hold one thing at a time).
>
> ☞ *When you shut off the computer, the Clipboard's contents disappear.*

To **cut** something, you select it (how you do that varies with the program you're using), then pick the *Cut* command from the Edit menu—or just hit ⌘X. Whatever you've selected disappears from its original location and is stored in the Clipboard. (The Finder and many other programs let you check the contents of Clipboard by choosing *Show Clipboard* from the Edit menu.) **Copy** (⌘C) works the same way as *Cut*, except that the selected material stays in the original location in addition to moving to the Clipboard.

To **paste** what you've cut or copied, you just indicate where you want it and hit ⌘V—or select *Paste* from the Edit menu. (How you indicate the spot to paste depends on the application you're in.) You can cut and paste both within and between most Mac programs. The amount of material you can transfer is virtually unlimited since, although the Clipboard is usually held in memory, it can also use disk space when it needs more room.

> Remember—*the Clipboard will hold only one selection at a time;* each time you cut or copy something new, the previous material disappears.

On the other hand, since things stay in the Clipboard until you flush them, you can paste the same thing many different places—as long as you remember not to cut or copy anything else in the interim.

If you simply want to get rid of something, you can just cut it and never paste it; it will disappear the next time you cut or copy. Or you can just hit the (Delete) key instead, and whatever's selected will disappear without even passing through the Clipboard.

🍎 *the Scrapbook*

While the Clipboard is a temporary holding area for cut or copied material, the **Scrapbook** is a permanent file that you access with a command on the 🍎 menu. What you put in the Scrapbook stays there not only when you add more stuff but also when you turn the machine off. (You can, of course, remove things from the Scrapbook whenever you want.)

Since you use *Cut, Copy* and *Paste* to get things into and out of the Scrapbook, they all pass through the Clipboard on the way. If you're just transferring a few things, it's easier to move them one at a time with the Clipboard—that is, to simply cut and paste them. If you have several things to transfer at one time, or if you want them to be available for pasting for more than one work session, the Scrapbook is more convenient. (For more on the Scrapbook, see Chapter 7.)

🍎 *the System Folder*

The *System Folder* is where the Mac looks for the basic software that tells it how to operate: the System file, the Finder, etc. The System Folder is treated specially by the Mac; to remind you of that, its icon has a little picture of a Mac on it.

You can modify certain aspects of the System yourself, by adding or removing fonts, sounds and specialized programs called **extensions** (called **inits** in System 6) and **control panels** (called **cdevs** in System 6). For details on thes, see Chapter 7, Chapter 9 and Appendix A.

🍎 *closing, quitting and switching*
between applications

When you're done working on a document, the File menu of whatever application you're using gives you two choices—*Close* or *Quit*.

Quitting takes you out of the application and back to the Finder (that is, to the desktop). *Closing* leaves you in the application, so you can open another document.

In System 6, Mac beginners often got lost when they closed a document (or the last document, if several were open) and were left with a blank screen with no icons on it. Arthur calls this the *nothing screen* (although nobody else does). If you're still using System 6, the thing to remember is that no desktop is completely blank—there's always the menu bar across the top. If you pop down various menus, you'll see that there are lots of things you can do. So here's the last basic principle—and it's a good one for people using System 7 too:

> **When in doubt, explore the menu bar.**

In System 7, there's another orientation aid—the Application menu. It appears at the right end of the menu bar and its title is an icon of the Mac (when you're in the Finder, that is; when you're in another program, the icon changes to represent that program). The Application menu lets you switch between programs, and hides clutter that belongs to programs you're not using at the moment. Here's how it looks when you have a few programs open:

To get back to the desktop from another program, choose *Finder* from the Application menu (or just click anywhere on the desktop).

Hide Finder
Hide Others
Show All

✓ 🖥 **Finder**
◆ **Microsoft Word**
RightWriter®
SuperPaint

🍎 *ejecting floppy disks*

There are several ways to remove a floppy disk. The best way is from the Finder—just drag the floppy disk and icon to the Trash. (Don't worry—nothing will be erased from the disk; it's just a way of telling the Mac you want to eject it.) You can also use the *Eject Disk* command on the Special menu, but disks ejected that way leave behind a **ghost** on the desktop, like this:

letters

The Mac keeps a record of the ejected floppy and may later ask you to reinsert it. (If it does, and you don't have the disk around, hit ⌘. —several times, if necessary—and the Mac should leave you alone. Then drag the ghost to the Trash.)

Y ou can eject floppies while you're working in an application too. Choose *Save As...* or *Open...* from the File menu, click *Desktop* in the dialog box that appears, select the floppy disk's name from the list and then click *Eject.* This works fine as long as nothing is open on the disk you eject. But if you've made changes to a file, folder or window that weren't saved to the disk, the Mac will demand that you reinsert that floppy at some later point, and will accept no substitutes. The Mac also ejects floppy disks when you shut it down.

🍎 *shutting down*

When you're done working and want to turn off the Mac, the first thing to do is to get back to the Finder. Then choose *Shut Down* from the Special menu. Depending on what Mac you have, it'll either turn itself off, or tell you it's OK to turn it off.

Special
Clean Up Window
Empty Trash
Eject Disk ⌘E
Erase Disk...
Restart
Shut Down

It's very important to shut down properly, and not simply turn the computer off. Shutting down gives the Mac time to do a little house-keeping and make sure everything you think is stored on the disk really is stored there. But it's OK to choose *Shut Down* even if you have files open—the Mac will ask you if you want to save your changes before it shuts down.

🍎 *the Help menu*

Anytime you can't figure out what's going on, you can turn to the Help menu (as long as you're running System 7). It appears next to the Applications menu on the right side of the menu bar; its title is an icon of a balloon with a question mark in it (see the top of the next page for an illustration of it).

Choose *Show Balloons* on the Help menu and, as you slide the pointer over items on the screen, balloons will pop up that briefly explain how whatever the pointer is on works. To get rid of the balloons, select *Hide Balloons* (which appears on the menu when balloons are turned on).

[?]
About Balloon Help...
Show Balloons
Finder Shortcuts

The last command on the Help menu is **Finder Shortcuts**. It presents you with 27 suggested shortcuts for working in the Finder. Try them out once you feel at home with the Mac. (To get rid of the short-cuts window, click on its close box.)

shortcut

summary

Here's a recap of the most important principles to keep in mind when using the Mac:

> ☞ *You have to select something before you can do something.*
>
> ☞ *By itself, selecting never alters anything.*
>
> ☞ *To open icons, double-click on them.*
>
> ☞ *When in doubt, explore the menu bar.*

To learn more about using the Mac's basic software, read Chapter 7. To learn more about the theory and principles *behind* the Mac's basic software, a good book is *Human Interface Guidelines: The Apple Desktop Interface*, written by people at Apple and published by Addison-Wesley ($15). Although it's primarily aimed at programmers, it's quite accessible and pretty interesting.

Part Two

Hardware

Basic Mac hardware

Choosing a Mac

We'll explain most of the terms we use here, but if there are still some you don't recognize, consult the glossary, the index and/or Chapter 2.

⌘ *types of Macs*

There are currently three basic types of Macintosh computers:

 Compacts. Compacts, like the Classic II and the Color Classic, have small built-in screens and are the same basic size and shape as the original Macs. They're the least expensive type of Mac, with a keyboard included in the price.

 Modulars. A modular Mac doesn't have a built-in screen—you have to buy a separate external monitor (the keyboard is usually extra, too). Modular Macs are generally more powerful and expandable than compacts, and more expensive (we discuss expansion possibilities below). At this writing, there are four families of modular Macs (listed here in order of increasing performance and price): the LCs, the Mac IIs, the Centrises and the Quadras.

 Portables. These Macs are built for traveling—they're like notebooks with a screen and keyboard inside. The original, 20-lb Macintosh Portable was replaced by the smaller, 7-lb PowerBooks and the 4-lb PowerBook Duos. The Power-Books offer the performance of low- to mid-range modular Macs at a somewhat higher price, and you sacrifice expandability (though you can buy "docks" for the Duos that give it back—see below). Compact and modular Macs are often called *desktop Macs* to distinguish them from the portables.

If you want to combine the functions of a modular and a portable Mac, consider getting a PowerBook Duo and a Duo Dock. The Duos are the smallest, lightest Macs. They've got all the brains of a normal Mac, but no floppy drive, and no *ports* (sockets) for connecting external devices like monitors, disk drives, etc.

A **Duo Dock** is like a modular Mac without a brain. The Duo slips into the Duo ▦➡

Dock like a videotape going into a VCR, providing ***very good feature*** the brains, and the pair becomes a modular Mac. When you need to take a Mac on the road, you just eject the Duo and bring it with you. (If you don't need a modular Mac's expansion capabilities, you can also buy adapters that let you hook a Duo up to floppy drives and other external devices, giving it the capabilities of other PowerBooks.)

The Performas are Macs that are sold at appliance outlets like

bargain

Sears, Circuit City and Office Depot, instead of just at authorized Apple dealers. They come with a basic all-in-one software package pre-installed, so when you buy a Performa, you get everything necessary to start computing, for about what you'd pay a Mac dealer for the same machine without the software.

They're Apple's way of making Macs more accessible to the seven million American households who could really use Macs (for their kids, if nothing else) but don't have time to figure out which model and what software to get, where to buy the darn things and how to use them.

🍎 comparing Macs

Aside from their obvious physical differences, Mac models differ from one another in three main ways: performance, expandability and built-in hardware support. (Once you've picked the model you want, you still have to decide how much RAM and what size hard drive to get, but that's a much simpler issue—simply get as much as you can afford.)

Performance is mostly a function of the processor chip—the Mac's "brain." Any Mac can handle word processing and other basic tasks, but Macs with faster, more advanced processors feel more responsive to use, and can take on more challenging jobs—like desktop publishing or sophisticated design work—that are impractical or impossible on lesser Macs (see *the processor chip* below).

Inside modular Macs (and some compact Macs) are **expansion slots**—connectors where you or a technician can plug in specialized **cards** that allow you to do things like add an external monitor, connect to other Macs with fast cabling, or increase your computer's speed. The type and number of expansion slots varies between Mac models (see *expansion slots* on the next page).

Most recent Macs also come with some of this specialized hardware built in. For example, most modular models include video support, which allows you to plug a monitor into the Mac without having to spend hundreds of dollars on a video card. Nearly all current Macs (except the Duos) include microphones, allowing you to record your own sounds. Some Macs also have Ethernet support, for high-speed networking; and by the time you read this, there should be one or two models that let you record movie clips from videotape onto your Mac's hard drive.

very good feature

If a Mac has everything you want built in, who cares how many expansion slots it has? On the other hand, it's silly to pay up front for capabilities (like Ethernet) you may never use, and an expandable Mac lets you add these functions later. Of course, if you want to have it all now *and* be able to add whatever comes down the pike, sell your car and buy an expandable Mac with built-in support for everything.

For some help finding the right Mac for your purposes, see *the right tool for the job*, below.

the processor chip

The **processor chip** is where the computer actually does its thinking and translates the results into images on the screen. It's also called the **processor,** the **microprocessor**, the **CPU** (for *central processing unit)* or simply the **chip**. (Be aware that the term *CPU* is also sometimes used to refer to the Mac itself, as distinct from the keyboard, mouse, external monitor, etc.)

At this writing, Macs use the 68030 and 68040 processors made by Motorola; older Macs used the 68000 and 68020 chips. In general, the higher the number, the more advanced the chip's capabilities. In terms of raw processing power, the 68020, 68030 and 68040 correspond roughly to the 286, 386 and 486 chips produced by Intel for IBM compatibles. Before long, there'll be Macs that use a new, faster type of chip called the PowerPC.

things to come

Different Macs using the same type of chip run faster or slower depending on their **clock speed**, measured in **megahertz**—millions of cycles per second (abbreviated *MHz*). A Mac with a 68030 chip running at 33MHz is generally faster than one with the same chip running at 25MHz; but a Mac with a 68040 chip running at 25MHz is much faster than one with a 68030 chip running at 25MHz, or even 33MHz.

The type and clock speed of a Mac's processor are a good general guide to its performance, but not an absolutely reliable one. For example, the SE/30 and Classic II both use a 68030 chip running at 16MHz, but the SE/30 is faster because it moves twice as much information at a time along an internal electronic pathway called the **data bus**. Ultimately, hands-on experience (yours, a reliable friend's, or a magazine's lab test) is the best measure of a Mac's speed.

⌘ *expansion slots*

As mentioned above, expansion slots are connectors inside the Mac that let you plug in cards that do special tasks, like accelerate your computer or record video clips onto your hard drive. There are two basic kinds—**processor direct** slots (PDSs) and **NuBus** slots.

As the name implies, a PDS connects directly to the processor chip, which makes PDS cards faster than NuBus cards. But a Mac can only have one PDS, and PDSs in different models are generally incompatible with each other, which is why there are far fewer PDS cards than NuBus cards.

By contrast, you can use virtually any NuBus card in any Mac's NuBus slot (space permitting—the Centris 610 can only take 7" cards) and a Mac can handle as many NuBus cards as it has NuBus slots (five on the Quadra 950, for example). The Quadras' NuBus slots can transfer data twice as fast as regular NuBus slots, but at this writing, the cards to exploit that potential speed don't exist yet.

very good feature

Some Macs (the IIci and IIvx, for example) also have slots that are specifically designed for accelerator or cache cards, which speed up the Mac's operations.

✎ memory, a.k.a. RAM

A computer's **RAM** is the working space in which you create and modify documents and do other work. *(RAM stands for random-access memory, and is often just called **memory**.)* Whenever you're working on a document (a letter, a spreadsheet or whatever), what you see on the screen is being kept temporarily in RAM. Anytime you shut down or restart your computer, whatever was in RAM is lost. That's what hard drives and floppy disks are for—to permanently store the files you're working with before you turn the computer off.

All Macs come with some RAM built in, but you can buy and install more—how much more depends on the Mac (for more on RAM upgrades, see Chapter 4). Increasing your Mac's RAM lets you open more and bigger programs and files at one time. It also keeps your Mac from slowing down when you've got all those files open.

At this writing, new Macs come with at least four megs of RAM. Less than that is inadequate for running more than one program at a time under System 7; in fact, you won't even be able to run one large application. If you buy an older Mac, you may have to upgrade its RAM to make it a useful machine.

important warning

On the other hand, older Macs and system software weren't designed to use more than eight megs of RAM. To handle more than that, Macs running System 6 need a special program called Optima (from Connectix); even with System 7, the Mac II, IIx, IIcx and SE/30 need a program called Mode32 (available free from Apple deal-

important warning

ers, users groups and online services). The Plus, SE and Classic can't handle more than four megs under any circumstances.

✎ the hard drive

The Mac's hard drive is where it stores the software you need to use your Mac, and the files you create. When your Mac is on, it sits ready to load a document or program into memory (which is what happens when you open a file) or to copy the revised version of a file you've been working on from memory back into storage (which is what happens when you give the *Save* command in an application). The bigger the hard drive, the more programs and documents you can store (see Chapter 4 for more on RAM and hard drives).

🍎 *the coprocessor*

A *coprocessor* is a second processor chip that specializes in math, graphics or some other specific kind of computation. Many Macs include math coprocessors (also called *floating-point units*, or *FPUs*) although they're generally helpful only to people who use the Mac for tasks like sophisticated financial analysis, scientific formulas or computer-aided design. You can often add a coprocessor to a Mac that doesn't have one.

Coprocessors often get built into the next generation of the main processor—for example, the 68030 chip incorporates a memory-management unit that was used as a coprocessor with the 68020, and the 68040 chip handles the functions of the 68882 math coprocessor that's often used with the 68030.

🍎 *names and numbers*

Some Mac models have numbers as part of their names—the PowerBook 180, the Quadra 800, the IIvx, etc. But when you see an arabic number before a *slash,* that generally indicates the number of megabytes of RAM in the machine, and an arabic number following a slash generally indicates how many megs are on its hard disk. Thus a Mac LC III 4/80 has four megs of RAM and an 80-meg hard disk.

The SE/30 violated that naming convention, since the *30* after the slash referred to its 68030 processor chip, rather than to a 30-meg hard disk. Apple typically used an *x* to indicate the 68030 chip—as in IIx, IIcx and IIfx—but they apparently didn't think we could handle a machine called the *Macintosh SEx.*

gossip/ trivia

🍎 the right tool for the job

The basic question to ask yourself is—**what will you use your Mac for?** The average computer user does mostly word processing—even on a Mac, with all its sound and graphics capabilities.

If you're typical, you probably don't need a super-fast chip, a math coprocessor, six expansion slots, 128 megs of RAM, a 21" color monitor and a hard drive whose capacity is measured in gigabytes (you may *want* them, but you don't need them).

Try to figure out what software you'll be using and try it out on the computer you're considering. Imagine yourself performing those activities day in and day out, for months on end. Will the time it takes for the screen to redraw drive you crazy? Can you really see what you're doing on a 9" screen?

If you can afford it, it's a good idea to buy an expandable Mac. Then, if your needs change, you may be able to upgrade your current machine, rather than buying a whole new one.

Consider the number of expansion slots (two or three are plenty for most people) and the maximum amount of RAM you can put in the machine. Here's a chart to help you figure out what kind of Mac you'll need for the work you plan to be doing:

☞ **pretty much any Mac is adequate for:**

- small databases (up to 2000 records)
- check-writing programs
- simple graphics
- e-mail
- using a modem
- word processing
- small spreadsheets

other requirements or limitations:

compact Macs' screens show only ⅓ page
compact Macs' screens show only ⅓ page

☞ **a Mac with a 68030 processor is best for:**

- page layout (flyers)
- page layout (manuals and books)
- simple color games/graphics
- high-end graphics, photo work
- large databases (2000+ records)
- basic music with a synthesizer

full-page monitor
25MHz, large HD, full-page monitor or bigger
color monitor
25MHz, large HD, full-page monitor or bigger
large, fast HD for 20,000+ records   ‖➡

☞ _**more things a Mac with a 68030 processor is best for:**_

• **CD-quality audio recording**	_25MHz, large, fast HD_
• **multimedia**	_25MHz, large HD_
• **video movies (QuickTime)**	_video digitizer card,[3] large HD_
• **many large files/programs open at once**	_8MB or more of RAM[1]_
• **advanced math formulas**	_math coprocessor_
• **heavy use of large files over a network**	_Ethernet card or built-in support[2]_
• **file server (light use, small files)**	
• **file server (medium use and file size)**	_Ethernet card or built-in support[2]_

☞ _**a Mac with a 68040 processor is best for:**_

• **page layout (large files, color graphics)**	_19" monitor or bigger, large HD_
• **3D graphics, modeling**	_large HD, math coprocessor_
• **file server (many heavy users, large files)**	_Ethernet card or built-in support[2]_

HD = hard drive
1. _The Mac IIx, IIcx and SE/30 require Mode32 software to use more than 8MB of RAM._
2. _Ethernet cards require expansion slots, but you can also get Ethernet for Macs without slots._
3. _Video digitizer cards require an expansion slot._

Monitors

🍎 _pixels, resolution and screen capacity_

The images on a Mac's screen are made up of tiny dots called **pixels**. When you're word-processing on a black-and-white monitor, the blank part of the page is made up of white pixels, and the letters you've typed are made up of black pixels.

Different monitors use different-sized pixels, so the same image will look larger or smaller depending on what monitor it's displayed on. This also means that two monitors of the same size won't necessarily fit the same amount of material on the screen. So to measure a monitor's screen capacity, you need to know its dimensions in pixels, not just whether the manufacturer calls it a 12", 13" or 14" monitor (those numbers usually aren't accurate anyway).

very
hot
tip

For example, the Classic II's 9" screen displays 512 pixels across by 342 down, at a **resolution of 72 dpi** (dots per inch, or in this case, pixels per inch). *[72 dpi was chosen because type has always been measured in points, and there are 72 points to the inch. This makes some sense, but I think 72 dpi is too coarse. Once you get used to finer resolutions, 72 dpi looks ridiculously big and clunky.—AN]*

◆ *the refresh rate*

One of the most important characteristics in a monitor is its **refresh rate**—how often it redraws the image on its screen. The refresh rate is measured in **hertz** (times per second)—abbreviated **Hz**.

If the refresh rate is too slow, you get **flicker** (also called *strobe).* Regular house current alternates at 60Hz (here in the US); if you can see the flicker in fluorescent lights, a refresh rate of 60Hz is probably too slow for you. 60Hz is the refresh rate on compact Macs, but their screens are so small, most people find it acceptable. (The larger the screen, the more flicker is likely to bother you. Some companies go up to 72Hz, 87Hz and beyond on larger monitors.)

Peripheral vision is particularly sensitive to flicker, so if you're in doubt about a screen, turn away from it and see how it looks out of the side of your eye. Another good way to accentuate flicker is to wave your hand in front of the screen.

◆ *black-&-white, grayscale & color*

On black-and-white monitors, what looks like gray—the standard desktop pattern, for example—is actually made up of alternating black and white dots.

On a **grayscale** monitor, however, each dot can be black, white or a shade of gray. (How many shades of gray depends on the video card or the Mac's built-in video support.) With real grays available, screen images can be of photographic quality. (Of course the grays on a grayscale monitor are *also* composed of black and white dots, but the dots are much smaller.) Both black-and-white and grayscale monitors are lumped together under the term **monochrome**, which means **one color**.

On **color** monitors, each pixel on the screen is composed of three tiny dots of color—red, green and blue. Your eyes merge them into a single, colored dot.

I f you have a color monitor, you also have a grayscale monitor. To turn it into one, go to the Monitors control panel and click the *Grays* button (instead of *Colors).* Then choose a number from the list

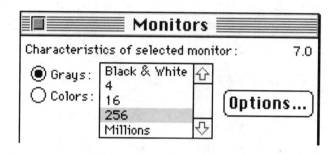

box (these numbers now represent shades of gray, not colors).

Scrolling (and other forms of screen response) take significantly longer on a color monitor than on a black-and-white monitor of the same size, and grayscale slows things down just as much (assuming you have the same number of colors and/or grays selected). To speed things up, choose *Black & White* in the list box.

◉ *built-in support and video cards*

All modular Macs being sold at this writing—and most PowerBooks—have some kind of video support on board, allowing you to attach an external monitor without having to buy any additional hardware. To run an external monitor on other Macs, you need a **video card** that plugs into a slot on your Mac. (Older Macs like the Classic II don't have slots, and require another kind of adapter).

M ost Macs' video support will handle 12"–14" monitors or Apple's portrait display, and the Centrises and Quadras support monitors up to 21". But some Macs require an upgrade to their **video RAM** (VRAM) to use the larger monitors. Also, not all non-Apple monitors can run off the Mac's built-in support, so be sure to ask before you buy.

On a color or grayscale monitor, the amount of VRAM in a Mac or the type of video card also determines how many colors or shades of gray can be displayed. Black-and-white is also called **one-bit** video because every pixel is controlled by one bit of memory (and since a bit can only be a zero or a one, the pixel can only be black or white).

Four-bit video means four bits of memory per pixel, which can represent sixteen different colors or grays on the screen; *eight-bit* video lets you display 256 colors or grays. And for photographic quality, you need *24-bit* video, which lets you display more than sixteen million colors or grays at once (or as many of them as will fit on the screen).

⌘ big screens (AN)

Back when I'd only used compact Macs, I never thought their 9" screen was too small. I loved its crisp, readable image. Still, it was annoying only to be able to see about a third of a standard 8½ x 11 page at a time, especially when trying to lay out two-page spreads. So I got a black-and-white two-page display.

After about a day, I could no longer work on a compact Mac without having to constantly repress the urge to grab the edges of the screen and try to pull them farther apart. After a week, I couldn't look at a compact Mac without feeling there was something *wrong* with it: *How come the pixels are so big? How come*

there's so little information on the screen? I don't think I've ever been more quickly spoiled by anything in my life.

External monitors are required with modular Macs, and you can also buy them for compact and portable Macs. But if you get one, remember—there's no turning back.

⌘ evaluating monitors

Your first consideration when buying an external monitor is which shape you prefer. The basic distinction is between tall and wide screens—or *portrait* and *landscape*, as they're often called.

For most purposes, wide screens are better. If you primarily do word processing, or lay out single pages, a tall screen will show you a whole page at once and cost much less than a two-page display.

The next consideration is how much data you want to display. A Classic II's screen has just over 178,000 pixels (512 x 342). Some monitors can display up to two million pixels—more than fourteen times as much material—although they usually display it at a higher resolution.

A good way to compare monitors is by pixels per dollar. Just multiply the number of pixels across by the number of pixels down, then divide the price of the monitor into that. The bigger the resulting number, the better (everything else being equal—which, of course, it seldom is).

Pixels per dollar can vary quite widely. But this measure should only be the beginning of your comparison—especially since some monitors give you a choice of resolutions. For example, a popular NEC color monitor displays 640 x 480, 800 x 600 or 1024 x 768, at various refresh rates, depending on what video card it's hooked up to.

If you plan on using your Mac's built-in video support, be sure to ask whether the monitor can run off of it. Otherwise, you'll have to buy a video card, which may cost more than the monitor! If you're thinking of using the monitor with something other than a Mac, make sure it's compatible with that computer.

⚠️
important warning

Monitors are a lot like speakers—you can look at technical specs all day long, but the only way to buy speakers is to listen to them, and the only way to buy monitors is to look at them, ideally side-by-side.

What you're looking for is a crisp, high-contrast, rock-solid image—one that isn't washed-out, doesn't waver or flicker, and isn't distorted around the edges. Getting that is more important than any other consideration, and worth paying more for. (For more specifics, see the next entry.)

Remember—you may be staring at the screen for *thousands* of hours, and anything less than a great image will really drive you nuts. Skimping on the quality of your monitor is like buying an uncomfortable bed—whatever you save won't be worth it in the long run.

🍎 *the test-drive*

Here's a checklist of what to look for when you've got the monitor(s) in front of you:

☞ **Is the screen image sharp?** Trust your eyes. With color monitors, sharpness depends partly on the ability of the display tube to aim its three color beams at the same spots on the screen (this is called **convergence,** and a few monitors let you adjust for it—a very good feature).

☞ **Is the screen big enough so that you don't have to scroll constantly?** Open a document in a word processor to see how much of an 8½ x 11 page fits on the screen at once. Some monitors let you change their resolution to show more on the screen, but that often makes text too small to read comfortably.

☞ **Does the monitor adhere to radiation standards?** Sweden's are the most restrictive, and several newer monitors conform with them. (No one's *proven* that sitting in front of a cathode ray tube all day, five days a week, causes problems, so our benighted country doesn't insist on monitor safety.)

☞ **Do you have room to view the screen from a comfortable distance?** This is especially important for very big screens. (John Kadyk recommends a distance of at least one arm's length.)

☞ **Is the screen image distorted?** Look for a lack of symmetry—lines that should be straight but aren't. (Some monitors have adjustments that let you correct distortion.)

☞ **Does the image flicker when you're at a proper viewing distance?**

☞ **Are controls easy to reach and use?**

☞ **Is the price right?** (Remember to figure in a video card, if necessary.)

☞ **Are the instructional materials that accompany the monitor understandable?** Useful? Comprehensive? An experienced user may not care, but a beginner or computerphobe may care a lot.

🍎 *if you want color*

Color monitors are beautiful, and they're a lot cheaper than they were just a couple of years ago. So why not buy one? For one thing, they don't display text nearly as well as monochrome monitors. For another, they still cost quite a bit more than black-and-white monitors. And finally, color may slow performance of normal operations beyond your tolerance, unless you spend extra money on accelerator cards.

But color is essential for many artists and designers, and it's a distinct advantage for games and graphics. So if you decide to shop for a color monitor, here are some things to consider:

☞ **Does the screen's color spectrum please you?** You may have noticed that some brands of color film look redder or yellower than the real world, while others are bluer or greener. The color balance of monitors varies the same way.

☞ **Is there a way to change the color balance if you want—for example, to match screen color to a particular color in a 35mm slide?**

☞ **Is the monitor too big?** Even the smaller ones are much bigger, front-to-back, than comparable monochrome monitors, and the biggest color monitors are monsters.

☞ **Will your table or desk support the weight of a big monitor?** *[Don't assume anything; my monitor eventually put a permanent curve in my table.—BB]*

Keyboards, mice and trackballs

🍎 *Apple's keyboards*

When you buy most modular Macs, the keyboard isn't included. You have a choice of buying the 81-key standard keyboard or the 105-key extended keyboard, which has a row of fifteen function keys (including *Undo, Cut, Copy* and *Paste),* a cluster of command keys—⌂Home⌂, ⌂End⌂, ⌂Page Up⌂, ⌂Page Down⌂, ⌂Help⌂ and ⌂⌫⌂ (forward delete)—and extra ⌂⌘⌂, ⌂Option⌂ and ⌂Control⌂ keys to the right of the spacebar. *[I personally can't stand the planklike size of the extended keyboard, but some people like them.—AN]*

Both of these *ADB (Apple Desktop Bus)* keyboards have jacks on either end, so you can plug the mouse into whichever side you want (you use the other jack for connecting the keyboard to the computer). Several companies make six-foot ADB cables that let you get your keyboard (and mouse) farther away from the Mac.

You can chain up to sixteen ADB devices together (assuming each device has an in and out port; a mouse would have to be the last device on the chain). This can be useful if you like using a mouse for some tasks and a trackball for others (trackballs are described on the next page), or if you're training people and want them all to have their own keyboards.

Don't connect or disconnect your keyboard—or any ADB device—without first shutting down your Mac. If you do, you may ruin the motherboard on your Mac.

important warning

♪ *cleanlimouse is next to smoothlimouse*

Cleaning your mouse occasionally will keep it working smoothly. Remove the ring at the bottom of the mouse by turning it, and drop the ball out into your palm. Clean the three little rollers inside the mouse with a Q-Tip dipped in alcohol. Rub the ball clean with a cloth before replacing it.

very hot tip

To give the rollers a more thorough cleaning, there's a kit from Curtis that's the epitome of simple yet elegant design. You put a drop or two of cleaning fluid onto a Velcro-covered ball that's resting on a Velcro pad, then put the mouse (with its regular ball removed) over the Velcro-covered ball and roll it around. It's easy, it's hygienic and...it's fun.

♪ *trackballs*

A *trackball* is like a mouse turned on its back. The ball (which varies widely in size) sticks out of the top, and you move it with your fingers, thumb or palm. Some people love trackballs and some people hate them.

Trackballs require less space than a mouse, and control the pointer more precisely (which is particularly important for graphics). All trackballs have a locking button that lets you drag things on the screen without having to hold the button down. Finally, most trackballs are easier to keep clean than mice.

Personal preference matters more with a trackball than it does with, say, a modem. If you decide to try a trackball, give it a fair chance. Ask for at least a few days to try it out, and your money back if you don't like it.

very hot tip

Protecting your Mac (and yourself)

● *basic Mac protection*

The Macintosh is a pretty sturdy computer, but it's not invincible, so take a few precautions when you set it up. Heat can shorten hardware's lifespan, so keep your equipment away from direct sunlight and from appliances that generate heat. *[I _thought_ there was a reason not to use my Mac II as an ironing board, and now I know what it is. Damn!—AN]*

important warning

Also make sure that the vents for the fans are not blocked. *[Yet _another_ reason not to iron on the II. I guess it really was a bad idea.—AN]* Dust can contribute to heat buildup and can cause other problems (especially if it gets into your floppy drive), so avoid dusty locations. *[What about lint?—AN]*

important warning

While heat may cause problems over time, a sudden surge of power can trash your Mac in an instant, so make sure you use a **surge protector**, especially if you live in an area where blackouts or thunderstorms are common (but don't depend on a surge protector for protection against lightning; see the next two entries for more on that). If you don't have a surge protector, unplug your computer *immediately* whenever the power goes out, because when the power returns, it will do so with a surge.

very hot tip

Route your Mac's cables carefully so nobody can trip on them. A jerked cable can jar a hard disk and jeopardize your data. If a cable comes loose while the Mac is on, it can create serious hardware problems. Always turn the power off before plugging or unplugging SCSI or ADB cables—otherwise you could cause a short that can damage the Mac or the data on it.

To keep your screen from burning out, use a screen saver (see Chapter 9 for more on them).

◉ *basic ergonomics* (AN)

If you put a compact Mac and its keyboard on the same surface, either the screen will be too low or the keyboard too high. Modular Macs also share this problem to some extent, but you can often tilt their monitors up or down to compensate for their actual height. (You can do this with compact Macs too, if you buy a swivel/tilt base for them.)

For comfortable typing, **your wrists should never be higher than your elbows, nor should they be bent** (*other than their slightly bent normal position*). Depending on your (and your chair's) height, this often means the keyboard should be on a surface 24"–27" from the floor.

That will be great for your wrists, but maybe not so great for your lower back. The 24"–27" typing surface height was designed for women (since most typists have traditionally been women) and their average height is about 5'4" or 5'5". If you're taller than 5'7" or so, typing on a surface this low will force you to sit on a chair that's too low for you, and that doesn't allow an open enough angle at your hips. *(To avoid lower-back problems, the angle between your legs and your trunk should usually be more than 90°.)* Even normal-height secretarial chairs can cause this problem.

very hot tip

Susan McCallister, who's 5'9" and has a bad back, solved this by putting her typing surface more than 30" above the ground, and getting a drafting chair (with a tilting seat) to bring her up to it. Sometimes she sits on it (with the seat at various angles), sometimes she leans on it and sometimes she stands at the keyboard.

In any case, whatever height your chair is, the critical relationship is between you and the keyboard, not between the keyboard and the floor. Again: your wrists should *never* be higher than your elbows, or bent beyond the relaxed postion, when you type (it's worth repeating).

very hot tip

The bottom of the screen should be 4–8 inches higher than the surface the keyboard is on, so that you can look at it comfortably without having to bend your head. And don't strain your eyes by putting it too close—allow at least a foot between the back of the keyboard and the front of the Mac.

However comfortable your workspace is, it's important to periodically change your position. Chris Allen says there's a highly rated ergonomic chair that slowly changes its position over the course of the day—automatically! It probably costs a fortune, but getting up and walking around every couple of hours (at least) is free—and very helpful.

Here's another tidbit from Chris: Just moving from the keyboard to the mouse can help prevent **carpal tunnel syndrome**, the painful wrist ailment caused by too much typing. It's the keyboard-only users who get it the worst (and I'm willing to bet that flexed wrists are a major factor in it).

[Mouse users can also get repetitive stress injuries (sometimes called RSI). In fact, certain mouse activities can be very stressful, since it's normally only a single finger that does all the repeated moving, and this motion occurs while the rest of the hand is partially flexed (to hold and guide the mouse).

It's worthwhile to experiment by alternating the hand you move the mouse with. The dexterity required is usually less than for normal writing, so even those of us who aren't ambidextrous can manage it.—DH]

Another vital issue is eliminating reflections from your screen. (Usually they're called **glare**, which is a misleading term.) You don't want any lights or windows behind the computer; in fact, it's much better to put a computer directly in front of a window than opposite one.

very hot tip

The best place for a light is on the ceiling (or bouncing off the ceiling) somewhere between you and the screen.

[I use one of those $10 swing-arm drafting lamps clamped to the shelf of a bookcase. The shade is turned to the ceiling and is about six inches in front of and three feet above my left ear. When I'm working on the computer, that's the only light in the room (except, of course, for the light from the screen). There are no reflections on the screen.

To block the light from the windows, I have solid wooden shutters on the windows (built especially for that purpose). It's not hard to do; just get pieces of wood or particle board the right size (plywood warps) and use door hinges to attach them. If that's too much of a project for you, go to a photographic supply store and get some of the blackout cloth used to light-seal darkrooms. It's easy to install it with duct tape or push pins, but a pain to take down when you want to let some daylight into the room.—AN]

radiation

Computer screens give off **VLF** and **ELF** *(very-low frequency* and *extremely-low frequency)* radiation, which research indicates can increase your risk of cancer. The strength of ELF radiation drops off rapidly as you move away from the monitor, but since there's no way yet to screen out ELF, no one should sit closer than four feet from the sides or back of a monitor (which produce the strongest radiation), or 28" (roughly arm's length) from the front of the screen.

important warning

This issue has gotten enough attention recently that several manufacturers are designing monitors that give off less radiation. Sweden has the tightest regulations governing ELF and VLF emissions, and monitors that meet their standards are the safest.

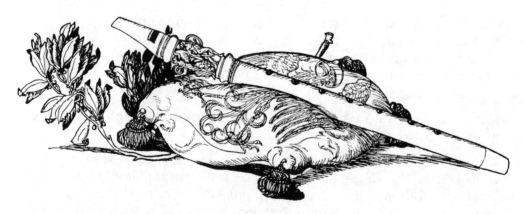

Chapter
4

Memory and storage

The basics

🍎 *storage vs. memory*

Even experienced Mac users are often confused about the difference between *storage* and *memory*. For example: why do you get out-of-memory messages when there's still plenty of room on your hard disk?

The confusion is understandable. Storage and memory are both ways of retaining information, and they're both measured in the same units—bytes, kilobytes, megabytes, etc. The difference is in how the information is retained.

> With **memory**, information is saved *electronically* on *chips*, and in **storage** it's saved on *media*, either *magnetically* on disks or tapes, or *optically* on disks or CD-ROMs. (If you're unsure about any of these terms, see the glossary and/or the index.) The distinction between memory and storage isn't as theoretical as it may seem; there are dramatic practical differences between the two ways of retaining data.

When people talk about *memory*, they're usually talking about *RAM* (which stands for *random-access memory*, because you can access different parts of it in any order—although, actually, that's true of all kinds of memory). RAM is where computers temporarily keep information you're working with.

Although the information in RAM can be accessed very quickly, RAM is usually *volatile:* its contents last only as long as power is being supplied to it. If you turn your Mac off without *saving* your work, what was in RAM during your work session vanishes.

important warning

That's where storage comes in. Using an application's *Save* command takes information from RAM and puts it onto storage media like *hard disks* and *floppies* (both of which are discussed in detail later on in this chapter). Once information is in storage, it's there permanently—or at least for a long time, assuming you take reasonable care of your disks.

It takes much longer to *write* (save information) to, or *read* (retrieve information) from, storage than memory. That's because storage devices involve mechanical moving parts, while the only things that move in memory chips are electronic impulses.

So memory is like your own memory—it's fast to put things in and out of, but when you die, everything in it disappears. Storage is like notes, letters, books and tapes—it takes longer to get information in and out of them, but they outlive you. That's the basic distinction, and it's a good, clear, useful one. But there are some exceptions—they're not critical to understanding the Mac, but if you're interested, see the next page.

bits, bytes, K, megs and gigs

A **bit** is the smallest possible unit of information (on a computer or anywhere else). It can represent one of only two things—on or off, yes or no, zero or one. A **byte** is made up of eight bits. In text, bytes are typically used to represent single characters (letters, numbers, punctuation marks and other symbols).

The smallest unit normally used to measure file sizes on the Mac is the **kilobyte**—known familiarly as a **K**—which equals 1024 bytes. Since the prefix *kilo-* means *thousand,* why 1024 bytes? Because computers are binary and normally increase their capacities in multiples of two: 2, 4, 8, 16, 32, 64, 128, 256, 512, 1024 (a very familiar series of numbers if you've been around computers for a while).

Despite the fact that a K is 1024 bytes and always has been, some companies call 1000 bytes a K. It's not a mystery why they do that—it makes their products appear to have greater capacities. We call these shortchanged, 1000-byte K *mini-K.*

very bad feature

Large files, RAM and hard drive capacity are usually measured in **megabytes** (usually called **megs**—after their inventor, the 14th-century Swedish adventurer Meg Holmberg—and often abbreviated **MB**). A meg equals 1024 kilobytes or 1,048,576 bytes (2^{20} bytes). As is the case with K, megabytes are sometimes rounded down to a million bytes, which we call *minimegs.*

As storage devices become more and more humungous, the next unit of measure is becoming common: ***gigabyte***, or ***gig***, which is 1024 megs. That's more than a million K and more than a billion (1,073,741,824) bytes. Marketing being what it is, we confidently expect gigs to be treated as an even billion bytes instead of as their true value—which, as you can see, is more than 7% higher.

⌘ *other types of memory*

ROM (read-only memory) is information that's built into the computer to tell it things like how to act when it's switched on. Although this information is stored on chips, like RAM, ROM retains its information permanently, because ROM chips can't be changed (at least not by mere mortals like us—there are machines that can change the data on certain kinds of ROM chips).

Information is stored in ROM permanently, but ROM is memory—no wonder people are confused.

There are also ways to put aside some of your RAM and treat it like a very fast hard disk (this is called a **RAM disk**) and ways to put aside some of a hard disk and treat it like RAM (this is called *virtual memory*). Both are discussed at the end of this chapter.

The analogy Chris Allen uses for all of this is interesting and may help clarify things. He says RAM is like the top of your desk and disks are like filing cabinets nearby. (To make the analogy more precise, imagine that the overzealous people who clean your office at night throw out everything they find on your desk.)

If you have a small desk (little RAM), you have to constantly run back and forth between it and your filing cabinets, because not many things will fit on top of the desk at one time. If you have a large desk (a lot of RAM), you have the luxury of not running over to the filing cabinets as often.

RAM disks are like drawers in your desk—smaller than filing cabinets, but convenient for some purposes because they're close at hand. ROM is like having some information permanently carved on your desk's surface so you can find it instantly (and so you'll never forget it).

Gigabyte and gig are both pronounced with hard *g*'s (as in *go*). We mention this because *gigawatt* (a billion watts) is often pronounced with a soft *g*, as in *giant*. For example, you may remember the scene in the movie *Back to the Future* when Doc Brown, in 1955, staggers into his living room, grabs a framed picture of Thomas Edison and yelps at it: "1.21 gigawatts! Tom! How am I going to generate that kind of power?"—followed a moment later by: "Marty, I'm sorry, but the only power source capable of generating 1.21 gigawatts of electricity is a bolt of lightning....Unfortunately, you never know when or where it's going to strike."

gossip/ trivia

Anyway, here's a summary of the main units of storage and memory capacity:

> 8 bits = **1 byte**
> 1024 bytes = **1 K** (1000 bytes = 1 mini-K)
> 1024 K = **1 meg** (1000K = 1 minimeg)
> 1024 megs = **1 gig** (1000 megs = 1 minigig)

⬤ *measuring RAM, disk capacity and file size*

To find out how much RAM a Mac has, go to the Finder and select About This Macintosh... from the ⬤ menu (with older system software, it's called About The Finder...). In the window that appears, divide the Total Memory figure by 1024 to get the amount of RAM in megabytes. (This window also tells you the Mac model and what version of the system software it's running.)

To find out the capacity of a hard disk, double-click on its icon to open its window. Then select *by Icon* or *by Small Icon* from the View menu. A bar below the window's title bar will indicate how many icons are in the window, how much data is stored on the disk, and how much space is still available to store files on. The sum of the last two figures is the drive's data capacity (because of the disk's formatting and invisible housekeeping files, it's a few percent under the overall drive capacity).

To find out how much space a file or folder takes up on disk, just select the item's icon on the desktop and hit ⌘I. You'll get a window that tells you the file's size in K—or megs, if it's that big—and in bytes, along with some other information. For most purposes, the K or MB figure is the one to use.

Hard disks

◉ hard disk basics

In the early days of the Mac, hard disks were luxuries—accessories lusted after by the great masses of computer users but owned by few. Now they're standard equipment—it's difficult to do any serious work on a Mac that only runs off floppy disks.

Unlike floppy disks, where the disk and its drive are two separate items, **hard disk** and **hard drive** are (typically) two names for the same thing—a metal case inside of which are one or more rigid disks, or **platters**, stacked on top of each other, a mechanism to spin them, and the **read/write heads** that put data onto, and take data off of, the disk(s).

One advantage of hard disks is capacity—they store a lot more data than floppies. It's convenient to put everything on your hard disk, so you don't have to wonder which floppy a particular file or application is on.

But the preeminent advantage of hard disks is speed—open the same file from a floppy and a hard disk and you'll see the difference right away. And since you can keep your system software, applications and documents all on one hard drive, you don't have to spend time looking for, inserting and ejecting a series of disks as you do with floppies.

If you buy a new hard drive, it'll probably be ready to use when you get it (the internal drives in new Macs always are). Otherwise, you'll need to run the **formatting** software supplied by the drive's manufacturer (which can be confusing). If a disk's icon shows up on the screen when you start your Mac, it's ready to use.

🍎 shopping for a hard drive

Most new Macs come with an **internal hard disk** (one that's mounted inside the Mac itself). If you want more storage space, you can either replace the internal drive with a bigger one or add an external drive that hooks up to the Mac's SCSI port.

Since you don't have to pay for a separate case, an internal hard disk is cheaper than the equivalent external hard disk. It takes up no desk space, and you don't have to lug a separate piece of equipment around when you're moving your Mac.

But if an internal hard disk breaks, you'll be without your Mac while it's being repaired (unless you pull it out of the Mac). When you need to diagnose whether your hard disk or your Mac is causing a problem, it's a lot easier to disconnect an external hard disk than an internal one. And if you use one Mac at work and another at home, you can just carry an external drive back and forth instead of having to remember what to put on floppies.

Next you need to decide how large a drive to get. With today's software, 40MB is the bare minimum for people who use their Macs a lot; unless you're broke, it's better to get at least an 80MB drive. For serious desktop publishing or video work, you'll need a much bigger drive.

Finally, you need to pick a particular vendor and model—here are some guidelines to help you in that process:

The manufacturer of the disk mechanism itself is more

very hot tip

important than the name on the case. Almost all hard drive vendors buy their disk mechanisms—the actual guts of the hard drive—from someone else.

They add a power supply, a case, cabling and some software, and put their name on the outside. The quality of these parts makes a difference too, but the mechanism matters most.

For several years, Quantum mechanisms

very good feature

have been among the fastest and most reliable for drives of up to about 220 megs.

From 300 megs on up, Maxtor and Seagate mechanisms are good, at least as of this writing—to be sure, check with a user group, or ▐▐▐➡

any knowledgeable people you know.

Although hard drives' speeds vary, for most purposes, they're all fast enough. A disk's speed becomes more important when you're using large databases or applications that access the hard disk frequently—like video and animation programs, high-end audio recording software, CAD (computer-assisted design) programs and some games—but it's noticeable even in a program like Word.

Speed is usually assessed in terms of a drive's **access time** (how fast it can find a certain piece of data, measured in milliseconds) and **transfer rate** (how fast it sends and receives data, measured in megs per second).

When selecting a vendor to buy from, **get the longest warranty you can** and **buy from a company with a good reputation for customer support.** The best source for the latter kind of information is, again, a knowledgeable friend or user group.

important warning

You also want to think about price, and the best way to evaluate that is dollars per megabyte of capacity. Just take the cost and divide it by the number of megs the drive holds (the lower the number, the better).

If you can, use the drive's *formatted* capacity for these calculations, since that's how much *useful* space it provides, and the amount of space taken up by formatting varies from vendor to vendor for a given size of hard drive.

cartridge drives

If you want to be able to increase your storage space bit by bit and don't need to have all your data accessible at one time, consider getting a cartridge drive. A cartridge drive is like a regular hard drive, but instead of having a single disk, it takes hard disk *cartridges* that you can insert and eject like floppy disks.

The most popular cartridge drives use the SyQuest mechanism. SyQuest drives can take either 44-, 88- or 105–megabyte cartridges (most drives read just one of these sizes, and 44-meg drives are the most common as of this writing). They aren't quite as fast as most hard drives, and they're also louder, so they're primarily used for backup and archiving rather than as primary units.

Like regular hard drive mechanisms, SyQuest mechanisms are sold under many manufacturer's names, but they all function basically the same, and their cartridges are interchangeable. While the drives themselves typically cost twice as much as regular hard drives of about the same size, additional cartridges only cost 30 to 50 percent of hard drive prices, and they're much easier to store or transport.

bargain

SyQuest drives are useful for desktop publishers—many typesetting service bureaus now have them, so that customers with large documents or complex images to print can bring in a cartridge instead of a raft of floppies. *[If you work with scans, color, EPS files or long page-layout documents, cartridges aren't merely useful when going to a service bureau—they're essential.—AN]*

very hot tip

⚫ *turning hard disks on and off*

You should always turn on your hard disk(s)—and any other peripherals—first, wait until the hard disk is up to speed, and then turn on the Mac. When shutting off the Mac, follow exactly the opposite procedure—first turn off the Mac (by choosing *Shut Down* from the Finder's Special menu), then shut off your hard disk(s) and other peripherals.

important warning

The reason for these procedures is to insulate the Mac from surges caused by turning peripherals on or off. If the Mac is off when you switch a peripheral on or off, it can't be harmed.

SCSI devices

SCSI basics

SCSI is a standard developed by certain computer companies (Apple prominent among them) for connecting hard disks and other devices to computers. It stands for *small computer system interface* and is pronounced *scuzzy.* (It was almost pronounced *sexy,* which is closer to how the letters actually read, but Apple chickened out.)

gossip/ trivia

M ost hard disks are SCSI devices, as are many scanners, CD-ROM drives and some non-PostScript laser printers. Since this is the storage and memory chapter, we'll focus on hard disks, but most of the information in this section applies to any SCSI device.

The Plus was the first Mac to have a **SCSI port** (a place for connecting a SCSI device). All Mac models since then have had at least one external SCSI port plus an internal SCSI connection for a hard disk. (For a chart of what all those ports on the back of a Mac are for, see Appendix B.)

SCSI cables

When you're setting up a SCSI chain, you need the right cable to connect each device to the next. Most SCSI devices have 50-pin connectors, and most Macs have 25-pin connectors (except some PowerBooks, which use a more compact 30-pin connector). So to connect a SCSI device to the Mac, you normally need a cable with a 25- or 30-pin connector at one end and a 50-pin connector at the other (called a **system cable**). To connect one SCSI device to the next, you normally need a 50-pin to 50-pin cable (called a **peripheral cable**).

🍎 rules for SCSI chains

Including the Mac's internal hard drive, you can link up to seven SCSI devices together in a **SCSI chain** connected to the Mac. But there are a couple of rules about how you do this:

RULE #1:
Each device on the chain must have its own SCSI ID number, from 0 to 6. The Mac itself is always assigned ID number 7 and the internal hard disk (if there is one) always gets number 0. If any two SCSI devices have the same num-

important warning

ber, your computer may not start up, or it may crash and possibly even wipe out data on one or more hard disks.

M ost SCSI devices have switches or dials on their back panels that let you

reset their SCSI IDs. A few allow you to set their SCSI ID numbers with software, but this is a terrible idea, because if you crash, it can be very difficult to get to the disk and change its number.

RULE #2:
The devices at both ends of the SCSI chain must be terminated, and none of the devices between them should be. A SCSI **terminator** is a little piece of hardware that keeps signals from echoing back and forth along the cabling, which can cause errors.

S ince internal drives are always first in the chain, they have terminators built in. A few external SCSI devices also have ***built-in terminators***, but more often they come with external terminators.

An ***external terminator*** looks like the

plug at the end of a SCSI cable. SCSI devices have two SCSI sockets, so when you've put a device at the end of a chain, one of the sockets is open. That's where you plug in the external terminator.

(We're assuming the device isn't internally terminated—check its manual to be sure. If a device is internally terminated, put it at one end of the SCSI chain, or have a technician remove the termination.

S ome SCSI devices also have a switch on the outside that lets you turn the internal termination on or off.)

If your Mac has no internal SCSI devices, you need to terminate the first external device in the chain—the one connected directly to the Mac. To do this, you need a ***pass-through*** ⫸

terminator, which goes between the SCSI device and the cable connecting it to the Mac.

EXCEPTIONS TO RULE #2:

According to the engineering department at MicroNet (one of the best hard disk manufacturers), there are some exceptions to the termination rules discussed above. If a SCSI chain is eighteen inches or less, it's generally best to terminate just one end. And if it's more than ten feet (as it usually will be if there are three or more devices in it), it should be terminated in the middle as well as at each end.

The fx is extremely vulnerable to bad termination. You must use the **fx's special black external terminator** at the end of the SCSI chain, and no device in the chain, including the last one, can be internally terminated.

However, if that last device has a 25-pin SCSI socket (like the one on the back of the Mac itself) rather than the more standard 50-pin socket, you're SOL (seriously out of luck).

You need **part number ¿∞#≠*£, the 25-pin fx SCSI terminator**.

It's over there in that bin, right between the sky hooks and the peace dividend.

Can't find it? That's not too surprising, since Apple neglected to make them (they don't make 25-pin terminators for other Mac models either). You'll have to dangle a 25-pin-to-50-pin SCSI cable (or adapter) off the back of the device and attach a 50-pin fx SCSI terminator to that. Not too elegant, but at least it works.

If you've set up your hardware according to the above rules and exceptions, and your Mac still won't work right, see Appendix A.

Floppy disks

⬤ floppy disks and drives

The Mac has used three types of floppy disks, each capable of holding a different amount of information: 400K **single-sided** disks use only one side of the disk; 800K **double-sided** disks use both sides of the disk; 1.4MB **high-density** disks use both sides and pack the information more tightly.

How can you tell these different types of disks apart? 400K and 800K disks look basically the same, but most of the latter are marked *800K* or *Double-sided* on the metal shutter or on the back.

High-density disks are easy to identify. In addition to the *locking hole* (described below) that all Mac disks have in the upper right corner, there's another hole in the upper *left* corner; unlike the locking hole, this left-hand hole has no sliding tab. In addition, high-density disks usually have a stylized *HD* symbol on the metal shutter or in one corner of the disk.

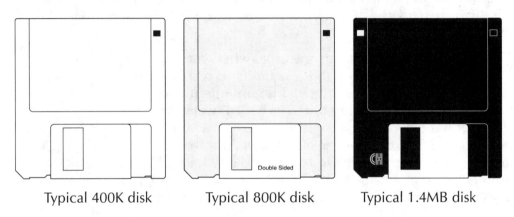

Typical 400K disk   Typical 800K disk   Typical 1.4MB disk

There are three kinds of floppy drives to match the three types of disks. The high-density, 1.4MB drive is called the SuperDrive. The 400K and 800K drives are called simply that.

All floppy drives that come with new Macs are SuperDrives; 800K drives aren't being made any more, but there are still a lot of Macs around that use them (unless they've been upgraded)—the Pluses, some older SE's and original Mac IIs. 400K drives came in the earliest Mac models and are now obsolete; unless you're running a very primitive system, you shouldn't buy a used 400K drive no matter how cheap it is. In fact, we know someone who was offered 20 of them *free* and refused.

Each of these drives can read disks up to its own capacity—so 400K drives can read only 400K disks, 800K drives can read 400K and 800K disks and SuperDrives can read 400K, 800K and 1.4MB disks. (For an exception to this, see the entry below titled *1.4MB disks initialized as 800K.)*

With the help of special software like Apple's Macintosh PC Exchange, Dayna's DOS Mounter or Insignia Solution's Access PC, SuperDrives can also read 3.5-inch floppies from IBM PCs running MS DOS.

⚫ *initializing floppy disks*

All disks, hard or floppy, have to be **initialized** (or **formatted**) before you can use them. When you insert a virgin floppy into a Mac, you get a dialog box that tells you *This is not a Macintosh disk* or *This disk is unreadable:* and asks *Do you want to initialize it?* Simply click either the *Initialize, One-Sided* or *Two-Sided* button. (To abort the process, click the *Eject* button.)

But beware: if you get this message when you insert a disk that already contains data, think before you respond, because initializing will permanently erase the disk's contents (i.e. beyond a recovery program's ability to retrieve it). Try ejecting and reinserting the floppy. If you get the message again, try inserting the disk in someone else's drive. If it works there, your floppy drive may need to be cleaned and/or realigned, or you may have a high-density disk that was formatted in an 800K drive (see below, or see Appendix A for more ideas).

important warning

⚫ *1.4MB disks initialized as 800K*

If you put a high-density floppy into an 800K drive, the Mac will offer to format it (whether or not the disk has already been formatted as a high-density disk). The disk will format as an 800K disk, and will work fine...in other 800K drives. But if you put it in a SuperDrive, you'll get a *This disk is improperly formatted for use in this drive. Do you want to initialize it?* dialog box.

If you need the information from a disk that's been formatted in this way and there's no 800K drive available, you can fool the drive by using tape to cover the hole in the upper left corner of the disk. Consider this a temporary fix only—the tape's bound to come off sooner or later, and Murphy says it will come off in the drive. *[I suggest you only try this in an emergency. Putting tape—or anything that might come off in the drive—on a floppy is just asking for trouble.—RS]*

very hot tip

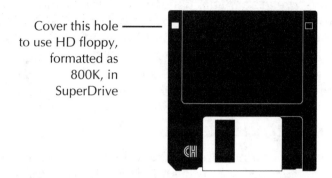

Cover this hole ————
to use HD floppy,
formatted as
800K, in
SuperDrive

important warning

If you don't need the data that's on it, you can try to reformat the disk as a 1.4MB, but since 800K drives use more magnetic power, a SuperDrive won't be able to thoroughly erase the disk and it's likely to be much less reliable. So— ***don't confuse 800K and high-density floppies.***

the paper-clip trick

The tiny round hole to the right

very hot tip

of a floppy drive slot lets you manually eject disks by inserting a straightened-out paper clip and push-

ing firmly. A heavy-duty paper clip is best; you have to feel around for the right place to push.

This is the only way to get a disk out when the computer's off, and it works in *emergency* situations while

your computer's on. But don't try this trick while the drive is working— you may damage the disk.

important warning

floppies with items that are "in use"

Sometimes, when you drag a floppy to the Trash to eject it, you get the message *The disk [disk name] could not be put away, because it contains items that are in use.* This usually happens because a file from the disk was just open, and either it or the application it runs on is still open. Quit any open applications this might apply to and try ejecting again. If the message persists, eject the disk using the Special menu's *Eject Disk* command, and then drag the disk's icon to the Trash.

*very
hot
tip*

locking disks and files

To lock a disk so nothing can be changed on it, and so it can't be erased accidentally, simply slide the little tab in the upper right corner so that the square hole is open.

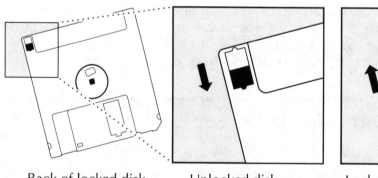

Back of locked disk   Unlocked disk   Locked disk

(In a masterpiece of counterintuitiveness, the disk is **locked** when the hole is *open* and **unlocked** when it's *closed.*) A disk that's locked shows a lock (what else?) in the upper left corner of its window:

It's a good idea to lock all your master program disks. To lock an individual file or application just select its icon, choose *Get Info* from the File menu and check *Locked* in the dialog box that appears.

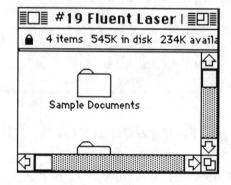

CD-ROMs

CD-ROM drives

CD-ROMs *(compact disk, read-only memory)* are a type of compact disk that stores data; but unlike floppy and hard disks, you can't change what's on them or add your own files—you buy them with data (like artwork, sample programs or fonts) already installed. (The exception is Kodak's PhotoCD technology, which allows photo labs to put your pictures into computer format on a CD-ROM, so you can display them on your screen, or print them. Not all CD-ROM drives are PhotoCD compatible, though.)

There's another little problem—CD-ROMs are *s-l-o-o-o-w.* *very bad feature* Hard disks can usually access a particular piece of information in 5–30 milliseconds (thousandths of a second), but even a fast CD-ROM drive takes about 200 milliseconds.

They store a lot of data, though. Depending on how they're formatted, one CD-ROM can hold about 550–600 *megabytes*, which is equivalent to more than seven hundred 800K disks and well over a quarter of a million typewritten pages. And there's a huge variety of art, movie clips, educational software and useful information available on CD-ROMs.

shopping for a CD-ROM drive

Here are some other things to look for when shopping for a CD-ROM drive:

very hot tip

☞ **Does the drive come with everything you need to run it with a Mac?** Some manufacturers sell the cables, and even—incredibly—the required drive soft-

ware, separately. Make sure the prices you compare include *everything* you need.

☞ **If you're networked with other computers,** ⫸

does the drive include software that lets you share the drive with others on a network, or will you have to buy separate software like DriveShare from Casa Blanca Works.

☞ **How fast is it?** Compare the average access speeds and transfer rates of drives you're considering and if you can, do a test in the store: load a big file, say a HyperCard stack of several megabytes, and time each drive.

☞ **How easy is it to use?** Does it have a power indicator of some kind or do you have to figure out by trial and error whether it's on? Can you set its SCSI address easily?

☞ **Can the drive use Kodak's multi-session PhotoCD technology,** so you can build your own CD-ROM photo album?

☞ **Does it give you ready access to audio CDs?** Many CD-ROM players let you play your music CDs, but most don't have a built-in pre-amp so you need headphones or an external pre-amp between the drive and your speakers.

Some drives have limited volume controls, like a three-level switch (quiet, medium, loud)

instead of the dial you might expect. Some have their own software that lets you select CD audio tracks from your Mac screen; others rely on Apple's CD Remote desk accessory.

☞ **What extras come with the drive, and are they worth it to you?** Does it have two SCSI ports on the back or just one? If just one, it has to be at the end of the chain.

Are there **audio-out** ports that let you connect the player directly to a stereo system? Does it come with sample CD-ROMs or other additional software?

Backing up disks

🍎 *about backups*

There are only two kinds of computer users: those who've lost data and those who are about to. The latter obviously haven't had their computers very long.

Since you're guaranteed to lose data someday, it's prudent to reduce the consequences of that by creating backups of your important files—copying them from the disk they're stored on to some other disk or tape. If you do that often enough, losing data is no big deal. For example, if you back up every ten minutes, you can never lose more than ten minutes' work. You can back up "by hand" (by simply dragging files to another disk) or you can have a backup utility program help you with the job. Either way, it's worth the time and effort.

🍎 *what to back up*

It's good to have at least one or two backups of everything on your hard disk. But once you've done that, all you really need to back up are files that have changed since the last time you did a backup. That generally means documents you're working on—whether they're letters, spreadsheets or databases—*not* applications or old documents that you've got backed up.

You may have also made other changes, like adding a font or control panel to your system or changing a preference in an application. To be sure you get all of these too, you can use the Finder's *Find* command to pick out all the files that were modified since the date of your last backup (for details on using *Find*, see Chapter 7). You can also buy backup utilities that will handle this for you (for more on them, see Chapter 9).

*very
hot
tip*

🍎 *what to back up onto*

In this entry, we assume you're backing up *from* a hard disk. You can back up data onto floppies, another hard disk, a removable cartridge, a tape or a **rewritable optical disk** (a high-capacity floppy-sized disk that needs a special kind of drive).

Floppies are the least expensive, but backing up a full 40-meg hard disk requires about fifty 800K floppies, or thirty high-density ones—just think of the time it will take. And that's if you make only a single copy; if you're really careful, you'll make two backups. And what about files that are too big to fit on one floppy? (One answer is in the next entry.) Of course, you don't have to back up your entire hard disk very often, but if you're regularly backing up large amounts of data, using floppies is tedious and time-consuming.

Removable hard-disk cartridges are probably the most popular backup medium. (For more about them, see the entry called *cartridge drives* in the hard disks section above.)

🍎 *fitting big files onto floppies*

If a file is up to about twice the size of the free space on a floppy disk, you may be able to compress it to a size where it will fit, using a program like Compact Pro (available from user groups and online information services) or StuffIt. If it's bigger than that, you'll need a backup program that's designed to split one file across two or more floppy disks, like Redux, DiskFit Pro, Fastback Plus or Retrospect.

very hot tip

Memory

🍎 *how much memory do you need?*

With today's system software and applications, you'll need at least four megs of RAM. If you want to have a lot of large files and/or applications open at once, you'll need eight megs or more. If you plan to use heavy-duty page layout, graphics or CAD programs, get as much RAM as you can afford.

System 6, and software that came out before System 7 existed, don't need as much memory. With an older Mac on System 6, you can get by with one meg if you use software that's fairly basic (not the latest version of Word or a color graphics program, for example). With MultiFinder, you'll need at least two megs to do anything useful, and you'll probably be happier with four or five.

🍎 *upgrading memory*

As mentioned in Chapter 3, the maximum amount of RAM you can install in a Mac depends on which model it is and what version of the system software you're using.

Macs running System 6 need a special program called Optima (from Connectix) to handle more than eight megs of RAM; even with System 7, the Mac II, IIx, IIcx and SE/30 need a program called Mode32 (available free from Apple dealers, user groups and online services).

RAM comes on little wafers that plug into slots inside the Mac. These wafers (most of which are called **SIMMs,** for *single in-line memory modules)* come in various sizes and types, and not all Macs can use the same types and sizes. The Classics, Centrises and the Mac IIfx all use different types of SIMMs from each other.

RAM chips also vary in their speed, measured in **nanoseconds** (billionths of a second, abbreviated **ns)**; Macs with faster processors require faster RAM. So when you buy RAM, be sure to tell the vendor what Mac you're using, so they'll give you the right type of upgrade.

On most modular Macs, it's fairly easy to install SIMMs yourself, if you've got steady hands and nerves. On most compact Macs, it's a bit dicier, and you need a special screwdriver to open the case (a **Torx T-15** with an extra-long shaft).

If you want to install your own RAM (which will save you money),buy your memory

bargain

from a vendor (like TechWorks, in Texas) that will include an instruction book and screwdriver with your order.

A Mac's maximum RAM depends on what kind of SIMMs it can use and how many SIMM sockets it has (some models have from one to eight megs of RAM soldered into place).

Manufacturers keep cramming more and more RAM onto memory chips; as of this writing, a single SIMM can have as much as 32 megs of RAM on it. (The more memory a SIMM contains, the **denser** we say it is.)

The PowerBooks don't use SIMMs at all; they only contain one slot, into which you can plug a memory upgrade card of up to 10MB (20MB for Duos) to add to the four megs that are soldered in.

If you've upgraded your RAM to more than eight megs, be sure to turn on the **32-bit addressing** option in the Memory control panel (select *Control Panels* from the menu, double-click the Memory icon, click the appropriate radio button and restart your Mac). ⌦➡

Without 32-bit addressing, your Mac won't be able to access all the memory you've installed.

But beware: some software (particularly programs from before 1991) don't work with 32-bit addressing on.

So if you find your Mac acting strangely when you use a certain program, and the problem goes away when you

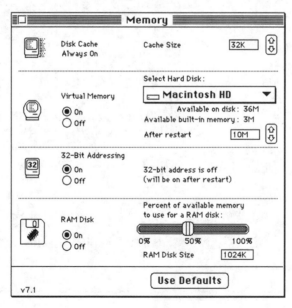

important warning

turn off 32-bit addressing, consider upgrading to a more recent version of the program.

(Before you buy it, ask the manufacturer if it's **32-bit clean**.)

RAM disks

A **RAM disk** is a portion of memory that's set aside to act as a temporary disk. With System 7.1 or later, you can create a RAM disk using the Memory control panel (shown below). Just click the *On* button in the RAM disk area and use the slider bar to adjust its size, then restart. It will appear as an icon on your desktop, and you can use it as you would any other disk, but when you shut off your computer, everything in the RAM disk disappears.

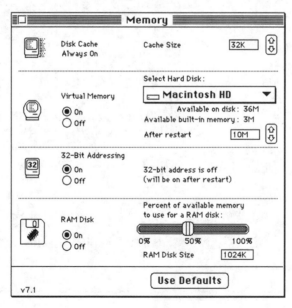

So what good is it? Well, what's stored on a RAM disk can be retrieved a lot faster than what's stored on a disk. Put an application there and you'll notice that virtually all its operations speed up. Put your System and Finder there and all the things they do will speed up.

shortcut

If you're not using System 7.1, you can get RAM disk utilities from user groups, bulletin boards and commercial information services.

🍎 *virtual memory*

Virtual memory is sort of the opposite of a RAM disk—it's a technique that lets the computer use part of the hard disk as if it were RAM. Portions of large files or programs get swapped from RAM to the virtual memory section of the disk and back again as needed. Virtual memory is useful for large graphics, long animations, complex sounds, lots of scanning and keeping a lot of files open at the same time.

Because virtual "memory" is actually on disk, it's a lot slower than real RAM. But it's also a lot cheaper (the bigger the drive, the cheaper it tends to be).

bargain

A s with a RAM disk, you turn virtual memory on in the Memory control panel (shown on the previous page). Choose the hard disk you want from a pop-up menu, click the arrows in the After Restart window to set the amount of memory, close the control panel and restart your Mac. However much virtual memory you request, the Mac takes twice that amount of disk space, and it's limited by the amount of physical RAM you have.

Virtual memory works best when you use it to run one program and one big file rather than a lot of smaller programs or files. *[In my experience, virtual memory slows things down considerably, particularly on faster Macs, and it makes a huge impact on the Plus, which has a slow SCSI port. Unless you're flat broke, buying more RAM is a better choice.—RS]*

*very
hot
tip*

Older Macs with 68000 or 68020 processors (except Mac IIs with a PMMU upgrade) can't use System 7's virtual memory (there are third-party alternatives that work with System 6, like Connectix' Virtual 3.0).

Printer basics

● *types of printers*

Three types of printers are commonly used with Macs—*dot-matrix*, *inkjet* and *laser*. You can also output from a Mac directly to an *imagesetter*.

Dot-matrix printers (like Apple's ImageWriters) usually form characters and images out of a pattern of dots made by pins pushing an inked ribbon against the paper (although there are other ways of producing the image). The quality of the output varies according to the number of pins used (a 24-pin printer's output is better than a 9-pin printer's), but it's generally inferior to the ouput of the other printer types discussed here, and they tend to be noisy and slow. Their main advantage is that the impact of the pins lets you make multiple copies using carbon or NCR paper.

very bad feature

Like dot-matrix printers, *inkjet printers* form characters out of little dots, but because the dots are created by tiny jets of ink, they're more like splotches, and blend together much more than the dots produced by dot-matrix printers.

Inkjets are also much quieter and somewhat faster than dot-matrix printers, and usually produce higher quality output. Apple's StyleWriter II and Hewlett-Packard's DeskWriter are two inkjet printers that are compatible with the Mac.

very good feature

Laser printers (like Apple's LaserWriters) create images by drawing them on a metal drum with a beam of laser light. The image is then made visible by electrostatically attracting dry ink powder (called *toner*) to it, as in a photocopying machine. The toner is then bonded (*fused*) to the paper by heat and pressure. Laser printers are more expensive than dot-matrix or inkjet printers, but their output is generally superior.

Imagesetters are digital typesetting machines; unlike traditional typesetters, they can produce graphics as well as text. These high-end machines output onto film or the kind of photosensitive paper used for photostats.

🍎 *relative resolutions*

It's primarily a printer's **resolution,** measured in dots per inch *(dpi)* that determines how clear and sharp its output will look. At best quality, an ImageWriter prints at 160 dpi across and 144 down, which gives you about 23,000 dots per square inch *(dpsi)*.

HP's DeskWriter inkjet printer produces 300 x 300 dots per inch, which gives you 90,000 dots per square inch—about four times the ImageWriter's resolution—and Apple's StyleWriter inkjet produces 360 x 360 dpi, which gives you almost 130,000 dpsi—about six times the ImageWriter's resolution.

Different laser printers print at anywhere from 300 x 300 dpi to 1200 x 600 dpi, so that, at the high end, they provide more than five times the resolution of the best inkjets. Some laser printers also offer various forms of **enhanced resolution**, which smooths jagged edges and/or sharpens grayscales to give the appearance of higher-dpi output.

But even laser printers' output doesn't compare to what a high-end imagesetter can do. For example, the 3386-dpi Linotronic 330 produces output that's more than 125 times a standard laser printer's resolution and almost 500 times the ImageWriter's.

🍎 *PostScript vs. non-PostScript*

There are two basic kinds of laser printers—those that have PostScript built in and those that don't.

(PostScript is a page-description programming language used by many laser printers and imagesetters, a few inkjets and no dot-matrix printers.)

You pay more for a PostScript printer, and here's what you get:

☞ PostScript printers can be shared by Macs on a network without having to funnel everyone's print jobs through one "host" Mac.

☞ Only PostScript printers can print PostScript graphics like those produced by Illustrator and FreeHand.

(Well... you can buy PostScript interpreters for other printers, but you'd be better ▥➡

off getting a PostScript printer if you're going to do that kind of work.)

very hot tip

☞ They print crisp, clear PostScript outline fonts without needing a special utility called ATM.

This is less of an advantage now that

there are plenty of TrueType fonts available, and you can get ATM for free.

(For more on PostScript and TrueType fonts and ATM, see Chapter 8.)

Printing tips

🍎 *the Chooser*

The first time you print something, you have to tell the Mac what printer you're using. You do that by selecting **Chooser** from the 🍎 menu and clicking on the icon of the printer you want to use (you're actually selecting a printer *driver*, not a printer—see *printer drivers* below for details).

If you click on the Laser-Writer icon, a list of available Laser-Writers will appear in the list box (as shown at the right). Just

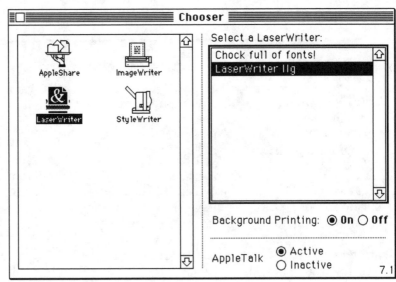

click on the printer you want (even if there's only one on the list).

If you click on the ImageWriter or Style-Writer icon, the Chooser will ask you if the printer is connected to the printer port

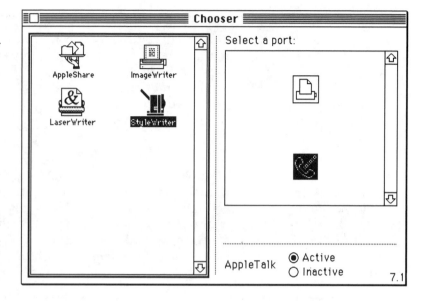

or the modem port (as shown above). Just select the correct port's icon.

● *printer drivers*

When you select a printer's icon in the Chooser, you're really selecting a **printer driver**. Drivers are programs that tell the Mac how to communicate with your printer, and generate the Page Setup and Print dialog boxes that appear when you select those commands from the File menu. Without them, each application woud have to contain information about every type of printer you might use.

The drivers for Apple's printers come with the system software and are named after the printers they're designed for (e.g. ImageWriter, StyleWriter and Laser-Writer). Some third-party printers have their own drivers, although many are designed to use Apple's drivers.

Sometimes a single driver works for several related printers. For example, Apple's LaserWriter driver works ▐▐▐▶

for all seven PostScript Laser-Writers (the Personal LaserWriter LS and Select 300 aren't PostScript printers and have their own drivers).

Printer drivers go in the Extensions folder in your System Folder; if you drag them onto the System Folder icon (not the window), the

Finder will put them in the Extensions folder automatically. (In System 6, printer drivers go in the System Folder, but not into any folder within it.)

Apple's printer drivers usually get updated along with other system software, so make sure you replace them

when you upgrade your System.

You can find the version of the printer driver you've selected in the Chooser by looking in the Page Setup or Print dialog box of any application; the number is just to the left of the *OK* button. Or you can simply Get Info on any printer driver icon from the desktop.

Page Setup

Different printers offer you different kinds of control over your print-out. The printer driver generates a basic set of options, and applications add others. All of the options show up in the Page Setup and Print dialog boxes that appear when you choose those commands from the File menu.

Different kinds of printers also use different print areas on the page—so when you use the Chooser to switch to a different type of printer—from a StyleWriter to a LaserWriter, say—you'll get a message telling you to select *Page Setup...* in any open applications. (Actually, you should only do this when you're in the document(s) you want to print on the selected printer.)

After you click *OK* in the Page Setup dialog box (you don't have to change any settings) you may notice your document looks different on the screen. Changing printer drivers often changes line breaks, page breaks and the like, so if you're printing drafts on a dot-matrix or inkjet

important warning

printer and printing final output on a laser printer, don't spend time arranging your document's page formatting until after you've selected the laser printer in the Chooser and selected *Page Setup...* from the File menu.

R eader Choong Han Chu told us a way to make one of those transitions a lot smoother if you're proofing on an ImageWriter—just select the *Tall Adjusted* option in the ImageWriter's Page Setup box before you start your work. This option gives you the same margins you get using the LaserWriter driver, so your ImageWriter drafts will match your final LaserWriter output.

very hot tip

🍎 *printing in the background*

Macs can send out information to printers much faster than printers can receive and process it, so the computer is tied up in the printing process much longer than is really necessary. A print **spooler** is a program that creates a special print file on disk that then gets fed out to the printer in chunks, at a rate the printer can handle. Since the Mac creates this print file quite quickly, you can get back to work and leave the computer and the printer to talk to each other in the background. *(***Spool** *is an acronym for simultaneous print operations online.)*

shortcut

K eep in mind that you need enough room on your disk to hold the print file (it will be at least the size of the document you're print-ing). On some Macs, the other work you're doing will be periodically interrupted as the print file is fed to the printer. If your Mac is fairly slow, you may find it less frustrating to just take a break during print-ing than to deal with a computer that ignores you for up to a full minute out of every three or four.

Backgrounder is a good print spooler for the StyleWriter and LaserWriters that comes with the Mac's system software; it works with System 7 and System 6's MultiFinder. (To use it with the StyleWriter, you need a StyleWriter driver that's more recent than version 1.0.)

Backgrounder works with **PrintMonitor**, a utility that keeps track of what document's being printed, how many pages are left to go, what other documents are waiting to be printed, etc. On a network, it will also tell you whose document is being printed and what other documents are in line to be printed.

P rintMonitor has another nice feature: when the printer needs attention (because it's out of paper, say), PrintMonitor flashes its icon in the upper-right corner of the screen, alternating it with the Application menu icon. (In System 6, it does the same with the menu icon in the upper-left corner of the screen.)

very good feature

To use Backgrounder, put it and PrintMonitor in your System Folder. Then go to the Chooser, select the LaserWriter or StyleWriter icon, and turn Background Printing on.

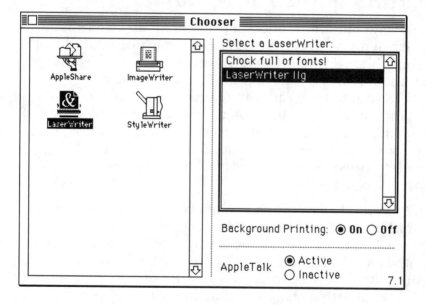

M any people will have both a third-party print spooler and Backgrounder running at the same time! Amazingly enough, this often works, but it costs you time, since everything is done twice. And it can cause problems, like locking up your Mac.

important warning

To give you an idea of how much more quickly a spooler gives you back the use of your Mac, we did a test. It took

SuperLaserSpool (a non-Apple spooler) two minutes to read a 27-page PageMaker file onto the disk, and another twenty minutes to actually print the file out. The eighteen-minute difference is time you get to work on the Mac that you otherwise wouldn't have.

¢ *cancelling printing*

When you print, a dialog box like this one below appears on the screen. Each application has its own kind (this one is from Nisus) and not all tell you which page is being printed. There's usually a *Cancel* button, but even if there isn't, **you can almost always cancel printing with** ⌘. , or sometimes the Esc or accent grave (`) key.

> **Press and hold "⌘." to cancel printing.**
> **Printing page 1 of 73.**

Don't expect instant compliance with your cancel command. If you've asked for 100 copies of a document, cancelling the print job won't stop a LaserWriter from spewing out 100 copies of the page it's working on. The only way you can stop it is by shutting the printer off.

important warning

very hot tip

Whatever the situation, remember: turning the printer off in the middle of printing isn't going to hurt anything. At worst, a LaserWriter will have a half-fed sheet of paper inside; if it does, just open the case and pull it out.

¢ *unclogging ink cartridges*

Sometimes ink clogs some of the fine holes in inkjet printheads, so you see blank stripes in whatever you're printing. To clear the holes, you can try pressing the Prime button on the DeskWriter, but that doesn't always work—and it shortens the life of the cartridge.

important warning

Instead, try printing a heavily inked page one or more times. You can make a suitable page to print by going into a graphics program, drawing a box that fills a whole page, and filling it with black (or a dark pattern).

paper for crisper print quality

If you look closely at an inkjet printer's output, you'll notice that the ink spreads a bit into the fibers of the paper, creating a fuzzy edge around everything. You can reduce this by using the right paper.

W hat's the right paper? To some extent, that depends on the printer and the kind of ink you use. See what the printer manufacturer recommends, and experiment.

If you're willing to pay for it, clay-coated paper made specifically for inkjets will give you the best results. It virtually eliminates spread, making output from an inkjet almost as crisp as a laser printer's.

*very
hot
tip*

naming your printer

The LaserWriter Utility program (it comes with LaserWriters) lets you name your printer anything you like. (The name appears in the Chooser desk accessory when you select the LaserWriter driver icon.) Renaming LaserWriters (they start out as *LaserWriter Pro 600* or whatever) is possible at any time, but it's absolutely necessary on a network that has more than one LaserWriter. Otherwise, your printout might end up in another room, on another floor, or even in another building.

LaserWriter Page Setup options

The LaserWriter driver gives you a number of useful features in the Page Setup dialog box. One of these is **Faster Bitmap Printing**, which preprocesses bit-mapped images before they're sent to the LaserWriter. Apple states that "in rare cases, some documents may not print with this option turned on," but we've never experienced that. If it happens to you, just turn the option off and try again.

The **Graphics Smoothing** or **Smoothing Bitmap** option removes some of the jagged look bit-mapped graphics might otherwise have—for example, the stair-step effect around curves turns into a slightly squiggly line. This option is only for Apple's LaserWriters, not for other brands of PostScript printers. Some programs (like Page-Maker) have smoothing routines of their own that work on all PostScript printers.

Clicking on the *Options* button gives you several additional choices. (The **dogcow**—a beast of indeterminate species—demonstrates the effect of each option as you select it.) For example, you can flip the

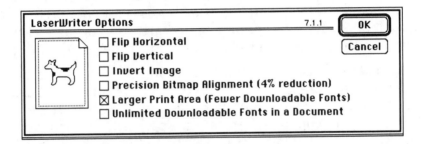

entire image on the page vertically or horizontally, or "invert" it (change whites to blacks and blacks to whites).

Precision Bitmap Alignment improves bit-mapped graphics by reducing the entire image on the page to 96% of its normal size. This gets around the incompatibility between the 72 dots per inch of the Mac's screen and the 300 dots per inch of the LaserWriter's output (300 divided by 72 is 4.1666, but 96% of 300 is 288, into which 72 goes exactly 4 times).

There's a neat trick that avoids having to reduce the whole document—just enlarge the graphic to 104% of its original size (of course this only works in documents that give you that precision). But be aware that neither this approach or *Precision Bitmap Alignment* will work if the graphic has already been reduced or enlarged from its original size.

*very
hot
tip*

Larger Print Area lets you cover more of the page. It tells you that the trade-off is fewer downloadable fonts, but even a font maniac like Arthur virtually never runs into that limit (and he virtually always checks that box).

⚫ *suppressing the LaserWriter's startup page*

Every time you turn on the LaserWriter, it spits out a rather attractive test page that tells you how many copies have ever been printed on the machine. While it's possible to get into this constantly mounting total as a measure of your productivity (and therefore your general worth as a human being: *I've printed 3217 pages on my LaserWriter—I must be doing something useful with my life*), it does cost you about 3¢ in toner, some fraction of a cent in paper and some hard-to-figure but probably significant amount of wear-and-tear on the machine.

So it's sometimes nice to be able to turn off the startup page, at least for a while. The easiest way to do that is to use the Laser-Writer Utility program (if you can't find the one you got with your LaserWriter, you can copy it for free at an Apple dealer). With your printer selected in the Chooser, start up the program, select *Set Startup Page...* from the Utilities menu, and click the *Off* button.

Hardware buying tips

This chapter was written by Arthur Naiman.

As with a car, the three most important things to look for in a piece of computer hardware are: whether it can do what you want it to do; how reliable it is; and (with a nod to Commandment IX) how easy it is to get it fixed.

One way to maximize your chances of getting a reliable (and repairable) piece of hardware is to buy from a company with a commitment to quality. Granted, that commitment can evaporate like the morning dew—and has, many times—but you still stand a better chance from a company that's had it in the past than from one that hasn't.

◢ *don't get mad—get even*

It's astounding how little some companies care about their customers. We could give you several examples of this, but it doesn't seem fair to single out just a few companies when there are so many bad ones.

If you do get screwed, don't waste a lot of time writing long letters. If people don't treat you decently, it's usually because they aren't decent, and your heart-wrenching appeals are going to fall on deaf ears and hearts of stone.

Make a few, good-faith efforts to get them to do what they're supposed to, then go *directly* to Small Claims Court. *(DO NOT PASS GO. DO COLLECT $200+.)* Marshals seizing their office equipment—that's the kind of thing these companies understand. (For how to do it, see *Everybody's Guide to Small Claims Court* from Nolo Press.)

very hot tip

◢ *some good guys*

On the bright side, there are a lot of excellent, caring, moral companies. For example, we've had great experiences at Goldstein & Blair with APS of Independence, Missouri. Because their prices are often the lowest around, we've bought several hard drives from them.

bargain

One drive we reshipped to an employee who worked in an outlying office. Although the drive worked at our office, it was broken when it got to her. She called APS and was immediately impressed with their competence on the phone. She was even more impressed with their service: in spite of the fact that we had reshipped

very good feature

the drive, they sent her a replacement drive overnight, at no cost. The morning after she called, she had the new drive.

APS didn't even ask her to return the old drive until she got the new one. (We should mention that the people she dealt with at APS had no idea who we were or that they could get some good publicity out of this. They thought we were just another customer.)

MacConnection keeps blowing people's socks off with the speed with which they ship orders. ComputerWare has a reputation for being very knowledgeable and great to deal with.

---

what to look for

First, look for a good long warranty—at least a year. Lots of companies offer two-year, three-year or even five-year warranties. (Of course these companies may not be around in five years, or even two, and that's definitely something else to consider.)

Another important consideration is good support. You want to buy from a vendor who will answer any questions and deal with any problems that come up, and who will make you feel like a colleague, not an annoying pest, while doing so.

Last—but not, needless to say, least—is price. How important it is depends on your budget, of course, but let me say this: Don't underestimate the Mac's importance in your life. This is not some trivial plaything—this is a very powerful tool for personal expression.

If you *want* something—a laser printer instead of a dot-matrix printer, say, or a big screen instead of a nine-inch one—you'll usually be happier if you figure out some way to justify having it.

We've seldom if ever heard anyone say, "I really shouldn't have bought this [expensive piece of computer equipment]. I really could have gotten by with [something simpler and less expensive]."

But we can't count the number of times we've heard people who've gotten some powerful new piece of hardware say, "How did I live without this?"

❡ *don't do today what you can put off till tomorrow*

On the other hand, don't buy something you plan to grow into; by the time you grow into it, you'll be able to buy something better for less. There's one exception to this rule: If you're about to buy your first hard disk, get twice as much capacity as you think you'll need. You'll fill it up before you know it.

very hot tip

It is possible to outsmart this rule, if you really jump in size. For example, when Arthur went from 144 megs to 315 megs, it took him a long time to fill up the new disk. But there's also an exception to this exception to the exception. If you start dealing with lots of TIFF files (typically from scanners), especially color TIFFs, virtually no disk is going to be big enough.

One person we know who does that kind of work bought a *1.2-gigabyte* drive. He said he never wanted to get a *disk full* message again. But he already has, just a few months after he got the disk. We also know a service bureau that works with hundreds and hundreds of scans. They have *two* 1.2-gigabyte drives and are always backing up onto cartridges and tape to make room on the disks.

Anyway—because computer technology is still on the steep upslope of its growth curve, technological advances that provide more power for less money have (so far) always greatly outstripped increasing material and labor costs. Sometimes prices go down a lot and sometimes they go down a little, but they almost always go down.

❡ *don't put off till tomorrow what you can do today*

Since prices are always falling, people will sometimes advise you to wait and buy later, when whatever you're buying will cost you less. This advice doesn't always make sense. For one thing, if you followed it faithfully, you'd never buy anything. For another, it fails to consider the value of owning and using the equipment, which, in our experience, has almost always outweighed whatever money we might have saved waiting for tomorrow's lower price.

So, if you have a use for something right now, and you want it, do without the new car—the Mac is more fun.

Part Three

Software

Basic Mac software

Tips for all applications

The tips in this section should work in virtually all Macintosh programs, from the Finder to obscure DA's. Don't blame us if they don't—blame the people who wrote the program, because they didn't follow the standard Mac interface.

basic terms

The entries in this chapter assume you understand the material in Chapter 2. If you have trouble with any of the terms or concepts here, either look them up in the glossary or index, or read *Learning the Mac* first.

escaping from hang-ups

In System 7, [Option][⌘][Esc] will usually free you from an application that's hung up, without your having to restart the computer. (This is almost reason enough all by itself to use System 7.)

very good feature

selecting multiple items

As mentioned in Chapter 2, shift-clicking lets you select more than one object at a time. It acts as a toggle—not only do things that aren't selected get selected, but things that *are* selected get *de*selected when you [Shift]-click on them.

You can also select multiple objects by dragging a selection rectangle around them (also described in Chapter 2), and you can combine the two techniques. For example, if objects you don't want fall into the selection rectangle and get selected, just [Shift]-click on them and they'll be deselected. Here's another way to combine them:

Let's say you have a single icon selected in a desktop window. If you hold down [Shift] while you drag a rectangle around four other icons, you'll have five icons selected when you're done. It also works the other way. If you have ten icons selected in a desktop window and then hold down [Shift] while you drag a rectangle around four of them, they'll deselect and you'll end up with six icons selected.

All these techniques work the same way in object-oriented graphics programs ("draw" programs) as they do on the desktop. (They don't work in paint programs because there are no objects to [Shift]-click on.)

[Shift]-clicking can also be used to select portions of continuous material like text. Let's say you want to select three paragraphs of a word processing document. You'd click in front of the first character in the first paragraph, then place the I-beam pointer after the last character of the third paragraph, hold the [Shift] key down and click again. This causes everything between the two clicks—all three paragraphs, in this case—to be selected. (Some word processors have easier ways to select a lot of text, but this basic technique should work in all of them.)

Some of these techniques may be a little hard to visualize, but when you use them a bit, they'll quickly become obvious, and then automatic.

◆ the double-click drag

To select text word-by-word, double-click on the first word and drag. The selection will be extended one word at a time.

very hot tip

◆ taking screen shots

You can capture anything that appears on your Mac's screen at virtually any moment by pressing [Shift][⌘][3]. You'll hear a sound like a camera shutter clicking and a file called *Picture 1* will appear in your hard disk's window in the Finder (if there's already a *Picture 1* file, it'll be called *Picture 2*, and so on). In System 6, there's no sound when you take the shot and the files are called *Screen 0, Screen 1*, etc.

very hot tip

Tips on icons, files and folders

🍎 *finding files and folders*

If you're not sure where a file or folder is on a disk, you can find it using the *Find* command on the File menu in the Finder. Just type the item's name (or as much of it as you can remember) into the Find dialog box and click the *Find* button.

There may be several items on disk whose names contain what you typed into the dialog box (which is called the *search string)*. If the first item that's found isn't the one you wanted, use the *Find again* command (⌘G) to search for the next one and so on.

Even if you know where a file is, the *Find* command can help you get to it faster than you could by manually opening all the folders that enclose it. And it only opens the folder that actually contains the item you're looking for, rather than littering your screen with the windows of all the folders enclosing it.

If you click the *More Choices* button, a larger window opens (like the one below); it lets you look for a file by many other criteria than just its name. For example, if you can't remember what a document is called but know it's one of a handful that you've worked on in the last

---

Find

Find and select items whose

| date modified ▼ | is after ▼ | 8/**12**/92 ⬍ |

Search | on "Macintosh HD" ▼ | ☐ all at once

[Fewer Choices]   [Cancel]   [**Find**]

few days, you can search for all the files whose modified dates are within that period.

Y ou can also narrow the search to a specific disk, folder or set of folders, or have the Mac display all the found files at once instead of using the Find again command. But we've found narrowed searches to be unreliable, and the *all at once* option can only display a limited number of items if they're in different folders (System 6's Find File DA handles this better). Third-party programs like DiskTop do a better job at both of these tasks.

bug

 *aliases*

Aliases are one of System 7's most useful innovations. An alias is a copy of an item's icon that looks just like the item itself but is

very good feature

really just a remote control; when you double-click on the alias, you open the original.

Y ou can make aliases of documents, applications, folders, even shared files on other computers. And since an alias isn't an actual copy, but just a

remote control, it only takes up about one K on disk, even though it may represent a file or application that's several megs in size.

M aking an alias is simple: you just select an item and then choose *Make Alias* from the File menu. The alias will appear next to the original, with its name in italics. You can then rename it or move it anywhere you want (the name stays in italics, though).

You can move or rename the original too, and the alias will usually keep track of where it went and

what it's called. (Obviously, the original has to be somewhere accessible to your Mac, or it won't be able to open it.)

You can make more than one alias for an item, and put them wherever they'll be handy. Since the  menu is almost always accessible, many people put aliases there.

E ven the system software does that, since the *Control Panels* command on the  menu is nothing more than an alias for the Control Panels folder in the System Folder.

⌘ using aliases

You can't always keep applications out on the desktop or in your main hard disk window, because they often demand folders of their own, containing dictionaries and other kinds of support files. But you can still access them easily through aliases.

shortcut

For example, you might have the Word application file inside a Word folder inside a Word Processing folder inside an Applications folder; but you can launch it without having to dig through all those folders by putting an alias of it on the ⌘ menu or out on the desktop.

What's good for applications is good for folders or documents too. So *if you*

frequently go back and forth between two folders, put an alias of each inside the other.

You can also make aliases for the Trash, so you don't have to hunt for it under open windows. Put Trash aliases inside any of the folders you use frequently, and you can just drag files into the Trash alias when you're in that folder window.

⌘ naming and renaming icons

When you create a new item in the Finder—either a new folder with ⌘N, an alias using *Make Alias*, or a copy of a file or folder with ⌘D—the new item's name is automatically selected; to rename it, just begin typing.

To rename an existing item in System 7, you have to click on its name and wait for a box to appear around it. You can minimize this wait by going into the Mouse control panel and setting the double-click speed to its fastest—that's what the delay is based on. Or, if the item is already selected, you can select its name immediately by pressing Return or Enter. When you've renamed the icon, press Return or Enter again to deselect the name.

If you rename an icon and change your mind while the icon is still selected, you can use the *Undo* command (⌘Z) to revert to the original name.

● *dragging duplicates*

To move a *copy* of a file to a different place on the
same disk (instead of moving the file itself) hold [Option]
while you drag it; the copy appears in the new spot
with the same name as the original—without *copy*
tacked on the end, as happens when you use [⌘D] to
copy a file. (We mentioned this in Chapter 2, but
thought it was worth repeating here.)

*very
hot
tip*

Tips on windows

● *pop-down folder hierarchy*

If you've got a folder's window open on the desktop, there's an easy way
to find out where it is in the hierarchy of folders on your
disk. Just hold down [⌘] and click down on the window's
name in the title bar. A pop-down menu like the one
below will appear, showing all the folders that contain the
open one. (This only works for the active window, so if the
window you're interested in isn't active, you have to click on it first.)

shortcut

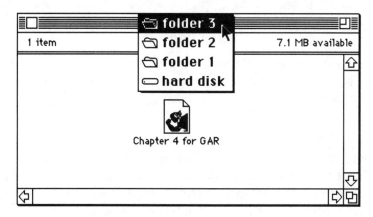

You can open any of the folders on the menu simply by selecting its
name. If you hold down [Option] while you do this, the first window will
close as the second opens.)

🍎 *hiding and seeking application windows*

System 7 offers several ways to hide application windows without actually closing them. To see what's behind the windows of the application you're currently using, select *Hide [application name]* at the top of the Application menu (the one at the right end of the menu bar—an example is shown below) and all the windows for that program will disappear. The command's name changes to show the active application's name (in the menu below, for example, Word is active).

very good feature

Hide Microsoft Word
Hide Others
Show All

![CEIAC icon] **CEIAC**
![Finder icon] **Finder**
✓![Word icon] **Microsoft Word**

If you want to hide the windows behind a document you're working on, select *Hide others*; the windows in the Finder and all other open applications will disappear, so you can focus on the file you're working on.

When you're switching between applications (including the Finder), holding down Option as you select the next application you're moving to will hide the windows of the application you're leaving.

To bring back a particular application's hidden windows, just select its name from the Application menu. To bring back all the hidden applications' windows, select *Show All.*

Hidden windows are still open, they're just not visible. So when you bring them back, they all reappear just as they were before being hidden, but much faster than if you'd actually closed them.

🍎 *using labels*

System 7 lets you attach labels to files and folders, so you can identify all the ones that belong to a particular project or that share some status the Mac wouldn't normally recognize. For example, people sharing a Mac can label their files with their own names to keep track of what's whose.

To give a file or folder a label, select it in the Finder and then choose a name from the Label menu. If you've got a color monitor, each label has its own color, which also gets applied to the selected item. You can change the names and colors to whatever you want in the Labels control panel.

When you choose *by Label* from the View menu, items in the active window are sorted according to the order their labels appear on the Label menu, not by the labels' alphabetical order. For example, if the top label on the menu is *Hot* and the bottom label is *Archive,* items with the Hot label will be sorted before items with the Archive label.

Misc. desktop tips

⌘ turning off the Trash warning

Normally, when you try to empty the Trash, you're asked if you're sure you want to do that; if you find this tiresome, you'll be happy to know that you can disable this dialog box. To do that, select the Trash icon, hit ⌘I and uncheck the *Warn before emptying* checkbox in the Get Info window that appears.

In System 6, you get warnings when you drag applications or system software files to the Trash and if you try to empty the Trash when it contains these items. To disable these warnings, hold down the Option key when you drag the items to the Trash or when you empty it.

*very
hot
tip*

⌘ escaping switch-disks nightmares

To escape from one of those interminable switch-disks nightmares (the kind that make you want to scream at your Mac, *You want that disk again? There's something sick about your obsession with that disk!),* press ⌘.. Sometimes you have to press it more than once and sometimes it won't work at all, but it's worth trying.

*very
hot
tip*

⌘ *finding Finder shortcuts*

There are a lot of very handy shortcuts in the Finder, and System 7 makes it easy to keep track of them. For a list, select *Finder Shortcuts* from the Help menu in the Finder.

The System Folder

⌘ *system software*

When you first buy a computer, it's the hardware that gets all the attention. But what really makes the Mac what it is—an easy-to-use and highly customizable personal computer—is the *system software.* Part of this basic software is written indelibly into your Mac's ROM; you never see it and can't modify it, short of buying a hardware upgrade.

The rest—the part you can control—is provided by the various programs that come with the Mac and are stored in the System Folder on the startup disk (the hard disk or floppy your Mac starts up from when you turn it on, and whose icon always appears in the upper right corner of the desktop).

⌘ *System 7 and System 6*

The Mac's system software has gone through many versions over the years—the latest is System 7, which comes with all new Macs. But there are still plenty of older Macs out there using its predecessor, System 6. Most older Macs can run System 7 (or can be upgraded to use it) but few current Macs can run System 6 (if any, by the time you read this).

System 7 and System 6 are major versions of the system software, each of which has gone through several minor versions that fixed bugs or added features (for example, System 6 went from 6.0 through 6.0.8). But to keep things simple, we refer to System 6 and System 7, unless we're discussing some feature or problem that's in System 7.0 (say) but not in 7.0.1 or 7.1.

Except where noted, the information in this chapter refers to System 7 (although much of it applies to both versions). See the end of the chapter for tips that apply only to System 6.

🍎 what System are you running?

To find out which System version your Mac is running, go to the Finder and look on the 🍎 menu—under System 7, the first item is *About This Macintosh...*; under System 6, it's *About The Finder....* Select whichever of these is on your Mac and a window will appear that tells you the exact System version.

🍎 System Folder basics

It's easy to recognize the System Folder's icon, because it has a little picture of a Mac on it:

You can rename the System Folder whatever you want; it just has to contain the *System,* the *Finder* and, on Macs introduced since Fall 1992, the *System Enabler.* Without these files—which must be the right versions to work with the particular Mac and each other—the Mac won't be able to start up normally and create the desktop, where you can open and use programs and documents.

Of course, normally a System Folder contains much more than these three files, so in System 7, it organizes the other system software into folders according to their different types. Here's what some of the other types of files do:

☞ **drivers**—These programs allow the Mac to communicate with peripherals like printers; examples are the StyleWriter and LaserWriter files. System 7 puts drivers in the Extensions folder and lists them as ***Chooser extensions*** in the Kind column when you view the Extensions folder's contents by name. In System 6, they're listed as ***Chooser documents*** or simply ***documents.***

☞ **extensions** (called **inits** under System 6)—These programs run automatically when you start the Mac, and keep running invisibly in the background until you shut down. System 7 places them in a folder called

Extensions and they're listed as *system extensions* when you view that folder by name. System 6 lists them as *Startup documents.*

☞ **control panels** (called **cdevs** under System 6)—These utility programs let you do things like set the volume level on the Mac's speaker, create a new desktop pattern or establish file sharing with other networked Macs. System 7 stores control panels in the Control Panels folder, and lists them as *control panels* in the Kind column. System 6 calls them *Control Panel documents* or simply *documents*.

☞ **printer font files**—These are the outline fonts that get downloaded to printers (typically PostScript printers; see Chapter 8 for more about them). System 7.0 and 7.0.1 store them in the Extensions folder and call them *system extensions;* System 7.1 (sensibly) keeps them in its Fonts folder and calls them fonts; under System 6 they're called *documents.*

☞ **suitcase files**—Inside System 7.1's Fonts folder are suitcase files, which store TrueType and bit-mapped fonts and open like a folder when you double-click them. Desk accessories and sounds are sometimes kept in suitcases, too.

Some programs put their own files in the System Folder when you install or use them. These support files include *temp files*, which applications create to store information while you're working, and *preferences files*, which keep track of your preferred settings, like Short or Full menus in Word—these normally go in the Preferences folder.

Besides the Control Panels, Extensions, Fonts and Preferences folders mentioned above, the System Folder contains three other folders:

☞ **The Apple Menu Items folder** stores the items that appear on the menu. You can put any DA, document, application or folder you want on the Apple menu by dragging it into this folder. Some of the items that come with the system software are described in the section about the menu below.

☞ **The PrintMonitor Documents folder** stores the temp files that are created when you print a document using *background printing* (described in Chapter 5). PrintMonitor puts files that are to be printed into this folder, and they're automatically fed from there to your printer.

☞ If you want a program or document opened automatically when your Mac starts up (as long as there's enough memory), just put it in **the Startup Items folder.**

🍎 installing system files

(This entry is about adding files like those described above to an existing System Folder. To install the System Folder itself, see *installing a new system* at the end of this section.)

It's easy to install fonts, sounds, DA's, control panels and extensions in System 7—you just drag their icons onto the System Folder's icon, and it puts them into the appropriate folders. If it's a font you're installing, quit any open applications and DA's first. If you want to put a file in the System Folder but don't want it placed in any of the folders within the System Folder, drag the file into the System Folder's open window instead of onto its icon.

very good feature

System 6 doesn't organize system files into folders, but you install extensions, control panels and printer font files the same way—by dragging them to the System Folder. To install fonts or desk accessories in System 6, you add them to the System file with Font/DA Mover or with a utility like Suitcase (for details, see System 6 tips below).

🍎 System vs. system

There's an important distinction between **system** and **System.** Capitalized, *System* always refers to the System file itself or a particular version of the system software (e.g. *System 7* or *System 7.0.1*).

Lowercase, system can refer to any of three things: a system set—the collection of system software files you're using; the customized environment you've created by adding fonts, sounds, printer drivers, etc. to—or subtracting them from—the System Folder; or the hardware setup you use—say, a Mac IIsi with a particular hard disk drive and a particular printer.

A *system file* (without caps) is any file in the System Folder that helps run your computer—control panels, printer drivers and the like, including the System file and the Finder.

◉ *the Finder*

The **Finder** is the program that creates the desktop and its menus (◉, File, Edit, etc.). Since the desktop is usually the first and last thing you see when you work on a Mac, it's hard to think of a Mac running without it; but it can actually be replaced with another program, like the one that generates the simplified desktop on Performas (see below). (The term **Finder** is often used instead of **desktop**, as in *Quit the application and return to the Finder.* It doesn't usually work the other way, though: *Rearrange the icons on your Finder.*)

In System 7, you can run as many applications simultaneously as your Mac's memory permits, and you can see the desktop in the background while you work. To run more than one application under System 6, you need to run MultiFinder (described in the System 6 tips below). Otherwise, you can only run one application at a time, and the desktop disappears while you're working in it (which saves memory).

◉ *At Ease*

At Ease is sort of a simplified Finder that comes with the Performa Macs and can be bought separately to run on regular Macs. With At Ease running, applications and documents show up as large icons that you click on *once* (instead of double-clicking) to open.

When you're in an application, all windows and icons from other opened programs disappear, so you can't accidentally leave the one you're in with a stray mouse click. To get back to another application, you just select its name from the Application menu. To help you keep from losing track of files you create, there's a Documents folder that sits on the desktop; whenever you save a new document, that's where it goes, unless you select some other location.

At Ease makes the Mac easier for beginners to use, helps parents keep their children and Macs from confusing each other, and provides a way for a Mac's owner to restrict other users' access to private files.

◉ *avoid multiple systems*

In general, it's best not to keep more than one System Folder (or System file) on any hard disk or floppy. Multiple systems can make the Mac schizophrenic and cause it to crash a lot.

important warning

M ost people don't purposely put more than one system on a disk, of course. This usually happens because you've inserted a floppy that contains a program you want to install and then dragged all the files on the floppy, including its System Folder, over to your hard disk.

Periodically, and especially whenever you're experiencing more system crashes than usual, use the *Find* command or Find File DA to search your hard disk for the word *System,* and remove any extra System files or System Folders.

an emergency startup floppy

If your Mac won't start up from its regular startup disk, you can start it up from the System 7 Disk Tools floppy (or, depending on which Mac you have, a System 6 System Tools or System Startup disk). Your Mac won't have a lot of its normal fonts, DA's and printing capabilities, but you'll usually be able to access what's on your hard drive.

where to get system software

All Macs except the Performas come with disks for reinstalling the system software that came with the Mac. But if you've lost them, or want to install a different system version, the cheapest and easiest source for installation disks for versions through 7.0.1 is probably your local Macintosh user group. You can also download the software from bulletin boards and information services, or copy it from a friend or an Apple dealer (most will let you, if you provide the floppies).

bargain

S tarting with System 7.1, Apple decided not to make the software so freely available, so if you want the most recent version, you'll have to buy it from an Apple dealer.

upgrading from System 6 to System 7

If you decide to upgrade from System 6 to System 7, you should be aware that the transition may not be entirely smooth, especially if you're using a lot of software that was made before 1991, when System 7 came out. Be sure to back up *all* your files before installing System 7. If you don't have Apple's upgrade kit, be sure to get a good manual like *The Macintosh Bible Guide to System 7.1* from Peachpit Press.

important warning

🍎 *installing a new system*

Before installing a new system, be sure to make backups of your important files. The best way to install a new System Folder, whether you're putting it onto a blank hard disk or upgrading from an earlier version, is to run the Installer program on the first disk in your set of system software disks (Install 1, System Startup or System Tools, depending on what version you're installing).

T hen start up your Mac with this disk in your floppy drive, and run the Installer. Click the *Drive* button to select the disk you want to install onto, then click the *Easy Install* button.

When you install onto a hard disk that doesn't already have a System Folder, *Easy Install* gives you all the software you might possibly need, including drivers for every Apple printer. To avoid loading up your system with extra files, choose the *Customize* option instead. Then select the software you want from the list box that appears. Shift-click to select more than one option (e.g. software for file sharing, for your printer model and system software for your model of Mac).

very hot tip

The 🍎 menu

🍎 *adding items to the 🍎 menu*

System 7's 🍎 menu gives you quick access to anything you need to have handy, whether it's a document, a folder or a program. To put an item on the 🍎 menu, just copy it into the Apple Menu Items folder in the System Folder; to remove it, just drag it back out. (Or, to put an item's name on the menu without moving it, create an alias of the item and move *that* into the Apple Menu Items folder.)

shortcut

S ince DA's are designed to go on the 🍎 menu, System 7 automatically puts them in the Apple Menu Items folder when you drag them onto the System Folder icon. In System 6, only desk accessories can go on the 🍎 menu, and you have to install them with Font/DA

very good feature

Mover or a third-party DA manager program (see *System 6 tips* below). Macs come with several items already installed on the ❡ menu—we've described a few of them in the following entries.

❡ *Alarm Clock*

The Alarm Clock desk accessory functions like a real alarm clock (albeit a feeble one). You can also use it to reset your Mac's internal clock and calendar, or just leave it open anywhere on the desktop to keep track of the time. When you click the little flag to the right of the time, the clock opens down to let you adjust its settings.

C lick on the bottom left square to set your Mac's clock, the bottom center to set the date, and the bottom right to set the alarm. The middle panel is where you actually adjust the settings—just click on the number you want to change, and then click the up or down arrow to increase or decrease it.

To turn the alarm on, click the weird little icon at the left end of the middle panel, and the alarm clock icon will look like it's going off. When it actually does go off, your Mac will beep once and an alarm clock icon will alternate with the ❡ at the top of the ❡ menu (until you turn it off). It won't rouse the dead, but it's adequate once you get used to looking for it.

❡ *Calculator*

You can use the Calculator DA either by clicking its keys with the mouse or by typing in numbers from the keyboard. (Using the numeric keypad makes it feel like a desktop adding machine, except that it doesn't print a tape.) You can also copy the number the calculator is displaying and paste it into the document you're working on. And you can paste things *into* the calculator—not just simple numbers, but also chains of calculations, like 15+17*92/3.

It's not the most feature-laden calculator around, but it's simple to use, and it can display large numbers by using exponents. *[I know it's uncool, but I find it simpler just to use a calculator on my desk.—AN]*

✎ Control Panels

These important programs get a section of their own. It starts on the next page.

✎ the Chooser

The Chooser is most often used to choose a printer (how to do this is described in Chapter 5). But when you're working on a network, it also lets you select disks, folders and files on other Macs (see *file sharing* in Chapter 13).

✎ Key Caps

This utility displays a keyboard on the screen that shows you what character—or symbol—you get in a given font for each key (or key combination). You select the font you want to view from the Key Caps menu. (See Chapter 8 for more on Key Caps.)

✎ the Scrapbook

As discussed in Chapter 2, the Scrapbook is a file that saves any text or graphics you paste into it, so you can copy and reuse them later. Although it's a standard Apple desk accessory, it doesn't follow the standard Mac interface. For example, when you cut or copy something from the Scrapbook, you don't have to select it first—you just get whatever's showing. Adding something to the Scrapbook isn't very intuitive either—it *feels* like you're pasting it on top of the item that's showing, but when you give the *Paste* command, the Scrapbook creates a new page to receive what you're adding.

The Scrapbook window isn't resizable, but even though you can see only part of a large graphic you've pasted in it, the entire graphic is stored. The things you store in the Scrapbook are kept in a file named *Scrapbook file* in the System Folder. If you change the name of that file or move it out of the System Folder, the Scrapbook will be empty the next time you open it.

Since the Scrapbook contents are in that file, you can transfer them from one disk to another. You can even have several Scrapbook files (with various names) on the same disk—just rename whichever one you want to use at the moment *Scrapbook file.*

The control panels

▲ *using control panels*

Choosing *Control Panels* from the ▲ menu opens a window like the one shown below. It contains a variety of utilities that give you control over various aspects of the Mac. (In System 6, choosing *Control Panels* from the ▲ menu opens a sort of dialog box with similar utilities. See the *System 6 tips* section for details.)

Wopens so you can adjust its controls. This section describes the control panels that come with the Mac's system software, but there are a lot of third-party control panels too.

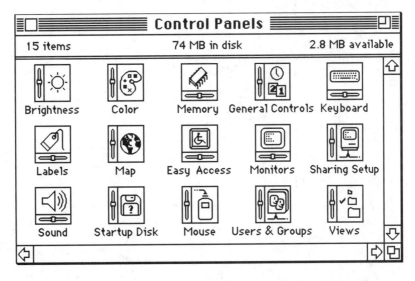

The basic Apple control panels are *General Controls, Keyboard, Mouse, Sound, Color, Map, Easy Access, Views, Labels, Startup Disk* and *Monitors.* In the entries below, we describe what they do and give you our recommended settings for them. The *Memory* control panel is discussed at the end of Chapter 4; likewise, *Sharing Setup, Users & Groups* and *File Sharing Monitor* have to do with file sharing on a network, which is discussed in Chapter 13.

recommended General Controls settings

The first General Controls setting (in the upper left corner of the illustration below) controls **the pattern on your desktop.** On a black-and-white system, you should probably stick with the default pattern, a medium gray, because it's quite pleasant for daily use. But if you want to change it, here's how:

In the square on the left is an enlarged view of the pattern; in the rectangle on the right is what the pattern looks like at actual size. As you can see, the default pattern is composed of alternate black and white dots.

You can make your own pattern by clicking in the left square to turn the squares on and off until you like the pattern you see in the right rectangle. There's also a whole slew of built-in choices; to cycle through them, click on the little arrows above the right rectangle.

If you're working in color, you'll see a strip of eight colored squares beneath the desktop patterns. Click on a color and then on a dot in the left square above it; the dot will change to the color you've chosen. (Clicking on the dot again returns it to the previous color.)

To change the choice of colors, double-click on any of them; that opens the Color Wheel (described below in the Color settings entry). Create the color you want, click OK and you'll be back in the General Controls control panel with the color changed. ▭▶

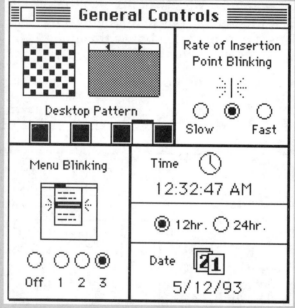

When you find or create the pattern you want—in black-and-white or in color—click in the right rectangle and the pattern will immediately be applied to the desktop.

Not surprisingly, *Rate of Insertion Point Blinking* controls how fast the insertion point blinks. This is a totally subjective mat-ter, so set it wherever you like—but do try *Slow* some time and see if you don't find it less distracting. Some people prefer *Fast*, because that makes the insertion point easier to locate. The default is the middle setting.

Menu Blinking controls how many times a command on a menu blinks after you choose it. If you don't think subtle feedback is important, try setting Menu Blinking to *Off*, but most people find it disconcerting to select a command and not have it acknowledged. Still, three times is overkill. If you have a nervous system, once should be plenty.

As for *the Time and Date settings*, let reality be your guide.

Keyboard settings

In the Keyboard control panel, **Delay Until Repeat** controls how long it takes before a key you're holding down begins to automatically repeat, and **Key Repeat Rate** controls how rapidly the key repeats after it begins repeating. Key Repeat Rate works best at either of the two fastest speeds and Delay Until Repeat at either of the two middle choices.

Keyboard Layout lets you choose a layout other than the standard US qwerty (boy, was that easy to type!) arrangement, if you've got the right keyboard and software installed. Apple makes keyboards for more than twenty languages.

❤ *Mouse settings*

The top setting in the Mouse control panel (shown below) is for **Mouse Tracking**. At the faster settings (on the right), a mere flick of the wrist moves the pointer a long distance (so it feels more like badminton than tennis). These faster settings are useful for large screens, when you really want to cover distance fast.

T he slower settings (on the left) make moving the pointer feel more like bowling than tennis. They're useful if you have a small screen, or if you always find yourself overshooting the mark when you move the pointer.

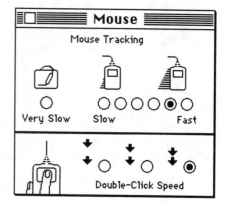

Mouse Tracking settings are very much a matter of personal taste. Play around with them until you find one you like.

T he bottom setting in the Mouse control panel tells the Mac how long it should wait after one click to see if you're going to double-click. With the longest interval set, the Mac will treat clicks that are fairly far apart as double-clicks; with the shortest interval set, you'll have to double-click pretty fast or the Mac will think you're giving two separate clicks rather than double-clicking.

[I recommend either the short interval (on the right) or the medium one (in the middle); if you use the long interval (on the left), you'll always be accidentally double-clicking on things and opening them when you only wanted to select them. But if you have some impairment of your fine motor skills, from age or illness, the long interval can be useful.—AN]

**very
hot
tip**

❤ *Sound settings*

The Sound control panel (at the top of the next page) lets you control how loud the Mac's alerts—and any other sounds it makes—will be. There are eight settings, from 0 to 7 (the loudest). When you slide the control to change the volume, the Mac gives you a demo of the new volume.

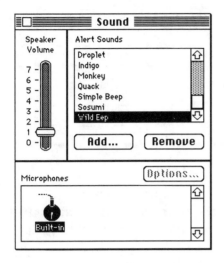

If you don't want to hear any beeps at all, slide the control to 0; instead of making sounds, the Mac will flash the menu bar when it wants your attention (except when starting or restarting—the Mac always makes noise then).

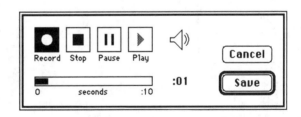

very hot tip

You can also choose which of several sounds the Mac will use to get your attention. When you click on a sound in the list, the Mac demos it for you (at whatever volume you've selected). Whichever sound is highlighted when you close the window is the one that the Mac will use as its alert sound (until you change it again).

You can add to this selection of sounds by installing new ones, as described under *installing system files* in the System Folder section above. Many sounds are available, especially on bulletin boards.

Most current Macs also come with a microphone, so you can also record your own sounds (to record onto a Duo, you need a MiniDock or Duo Dock). Just click the *Add* button and you'll get a set of controls like the ones on a tape recorder (shown above). Click the *Record* button and start making noise.

Color settings

On Macs with color monitors, the Color control panel (shown at the top of the next page) lets you change the color of window borders and the color of the background that surrounds highlighted text. (You change the color of the desktop itself in the General Controls control panel.) A list of colors appears on pop-up menus, and you can mix your own highlight color.

To do that, select *Other...* from the Highlight color pop-up menu. That opens the Color Wheel dialog box (shown below). The wheel has a dot in it that shows the currently selected color. You can click anywhere in the wheel to move the dot, or you can drag it around.

> **Color**
>
> **Highlight color:** [Black & White ▼]
>
> [Sample text]
>
> **Window color:** [Standard ▼]

To change the hue (the actual color), move around the circle. To decrease the saturation (the intensity of the color), move in towards the center of the circle. To change the brightness, use the scroll bar to the right of the wheel. (When you move the scroll box all the way to the bottom, you get black no matter what the hue or saturation is.)

There's a two-toned square of color in the upper left; the lower half shows the current color and the upper half the new color. Below that are numeric representations of the

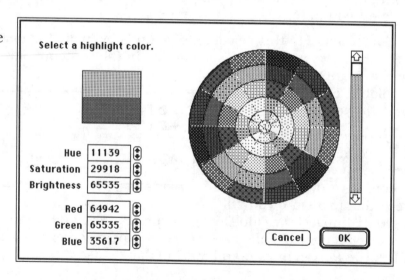

Select a highlight color.

Hue	11139
Saturation	29918
Brightness	65535
Red	64942
Green	65535
Blue	35617

[Cancel] [OK]

current color. You can work directly with them if you like, either by typing in new numbers or by using the arrows.

Click *OK* when you have a color you like. Keep the color relatively light—selected text doesn't invert to white against a highlight color, so dark colors make selections unreadable.

🍎 *Monitors settings*

The Monitors control panel lets you specify how many colors or shades of gray appear on your monitor.

If you have more than one monitor connected to a Mac, this control panel also lets you decide which one gets the menu bar and the desktop windows, and how you want the screens positioned in relation to each other. You can position them the way they really are on your desk, or any other way you want—as long as they're touching.

[I only use monitor 1 for color programs, and usually leave it turned off. But the pointer still travels into the part of the desktop set aside

for monitor 1 (to get it not to do that, I'd have to actually remove monitor 1's video card from my Mac).

It's quite annoying to have the pointer keep disappearing into a black screen, so I position monitor 1 so that it's just touching the least-used corner of monitor 2 (away from both scroll bars), as shown above. Amazingly, I still lose the

pointer a fair amount, but less often than if I positioned monitor 1's desktop anywhere else.—AN]

To change which monitor the menu bar shows up in, you just drag the miniature menu bar (shown at the top of monitor 2 in the illustration on the left) to the other monitor's icon.

The Mac assigns a number to each monitor, depending on which slot its card is in; if you're not sure which screen is which, click the *Identify* button and the numbers will flash on the screens themselves.

The list box at the top of the control ⫘➡

panel shows the number of colors or shades of gray that the selected monitor's video board can produce. When you click on the other icon to select the other monitor, the list box will change to display that monitor's capabilities.

Labels settings

System 7 lets you place files and folders in groups, by assigning names and colors to them (see the *Tips on windows* section of this chapter for details). The Labels control panel comes with seven preassigned labels (names and colors); you can change them however you want.

Just select any name and type a new one, or click on any color and select a new one from the Color Wheel that appears. When you close the control panel, the new names and colors will show up on the Labels menu in the Finder.

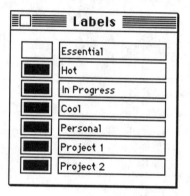

Views settings

The Views control panel was also introduced in System 7; it lets you customize the appearance of Finder windows to some extent. You can change the font and size of the text in windows and icon names (although menus and window titles stay in the Chicago font).

If you view windows *by Icon* or *by Small Icon,* you can keep your icons neatly arranged by having them snap to a grid that is either straight or staggered. (To tidy up windows that already contain files, you have to open them and choose *Clean Up Window* from the Special Menu.)

You can tell the Finder what types of information to display in windows that are viewed as lists. The only category you can't eliminate is an item's name.

The categories you leave checked are also the ones that will show up as choices on the View menu. (Three categories are permanent and always show up there— *by Icon, by Small Icon* and *by Name.)*

very hot tip

The version and comments boxes come unchecked, and you should leave them that way. Most people rarely need this information, and if you do need it for a particular file, you can get it by selecting *Get Info* from the File menu.

[Consider eliminating label and kind as well; you'll be able to get a lot more information on your screen. There are much better ways to organize files than by labels, and you can get the kind information (what program created the document) with Get Info.*—AN]*

very hot tip

You're also given the choice of having the Finder calculate and display folder sizes, but unless you need this information all the time, leave the box unchecked—it can really slow you down when you're moving or copying files.

The *Show disk info in header* option keeps you aware of how much space is on your hard disk (information that icon view windows automatically supply). But you don't need this information in every window. Instead, just create a folder called *disk space,* set its window to display by Icon, and copy it into the Apple Menu Items folder. Then, whenever you want to know how much disk space you've got, select *disk space* from the menu and the window that opens will tell you.

The characteristics you select in the Views control panel apply to all the windows on your desktop, so you can't set a font for text in one window and a different font for another window.

● *Startup Disk settings*

This control panel is so simple, it doesn't require an illustration. If your Mac uses two or more hard drives with System Folders on them, you can choose which one it will start up from in this control panel. Once chosen, that drive will remain the startup drive until you choose a different one.

● *Easy Access*

Easy Access is designed for people with disabilities who have diffi-culty using the mouse or issuing multiple key commands. The top item on its con-

very good feature

trol panel (shown at the right) is **Mouse Keys,** which lets you use the numeric keypad as a mouse.

S *low Keys* makes the Mac wait until you've held a key down for a bit before it gets registered as a keystroke; **Sticky Keys** lets you press keys one at a time that would normally have to be pressed together (like ⌃⌘S for *Save).* For more details on how to use Easy Access, see Apple's manuals.

```
┌────────────────────────────────────┐
│ ▣ ▢══════ Easy Access ══════        │
│ ⊠ Use On/Off audio feedback         │
│ ··································· │
│ Mouse Keys:    ○ On   ◉ Off         │
│    Initial Delay : ○○◉○○            │
│                   long    short     │
│                                     │
│  Maximum Speed : ○○ ◉○○○ ○○         │
│                  slow  medium  fast │
│ ··································· │
│ Slow Keys:     ○ On   ◉ Off         │
│  Acceptance Delay : ○○◉○○           │
│                    long    short    │
│  ⊠ Use key click sound              │
│ ··································· │
│ Sticky Keys:   ○ On   ◉ Off         │
│  ⊠ Beep when modifier key is set    │
└────────────────────────────────────┘
```

● *Map*

If you travel with a PowerBook, you may have a use for the Map control panel (shown at the top of the next page). Enter the name of a city and click *Find,* and Map will display its latitude and longitude, the local time there and how far it is from your home location. Probably the Map's most useful feature is the *Set* button, which resets the Mac's clock to the local time and changes the home location.

To see which cities Map recognizes, hold down the Option key and click on the *Find* button. This scrolls you through the list in alphabetical order, click by click.

There are some cities on the list you wouldn't expect (like Cupertino) and some we'd never heard of (like Bamako and Bangui). *[But not, say, Phoenix or Tucson.*

As a map-lover, the shoddy execution of this utility really annoys me. It could be quite useful, if the people who

rant

put it together cared about that, instead of treating it as some sort of gimmick.

It needs many more US cities—not just the home towns of everyone who worked on it, where they all live now and a few megalopolises. It needs a way to show (and print out) the whole list of cities the program knows about, and a way to expand the map to fill the screen, so you can see some detail on it. And it should tell you what state and/or country a city is in (where the hell is Bamako or Bangui—or, for that matter, Springville, a US "city" that Map lists?).

In its present state, Map is the kind of thing you'd expect to find as a free public-domain trifle on a bulletin board somewhere, not distributed by Apple with every computer it sells.—AN]

v 7.0

Add City   Remove City

San Francisco   Find

Latitude	37 °	48 ′	☒ N
Longitude	122 °	24 ′	☐ E
Time Zone	8 h	0 m	☐ +

mi 0   6:27 PM   Set

System 6 tips

❡ *using Find File*

Find File is a DA that comes with System 6. When you select it from the ❡ menu, you get a dialog box like the one below:

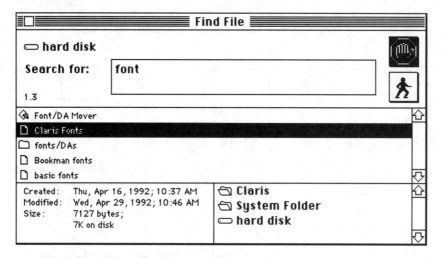

    To search for a file or folder, type any part of its name in the text box. The Mac will list everything it finds whose name includes what you typed. When you select a particular item from the list, Find File shows the path to its location in the lower right-hand corner of the dialog box.

    Once you've found what you were looking for, you don't have to dig it out of whatever folder it's in—just choose *Move to Desktop* from the Find File menu on the menu bar. When you're through using the item, select it and choose *Put Away* from the File menu, and it'll return to the folder it came out of.

❡ *System 6's Control Panel*

In System 6, control panels are called **cdevs** (for control panel *devices*) and Control Panel is the name of the DA that lets you access them.

(continued on page 148)

🍎 using Font/DA Mover

Font/DA Mover is a utility for moving or removing fonts and DA's between or from suitcase files and the System file. When you run the program, you get a dialog box like this:

Select *Font* or *Desk Accessory* from the top of the box, depending on what you want to move. The program automatically opens the System file in the

button's name changes to *Open* after the first click).

If you're moving items between files, click the button under the right-hand

click the *Copy* button and they'll be copied to the file shown in the other box.

If you're removing items from a file, just select them and then

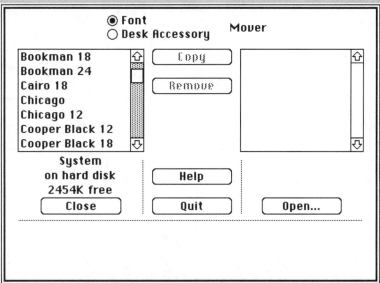

left-hand list box, but if you're not moving anything into or out of it, click the *Close* button below the box and then click it again to open whatever file you do want to use (the

list box to open the other file (or to create a new one). Once it's open, select the items you want to move (you can shift-click or drag through them to select more than one),

click the *Remove* button. There are also third-party programs, like Fifth Generation's Suitcase, that make it easier to load and unload fonts and DA's from your System.

When you select *Control Panel* from the menu, you get a window like this, with a scrolling list of icons displayed on the left side. When you click an icon on this list, its controls appear in the area to the right.

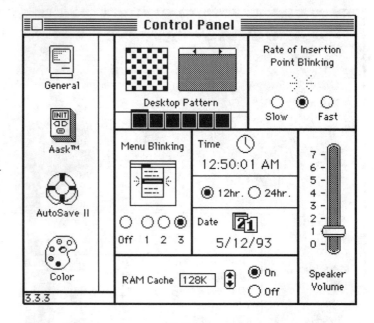

Because System 6 has fewer features than System 7, it has fewer control panels. System 6 includes the speaker volume and RAM cache controls in its General cdev, whereas System 7 handles them in its Sound and Memory control panels. Apart from these minor differences, though, cdevs/control panels work the same whether you're running System 6 or System 7.

Fonts

Font basics

⬢ *what is a font?*

In traditional typesetting, a ***font*** is a particular typeface in a particular size and a particular style. Among Mac users, however, *font* has come to mean a typeface in every size and every style (what a traditional typesetter calls a ***type family*** and Apple's LaserWriter manuals call a ***font family***).

For example, Geneva can be scaled to any point size and can be transformed into various type styles (bold, italic and so on). A regular typesetter would consider that many different fonts; to a Mac user, it's all one font—Geneva. So, throughout this book, we use *font* to mean a typeface in every size and style.

⬢ *bit-mapped, outline, screen and printer fonts*

When the Mac was first introduced, fonts came only in one format: ***bit-mapped***. Each character in a bit-mapped font is made up of a pattern (or map) of dots; each of these dots is represented by a *bit* in the computer's memory. Because of this one-to-one correspondence, the Mac needs a different bit-map for each font size you display on the screen (so Apple calls them ***fixed-size*** fonts). If you use a size that isn't installed, the Mac rescales the bit-map from a size that is installed—with mixed results (see *bit-mapped font sizes* below).

There are 72 dots per inch in the characters that make up a bit-mapped font—or, to put it a different way, they have a resolution of 72 dpi. (It's no coincidence that the standard Mac screen also has a resolution of 72 dpi.) You get several bit-mapped fonts with the system software, including Chicago and Geneva, but most of these come as outline fonts too.

The characters in ***outline*** fonts aren't made up of dots—they're composed of instructions for forming an outline of each character, which is then filled in. This means they can be scaled to any size, and look smoother and crisper than bit-mapped fonts.

When you send an outline font to a printer, the printer draws the characters in as much detail—at as high a resolution—as it's capable of. (For some comparative printer resolutions, see the second entry in Chapter 5.)

Most outline fonts come in one or both of two formats: PostScript or TrueType. **PostScript** is more than just a font format—it's a programming language specifically designed by its developer, Adobe, to handle text and graphics and their placement on a page.

At this writing, the Mac's system software can't display PostScript fonts on the screen, so they come in two parts: the actual outline font, which gets sent to the printer (and is therefore called the ***printer font***) and a bit-mapped version to represent it on the screen, called the ***screen font***. Sending a printer font to a printer is called ***downloading*** it, and that gives us another name for this kind of font—***downloadable***.

Not all printers are designed to handle PostScript fonts—only those with PostScript, or some emulation of it, built in (at this point, that includes most laser printers, but virtually no inkjets or dot-matrix printers). To address this problem, you need **ATM** (Adobe Type Manager), a utility that interprets PostScript printer fonts for the screen and for non-PostScript printers. (ATM is covered in the Font utilities section later on in this chapter.)

Like any bit-mapped font, a screen font will print out if the printer font isn't there, but it won't look a whole lot like the actual outline font does—both because of the lower resolution and because the person who designed the screen font knew it was only going to be used as an approximation of the font on the screen, and therefore probably didn't spend a lot of time fine-tuning it for printing.

TrueType fonts don't require separate screen and printer fonts—TrueType support is built into System 7, so the same font works both for displaying and printing. (TrueType capability can also be added to System 6.0.7 or 6.0.8 using a special installer available from Apple dealers.) You get nine TrueType fonts with System 7, and many others are available, but PostScript fonts have been around a lot longer, so there are more of them.

very good feature

There are other outline font formats too—the DeskWriter printer comes with fonts in Hewlett-Packard's own format, for example—but they're usually very limited in the variety of fonts available and the number of printers they'll work on.

For more information on the differences between PostScript and non-PostScript printers, see *PostScript vs. non-PostScript* in Chapter 5.

⚫ *basic font terms*

☞ ***Monospaced fonts***, like Monaco and Courier, give all characters an equal amount of horizontal space—an *i*, for example, gets as much room on a line as an *M*, even though it may be only 20% as wide. This is a throwback to the days of typewriters, when the carriage moved a fixed distance after each character was typed, but it can still be useful—for example, monospaced fonts let you set the size of a field in a database to consistently show a certain maximum number of characters, whatever the characters may be.

☞ ***Proportional spacing*** gives characters different amounts of horizontal space, depending on their actual widths.

☞ ***Baseline, cap height, ascender, descender*** and ***x-height*** are easier to show than describe:

☞ ***Leading*** (pronounced *LEDD-ing*) is also called *line spacing*—it's the distance from the baseline of one line of text to the baseline of the next. (In typesetting, it's actually the *extra* distance added to the spacing, but that meaning is dying out, and *leading* is coming to mean exactly the same thing as **line spacing**.)

☞ Both leading and the size of a font are measured in ***points*** (both on the Mac and in regular typesetting). Points are 72nds of an inch. (Actually, to be more precise, a point is .0138" and a 72nd of an inch rounds to .01389". But since the difference between them is less than one ten-thousandth of an inch, the distinction is...well...pointless.)

gossip/ trivia

☞ **Kerning** is adjusting the horizontal space between letters. Normally, each letter lives in its own little rectangle and letters on either side of it don't encroach on its space. But type is easier to read, and looks better, when certain letter combinations nestle into each other—like a lowercase vowel tucked under the overhang of a capital T, or the letters in the following illustration:

Vow   # Vow

Normal spacing   *Kerned*

☞ Some fonts contain **kerned pairs**—built-in kerning between certain pairs of letters (*Ta, To, Tr, We*, etc.). But kerned pairs work only if the program you're using supports them (most word processors don't, but most page-layout programs do). You don't have to worry about kerned pairs—you just type as usual and the software substitutes the kerned pairs for the plain pair you typed.

☞ **Serif** fonts have serifs—little hooks, lines or blobs—added to the basic form of their characters; **sans serif** fonts have none (*sans* is French for *without*).

The   ## The

Serif   *Sans serif*

🍎 *installing font files*

Under System 7, it's easy to install fonts—just drag them onto the System Folder icon (*not* into its window) and they'll be put where they belong. Under System 6, that works for installing printer fonts; to install bit-mapped fonts, see *using Font/DA Mover* at the end of Chapter 7. (TrueType fonts don't work under System 6 without a special extension—ask an Apple dealer.)

🍎 *recognizing TrueType fonts*

Both bit-mapped and TrueType versions of the same font can be stored in the same suitcase file, so how do you know which is which? There are two easy ways to tell. First, the TrueType font names don't have a size number after them, and bit-mapped fonts always do. Second, TrueType font icons show the letter *A* in three sizes (in icon views), while bit-mapped font icons just show a single *A:*

Helvetica   Helvetica 9

❡ *font styles*

On the screen, every font can be made bold, italic, outline, shadow and any combination thereof—sixteen possible variations in all: bold italic, bold outline, bold shadow, italic outline, italic shadow, outline shadow, bold italic outline, bold italic shadow, bold outline shadow, italic outline shadow, bold italic outline shadow and, of course, plain (which is called *Roman* in regular typesetting).

With PostScript fonts on paper, you don't get all sixteen combinations; for example, it's common for outline shadow to look just the same as shadow. How many variations you get depends on the font, the application and/or the printer.

❡ *bit-mapped font sizes*

Bit-mapped fonts come supplied in various sizes and, unless you've got a TrueType or PostScript version of the same font, they should be used only in the sizes you have installed, or in halves or quarters of those sizes. ***Scaling***—shrinking or enlarging—a bit-mapped font can result in some pretty horrendous characters, both on the screen and in printouts.

Picture a bit-mapped character as a series of filled-in squares on a piece of graph paper; each square represents one pixel (one of the dots that make up the image on the screen). To double the size of the character, you'd take a larger area of the graph paper and color in four squares for every one that was filled in the original. To double the size again, you'd take every square in the second grid and fill in four on the third grid (so every square from the original grid is now represented by sixteen squares on the third grid).

The illustration at the top of the next page shows the letter *b* being enlarged on just such a grid. (The smallest letter is actually using a grid that's half the size of the one shown; if we'd included all the lines in the illustration, the shape of the letter would have been hard to see.)

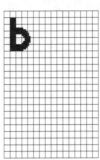 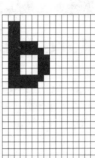 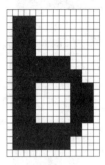

Y ou can see that what was an acceptable curve in the small letter gets worse with each size increase, producing the dread jaggies (staircasing like that on the right side of the rightmost *b).*

Scaling to a size that's not double, quadruple, half or a quarter the size of the original creates even more jaggies. It's not so bad if you're tripling the size, since each original square can translate into nine new filled squares, but let's say you're going from 12-point to 30-point (2.5 times bigger). You can't use half-squares (since each square on the grid represents a single pixel on the screen, and pixels are the smallest unit the

12-point (installed)
17-point (not installed)
24-point (installed)
33-point (not)

screen can display). So each original filled square will sometimes get replaced by four squares (twice the original size) and sometimes by nine squares (three times the original size). This produces the messes like the 17-point and 33-point type shown above.

T he installed sizes of bit-mapped fonts (including screen fonts) are shown in outline type on the font size menu (which is sometimes part of another menu), as shown here: (If you're using TrueType fonts, every size in your font menu will be shown in outline type, because they scale smoothly to any size.)

Font
9 Point
10 Point
✓ 12 Point
14 Point
18 Point
24 Point

Special characters

the standard special characters

There are some characters on computer keyboards you won't find on typewriter keyboards—the backslash (\), the vertical bar (|), the lesser than and greater than signs (< >) and so on. But when people talk about special characters on the Mac, they mean ones that aren't shown on the keyboard at all. To get one of these special characters, you hold down the Option key (with or without the Shift key) while pressing another key.

Let's say you want to type: *Hein, salopard! Parlez-vous français?* To get the special character ç in *français,* you hold down Option while hitting C. To get certain other special characters, you have to hold down the Shift key as well. For example, if you hit Shift Option C you get an upper-case Ç instead of a lowercase one. (In this case, the two characters are related, but sometimes the Option and Shift Option characters have nothing to do with each other.)

Some fonts have idiosyncratic special characters of their own, but there's a set of standard special characters that virtually all fonts share. No bit-mapped font contains all of them—Geneva and Chicago seem to have the most—but most outline fonts have the full set. The diagrams on the right show where they appear on the keyboard under System 7 (some of them are different

Standard Option characters

Standard Shift Option characters

under System 6 and earlier versions; if you've got System 7.1, you can choose between the two System's layouts in the Keyboard control panel.) For more on generating special characters, see the *Key Caps* entry in the *Font utilities* section of this chapter.

❡ *creating special typographic effects*

To distort a headline or other piece of display type for special effect, type it first in any draw program (but not a paint program; you need object-oriented graphics). Then paste it into a word processor or page-layout program, either through the Clipboard or the Scrapbook.

very hot tip

Once it's there, select it and reshape it to stretch the type horizontally, vertically or both. It will look terrible on the screen but when you print it out on an inkjet or laser printer, the characters will have the same crisp, clean edges that outline fonts normally do. (If you're using a PostScript font, you'll need ATM to get good quality from non-PostScript printers.) Here are some examples of the kinds of effects you can get:

Gloria Zarifa

Gloria Zarifa

(The fonts being distorted are Adobe's Cooper Black italic, Casady & Greene's Kells and their Gazelle.)

Gloria Zarifa

If your word processor doesn't let you reverse type—that is, make it white instead of black (usually on a dark background, so you can see it)—you can use a draw program to get it. First create a ⫸

solid shape filled with black (or gray, or any other pattern you want for the background). Then either drag some outline type on top of it or, with the filled-in shape selected, choose *Outline* from the Style menu and start typing. You can combine both these techniques, creating white writing on a dark background and stretching it once it gets into your word processing program. These typographic special effects also work on dot-matrix printers, but you don't get smoothing and the results don't look anywhere near as good.

Programs like TypeStyler, LetraStudio and Effects Specialist give you much fancier effects than these, and much more control over them. Check out the samples below:

Font utilities

🍎 Key Caps

It's often hard to remember which key combination to hit to produce the special character you need, or even whether the font you're using has that character. That's what Apple's Key Caps desk accessory is for.

When you choose Key Caps from the 🍎 menu, it displays a representation of the Mac's keyboard and puts a new menu title, Key Caps, at the right end of the menu bar. You select the font you're interested in from that menu and the Key Caps display switches over to it (Bookman, in the illustration below).

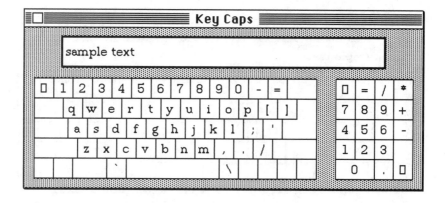

When you hold down the [Shift] key, Key Caps darkens the [Shift] keys on its display and shows you the characters you get in the selected font when you hold down [Shift] and press another key. But you already know what the [Shift] characters are (except in fonts composed entirely of pictures and symbols). Where Key Caps really comes in handy is in showing you the characters generated by the [Option] and [Shift][Option] keys.

When you hold down [Option], Key Caps displays a keyboard like the one shown at the top of the next page. System 7's Key Caps also shows which keys give you accents you can apply to other letters (they're out-

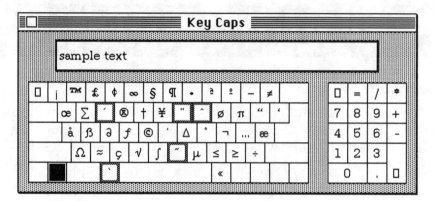

lined in gray). When you choose one of these keystrokes (on the keyboard below, we chose Option E), the display changes to show which letters you can apply the selected accent to (they're outlined in black).

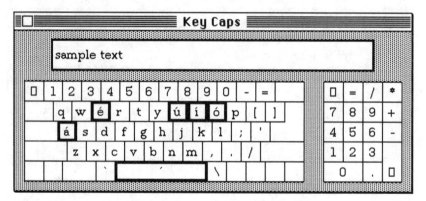

Y ou can enter text in the sample text area by typing on the keyboard or by clicking on the key you want in the Key Caps window. You can cut or copy this text from Key Caps into any document. (It won't appear in the

very good feature

very hot tip

font you chose in Key Caps, but it's easy enough to change the font once you're back in your document.) If you need a string of special characters, it's usually easier to type them in Key Caps, copy them to your document and then change the font, than it is to remember where each symbol is on the keyboard and type them directly into your document.

⬤ *ATM*

Adobe Type Manager draws PostScript Type 1 fonts on the screen based on the information in their printer files rather than in their bit-mapped screen fonts. This lets you display type at even the largest sizes without the dreaded jaggies. ATM also lets you print Type 1 fonts on dot-matrix, inkjet or non-PostScript laser printers, with quality comparable to what a PostScript printer would produce (depending on the resolution of the printer, of course).

[You can buy ATM in the store, but for you, seeing as you're Becky's niece and your zayda and my zayda were landsmen (Feeling confused? You need Every Goy's Guide to Common Jewish Expressions by Arthur Naiman, available at fine bookstores every-where)—for you, as I was saying before that unseemly interruption, we'll only charge for shipping and handling. Just call 800 521 1976 and ask for Saul.—AN]

bargain

Actually, you don't have to ask for Saul. This super deal is the result of an agreement Apple made with Adobe as "an interim step" while they work on adding ATM's capabilities to the Mac's system software (which may have already happened by the time you read this). The only difference is that the less expensive version comes with one font, Garamond, instead of Times, Helvetica, Courier and Symbol (and if you're using System 7, you've already got TrueType versions of those four anyway).

Here's how 48-point Bookman looks on the screen without ATM:

Bookman

Here's how 48-point Bookman looks on the screen with ATM:

Bookman

ATM is now much faster than the original version was, but it can still bog down work on a Classic or a Plus, or printing on an Image-Writer. To get rid of the slowdown while you're working on a document, make sure you've got screen fonts installed in the sizes you're using; it's only when you're using sizes that aren't installed that ATM has to create them for the screen.

One problem with ATM is that it forces you to keep printer files in your System Folder, even for fonts that are built into your laser printer or that you've downloaded permanently to a hard disk attached to the printer. ATM also makes some smaller fonts in certain styles virtually unreadable. Bold, italic and bold italics suffer the most. For example, compare the two samples of Bookman bold italic below:

Here's 12-point Bookman Bold Italic with ATM on.

Here's 12-point Bookman Bold Italic with ATM off.

Plain text looks more readable with ATM, but it doesn't always supply all the characters (there's not always a curly apostrophe, for example)—compare the samples shown.

Here's 13-point Bookman with ATM on.

Here's 13-point Bookman with ATM off.

Here's 9-point Benguiat with ATM on.

Here's 9-point Benguiat with ATM off.

Chapter
9
Utilities

Utility basics

🍎 *what's a utility?*

Utilities are programs that perform relatively simple tasks—like searching for a specific file on a disk, setting an alarm, clipping a picture or counting the words in a document. (Some utilities perform relatively complex tasks, but in that case, they're support tasks for the creation of documents—managing fonts, for example.) Utilities come in various forms—most commonly as *stand-alone programs, desk accessories* (usually called *DA's), extensions* and *control panels.*

🍎 *freeware and shareware utilities*

Many utilities are available as free software (known as *freeware)* or as **shareware** (try it and pay for it only if you like it and continue using it). A lot of these programs do things too minor to interest a commercial publisher, yet are quite useful. (We urge you to always send in the fee for shareware you use regularly; it encourages the author to come up with more goodies, and you sometimes receive documentation or upgrades not available to nonregistered users.)

One advantage of freeware and shareware, besides its low price, is that it tends to get updated more often than commercial software (most authors are very responsive to user feedback). Its major drawback is that it's tested much less than commercial products, and therefore more likely to crash your system or to clash with other programs.

important warning

Freeware and shareware programs also sometimes have quirky interfaces that make them hard to learn and use. And since there's no formal technical support, you're on your own.

You get freeware and shareware through user groups, online services and bulletin boards. (Peachpit Press offers a collection of the best freeware and shareware called *The Macintosh Bible Software Disks.* See the order form at the back of this book or call 800 283 9444.)

🍎 *extensions and control panels*

Extensions (called **inits** in System 6) are loaded automatically into memory when you start up your Mac; as that happens, their icons appear at the bottom of your screen.

Extensions use anywhere from 2K to 200K of memory (we haven't seen one larger than that), so if you don't have a lot of RAM, be careful how many you use.

Another potential problem with extensions is that they can clash with other system software or with an application.

☞ For more on this, see the entry called **extension and control panel conflicts** in Appendix A.

Some **control panels** (called **cdevs** in System 6) also load at startup; they have the same drawbacks as extensions, and

the term *extension* is often used (in this book and elsewhere) to include them.

But unlike extensions, when you double-click any control panel, you get a window where you can configure some aspect of your Mac or a peripheral device.

(Some even allow you to choose which control panels and extensions load at startup.)

Types of utilities

🍎 *substitutes for Apple utilities*

A number of utilities come with your Mac's system software—the Calculator DA, the Sound control panel, etc.; they're discussed in Chapter 7. But there are also commercial substitutes for many of these that offer more features.

For example, you can create a custom calculator with Dubl-Click's Calculator Construction Set, keep material on several Clipboards at once using Olduvai's MultiClip, or organize your Scrapbook material with Portfolio Systems' SmartScrap. FlashWrite is a shareware notepad DA that's much more useful than the one that comes with the Mac.

very good feature

There are also faster and more functional alternatives to the *Find...* command, like Softways' Mr. File, CE Software's DiskTop, Fifth Generation's FileDirector and Working Software's Findswell. (Another, cheaper alternative, if you want a convenient way to find a group of files all at once, is to install System 6's Find File DA on your System 7 Mac.)

shortcut

● *disk- and file-recovery utilities*

These utilities usually come as a package of programs designed to recover accidentally deleted or damaged files and repair damaged hard drives and floppies. Some of them also perform tasks like optimizing hard disks (reorganizing their contents so they'll work faster) and protecting files against computer viruses (for more on viruses, see Appendix A).

Three of the most popular are Central Point Software's Mac Tools Deluxe, Microcom's 911 Utilities and Symantec's Norton Utilities.

● *PowerBook utilities*

PowerBook users tend to be obsessed with finding ways to make the charge last longer on their battery-powered Macs. PowerBooks come with a control panel that allows you a crude level of control over three main drains on the battery: the spin of the hard disk, the screen's backlight and the processor's activity.

Third-party PowerBook utilities give you much more control over these functions, as well as indicators that show their status and the amount of charge left in the battery. Some programs also correct for disappearing pointers—a common annoyance with some PowerBooks' screens.

Some programs have a feature that compares files and folders on your PowerBook with those on your desktop Mac and offers to replace old versions of files on one Mac with more recent versions from the other Mac. This function is called **synchronization,** and there are programs that specialize in just that.

very good feature

There's a large selection of freeware and shareware PowerBook utilities, as well as at least two commercial packages: Connectix PowerBook Utilities (CPU) and Symantec's Norton Essentials for the PowerBook.

◉ *compression utilities*

When you're sending files over phone lines, or trying to squeeze them onto crowded disks, it's a good idea to use a compression utility. These handy programs compress (or compact) files into archives that are much smaller than the originals.

Compression utilities work by removing the redundancy present in most documents. For example, in this book, the word *and* appears thousands of times. If you replace each *and* with a single character, you save 67% of the space they took up. Using techniques like that, compression utilities can typically squeeze a 100K word processing document down to about 33K, and a 100K graphics scan in TIFF format to as little as 7K. Applications usually don't condense as much, because programs are partially compressed when they're written.

very good feature

Compression utilities can also fit a very large file or group of files onto a series of floppies by splitting it into as many archives as necessary. When you want the data back, the program expands (or *extracts)* the split-up information from the various archives and reassembles it.

The names of archives often end with a three-letter tag that identifies the program that compressed it and/or the sort of file it is. For example, a *self-extracting archive*—one you can expand simply by double-clicking on it, without the compression utility that created it needing to be around—often bears the tag *.sea* at the end of the file name.

The most popular commercial compression program is StuffIt Deluxe. There's also a shareware version of StuffIt, and another good shareware compression program called Compact Pro. Finally, there's at least one program—Salient's AutoDoubler—that compresses all the files on your hard drive, but allows you to open and use them in the normal way (they just take longer to open and close).

⌘ *text tools*

There are many text-related utilities available:

☞ **for making quick notes or taking word counts,** DA's like FlashWrite and miniWriter (shareware) and Casady & Greene's QuickDex.

☞ **for spell-checking in various types of documents,** Baseline's Thunder or Working Software's Spellswell or Lookup.

☞ **to find a string of text when you're not sure what file it's in,** Microlytics' GOfer

☞ **for printing addresses on envelopes,** Kiwi's KiwiEnvelopes!

☞ **to print anything onto standard Avery labels,** Avery-Dennison's MacLabel Pro

☞ **to turn your straight apostrophes and quote marks into curly ones** (so you can tell them apart from foot- and inch-marks and can tell an open quote mark from a close one), Quote Init or SmartKeys (or the *Preferences* command in whatever program you're using).

⌘ *screen savers*

Most computer monitors (like most TVs) are cathode ray tubes. They're coated on the inside with phosphor that glows when a beam of electrons hits it, creating the image on the screen. Leaving the same image on the screen for a long period of time can exhaust the phosphor in certain areas, causing it to shine less brightly, or not at all. That's where **screen savers** (also called **screen blankers**) come in.

They keep track of how long it's been since you hit a key or the mouse button and automatically black out the screen after a certain amount of time (which you specify). Hitting any key or moving the mouse brings back the image that was there before the screen saver kicked in.

You can turn most screen savers on immediately—the *Sleep Now* feature—by moving the pointer to a particular corner of the screen, which is useful when you're working on something you don't want everybody to see. And you can temporarily turn most screen savers off as well—the *Never Sleep* feature—by moving the pointer to a different corner of the screen, as you might want to do if you needed to watch something on the screen but weren't going to touch your keyboard or mouse for a while.

Today's screen savers don't merely black out the screen—they put moving images on it. And what images they are! *[Just as Greek drama arose out of religious choruses, so a whole new art form is rising out of the pedestrian task of protecting the phosphor on monitors. There are times when I sit hypnotized by my screen saver, unable to move the mouse to get back to work. And I'm sure the best is yet to come.—AN]*

very good feature

Berkeley Systems' After Dark, which Arthur uses, is easily the most popular screen saver around. There are also a number of shareware screen savers available, but not many of them activate automatically. John Lim's program Moiré is one that does.

🍎 *graphics tools*

Here are some of the graphics-related utilities available:

☞ **for applying artsy texture effects to bit-mapped graphics,** Aldus' Gallery Effects

☞ **for measuring objects on the screen,** Super Ruler (freeware)

☞ **for cataloging graphics files so they can be located using descriptive keywords and thumbnails,** Symmetry's Mariah, Loop Software's PictureBook+ and Multi-Ad Services' Multi-Ad Search.

🍎 *capturing screens*

Sometimes you need a picture of something on the screen to include in a document. The Mac's basic command for this function, ⇧⌘3, saves a picture of the entire screen image in a TeachText document, but you can't take a picture of part of the screen, or of an opened menu. Fortunately, third-party screen capture programs like Mainstay's Capture, Wildflower Software's SnapJot and Baseline's Exposure overcome all these limitations, and then some.

macro programs

A **macro** is a command that incorporates two or more other commands or actions. (The name comes from the idea that macro commands incorporate "micro" commands.) A macro can be as simple as a keyboard equivalent for a menu command—using ⌘S for *Save,* for example—or so complex that it really amounts to a miniprogram.

shortcut

Macro programs create macros by recording your keystrokes and/or mouse clicks, or by giving you a sort of pseudo programming language to write them in. Two of the more popular ones are CE Software's QuicKeys and Affinity Microsystems' Tempo.

miscellaneous utilities

We could fill the rest of the book describing all the types of utilities available. Instead, here are just a few more for:

☞ **automatically saving your files at regular intervals,** Bruce Partridge's shareware Sav-O-Matic

☞ **making your screen function like a window onto a bigger screen** (so that when your pointer reaches the edge, the view automatically scrolls over), Berkeley Systems' Stepping Out

☞ **putting a digital clock on your menu bar,** Steve Christenson's freeware SuperClock!

☞ **diagnosing hardware problems,** Maxa's Snooper

☞ **diagnosing software problems,** Teknosys' Help!

☞ **recording every keystroke you make** in a text file, so you can salvage your work even if your Mac crashes before you've saved it, Working Software's Last Resort

☞ **protecting your files from unauthorized access,** or "shredding" files you want to permanently dispose of, Microcom's Citadel and Kent• Marsh's FolderBolt.

Chapter
10

Word processing

Word processors and outliners

🍎 word processing features

The purpose of **word processing programs** (also called **word processors)** is to let you enter, edit and format text. To do that job well, there are some features that any word processor should have:

☞ **Headers** and **footers** are pieces of text that automatically print at the top (or bottom) of all (or a range of) pages. You should be able to easily place page numbers into either the header or footer.

☞ You should be able to specify different margins, headers and footers for *left and right pages.*

☞ **Leading** lets you vary the spacing between lines independently of the size of the font, in increments of one point or less. (It's pronounced *LEDD-ing,* not *LEED-ing;* in the old days of metal type, the lines were spaced apart with strips of lead.) Leading is an essential feature for all but the most basic documents, so don't buy a word processor that only gives you choices like single-spaced, space-and-a-half and double-spaced.

very good feature

☞ **Spelling checkers** go through a file and look for words that aren't on its list of correctly spelled words. If it can't find them on the list, it assumes that they're misspelled and asks if you agree. Since any spelling checker's dictionary is bound to be incomplete, make sure you can add your own words to a user dictionary.

☞ **Word count** is a very useful feature, and you should be able to do it for just the text you've selected, not merely for the entire document. Most word count utilities also give you the number of characters, paragraphs and lines.

☞ **Import/export.** What formats a word processor will accept files in, and what formats it's capable of exporting files in, is a very important but often overlooked feature. Some word processors can take text from (and transfer text to) just about any other program. Others make you jump through hoops to export and import, or only recognize a limited number of formats.

very hot tip

☞ You should be able to **preview** what your printout will look like on the screen.

Below are some other word processing features that aren't essential for all users but may be just what *you* need:

☞ **Page layout** features aren't found only in page layout programs. Many word processors give you drawing tools and most let you place graphics anywhere you want on a page.

very good feature

☞ The ability to format in **multiple columns** is very handy if you need it, but useless if you don't (although if you have it, you're bound to find a use for it). In most programs, unfortunately, the columns all have to be the same width; to get variable-width columns, you'll probably have to go into a page layout program.

☞ **Outlining** capabilities are sometimes built into word processors, as is the ability to automatically generate **tables of contents** and **indexes.**

☞ **Footnotes.** If you need them at all, make sure you can get them in the format you need (on each page, at the end of a document, with repeating numbers, or whatever). Whatever your basic requirements are, don't assume that they're the norm for footnoting.

☞ Some word processors (Microsoft Word, most prominently) have a feature called **Glossaries.** The name is confusing, since what's referred to isn't the everyday meaning of the word—a list of definitions like the one at the back of this book. These Glossaries—with a capital G—are collections of often-used words, phrases, paragraphs or graphics that you can recall with a keystroke and place in your document. (Sometimes they're called *Libraries.*)

☞ **Styles,** which are explained on the next page, are another very useful feature.

Remember, just because you can get all these features doesn't mean you need them. For example, if most of your word processing is business correspondence, or straightforward manuscripts, you won't need a program that lets you work in multiple columns. It's silly to pay for what you don't need and, almost inevitably, a lot of features you don't need will get in the way of the ones you do.

very hot tip

As of this writing, the most widely-used Mac word processor is Microsoft Word; other popular programs include MacWrite, WordPerfect and WriteNow. Personally, we use Nisus.

Styles

A **Style** is a collection of paragraph and character formats you can apply in one fell swoop to selected text. *(**Style** is capitalized to differentiate it from **type styles** like italic and bold. It's really a pain how Microsoft appropriates words that already have meanings, like *style* and *glossary*, and assigns them new, contradictory meanings.)*

A **style sheet** is a collection of Styles you use in a particular document, but since you can't capitalize in speech, most people refer to Styles as *style sheets* when talking. Styles were introduced to the Mac by Microsoft Word, and are probably that program's best feature.

If you change a Style, every paragraph defined as that Style changes automatically. For example, let's say that, as Arthur edits this, he's using a Style called *text*, whose definition includes the font Moulin Rouge in 18-point. In the book

very good feature

itself, however, the text will need to be 11-point Bookman. To make that change, you merely have to call up the Style called *text* and change the font definition from 18-point Moulin Rouge to 11-point Bookman. Everywhere the *text* Style has been applied, the text will automatically be changed to 11-point Bookman. You won't have to tediously go through the chapter and change all the body text by hand, carefully avoiding section heads (which are larger than 11-point), tables (which need to be in Optima, not Bookman) and so on.

outliners

An **outliner** is, in effect, a specialized kind of word processor with graphic features that make it easy for you to reorganize your material. You enter text on indented **levels** or in **headlines,** and then you drag it around. If you're thinking that you can do that in a regular word processor, by using tabs for indenting and then cutting and pasting to reorganize—you're wrong. Picture yourself cutting and pasting icons on the desktop every time you want to move something, and you'll get an idea of the difference in convenience.

The various levels or headlines don't have to be single words or phrases—they can be multiple paragraphs of text or even graphics. And best of all, you can **collapse** or **expand** the outline—looking at, for example, only all of the first level headlines, or everything up to the third level, or all the levels that are subordinate to the third first-level headline. Being able to get an overview of your document's structure, and to zero in on any section of it, is invaluable.

The usefulness of outliners isn't limited to organizing large text documents. You can, for example, use them to create calendars, or to-do lists on which you can reprioritize items simply by dragging them to a different spot. In fact, both outliners mentioned below have phone dialers built in, for the people who use them as address book organizers.

Symantec's full-featured More stretches the definition of an outliner into the category of a presentation program (for more on these, see Chapter 14). Symmetry's Acta is more economical, and comes as both a DA and an application.

bargain

General word processing tips

⌘ *two basic word processing rules*

No matter what program you're using, here are a couple of basic rules to follow:

☞ Only hit the [Return] key at the end of paragraphs, not at the end of each line.

☞ Don't use spaces to align words horizontally; they won't line up straight on paper, even if they look straight on the screen. Instead, use [Tab] to create columns, the *Center* command (or whatever it's called in the program you're using) to center text, and margin or indent settings to move text in from the margins.

❡ *insertion point vs. I-beam pointer*

Beginning Mac users—and even experienced ones—often confuse the **insertion point**—the thin, blinking, vertical line that indicates where the next character of text will appear (or disappear)—and the **I-beam pointer,** which looks something like this: I.

Basically, the I-beam pointer *places* the insertion point. You move it to where you want the insertion point to be and click once. To chainge the insertion point's location, you simply move the I-beam to another place and click again.

Unlike more primitive machines, the Mac has no **cursor**. This term from the world of the PC—and, before that, CP/M—is sometimes incorrectly applied to either the pointer or the insertion point.

❡ *importing word processing files to the Mac*

If you need to import a word processing document to a Mac from another type of computer (and you don't have a *filter* for translating the file), you have to first save the file on the foreign computer as a *text*, or **ASCII**, file.

If you neglect this step, the document will be a mess when it gets to the Mac, because word processing programs embed formatting codes in the text that will appear as gibberish on the Mac's screen. The same goes for exporting Mac files to non-Mac computers.

Word tips

Unless otherwise indicated, all these tips work in Word 5, and many of them work in Word 4 and Word 3 as well.

❡ *the "selection bar"*

Microsoft uses a very confusing term to refer to the narrow, invisible column to the left of the text in Word that you use for selecting text. Although *bar* virtually always implies a horizontal line—as when Microsoft Excel distinguishes a *bar chart* (horizontal lines) from a *column chart* (vertical lines)—Microsoft calls this vertical column the **selection bar.**

✿ using the Ruler

There are two triangular markers at the left end of Word's Ruler. The bottom one controls the left margin and the top one controls the indentation of the first line. If you drag the bottom marker (the margin), the top one (the indent) moves with it, but the top marker moves separately—that's how you change the distance between the two. (To move the bottom marker separately, hold down Shift while you drag it.)

To set a margin or indent to the left of the zero mark on the Ruler, just slide the marker to the left; after an initial hesitation, the window scrolls so you can get to the negative numbers. (To scroll to the left of the zero mark without moving anything on the Ruler, just hold Shift down while using the left scroll arrow at the bottom of the window.)

The default unit on the Ruler is inches, but you can change it with the General window of the *Preferences...* command (on the Tools menu, or the Edit menu in versions before 5.1). To change the default tab stops, use the *Document* command and type the new distance you want in the Default Tab Stops box.

✿ basic selection commands

To select:

a word	double-click anywhere in it
a sentence	⌘-click anywhere in it
a line	click in the selection bar
a paragraph	double-click in the selection bar
the entire document	⌘-click in the selection bar or press ⌘A

(And, of course—as with virtually all Mac programs—you can also select any amount of text either by dragging across it or by clicking at one point and then Shift-clicking at another.)

✿ using Shift to select

Moving the pointer with the Shift key held down selects the area the pointer moves across. So, for example, Shift⌘← selects the last word you typed. To extend the selection, just hold the keys down. The selection will continue backward, word by word (or whatever), until you release the keys.

shortcut

Note that [Shift]-clicking to extend a selection works in the original unit of the selection. So if you [⌘]-click to select a sentence (say), [Shift]-clicking someplace else extends the selection to include the whole sentence you've [Shift]-clicked on, regardless of where in that sentence you [Shift]-clicked.

● *line spacing and paragraph spacing*

There are two sets of spacing icons on the Ruler, with related commands in the Paragraph Format dialog box—***line spacing*** (the space between the lines within paragraphs) and ***paragraph spacing*** (the space before and/or after paragraphs). They're completely independent of one another.

● *leading control*

To control leading in Word, go to the Paragraph dialog box (the keyboard shortcut is [⌘M]), select *Exactly* under *Line:* and then type the number of points of leading you want into the *Line* box. (You don't need to type *pt* or anything after the number; Word knows you mean points if you don't specify inches or anything else, and in fact automatically puts *pt* after the number the next time you open the dialog box.)

So, for example, to print out text 11/13 (11-point type on 13-point lines, which is what you're reading now), first select the text, then go to the Character dialog box and type *11* in the *Size* box, then go to the Paragraph dialog box, choose *Exactly* and type *13* in the *Line* box.

● *sizing and cropping graphics*

Dragging the handles on the frame that surrounds a selected graphic resizes the frame, but not the picture. Making the frame smaller than the graphic crops the image, leaving the upper left part of it showing. Making the frame larger centers the picture in the frame.

To change the size of the picture instead of cropping it, hold the [Shift] key and drag on the frame. To return a graphic to its original size, hold down [⌘] and double-click.

very hot tip

Chapter
11

Handling data

Databases

⚫ *database terms*

Here are some basic terms you need to know when using a database program. To help make them clearer, we'll compare each with a concrete, real-world example that you're undoubtedly familiar with— a Rolodex file.

☞ A ***field*** is a single item of information, like a name or an address. It's the equivalent of a single line on a Rolodex card.

☞ A ***record*** is a grouping of related fields, like a person's name, address, phone numbers, etc. It's the equivalent of a single Rolodex card.

☞ A ***database file*** is a collection of related records. It's equivalent to all the cards on a given Rolodex file.

☞ A ***database program*** (or ***database manager***) is the application that creates and handles database files. It's partly equivalent to the Rolodex file itself— the wheel, the knobs, the dividers, etc.—but because computer software has more intelligence than physical objects, another part of what a database program does is equivalent to what you do when you put cards on a Rolodex file, rearrange them and so on.

Just to make things confusing, both *database files* and *database programs* are also sometimes called simply *databases*. So you might say, *which database do you think is best for a small business?* (referring to a program), but you'd be just as likely to say, *which of these databases has your customer data on it?* (referring to a document). In this chapter, we tend to use *database* to refer to the software and *database file* or *document* to refer to the information itself—but, here as elsewhere, only the context will ultimately tell you which is meant.

Other basic terms aren't so easily related to the physical world, since they relate to the computer's special capabilities:

☞ A ***field name*** is a label you use to refer to the field—*First Name, Last Name,* etc. The ***field data*** is the information you put into the field—John, Smith, 123 Elm St, etc.

☞ A *calculated* or *computed* field contains a formula that computes data from other fields in the same record. For example, you might have a field called *subtotal* that adds up several fields that have prices in them, a second field called *sales tax* that indicates what percentage to add to *subtotal* and a third field called *grand total* that multiplies *subtotal* by *sales tax* and then adds the result to *subtotal*.

☞ A *report* is a printout of information in a database (or based on it). It can be a simple list, like a bunch of mailing labels, or it can include computations. These **report calculations** differ from calculated fields in that they gather data from more than one record—a calculated field might total all the items on a single invoice, while a report might total your sales for the month.

☞ **Sorting** lets you arrange records alphabetically, numerically or chronologically (forwards or backwards). Most databases let you do **multilevel sorts,** so you might have your customer file sorted by zip code, and within each zip code, by the customer's last name.

☞ **Selecting** finds records that match certain criteria. For example, you might look for all invoices that have outstanding balances more than 60 days old. Or you might select all customers in Colorado with total sales of $500 or more.

☞ A *multiuser* database is one that can be used on a network by more than one person at a time (although only one person can *change* a particular record at any given time).

🍎 *flat-file vs. relational databases*

There are two main types of database programs. *Flat-file* programs (also known as *file managers*) create database files that are independent of one another. Some examples are FileMaker,

Panorama and the databases that are part of integrated programs (see *integrated programs* below for more on them).

Relational database programs (like 4th Dimension,

Omnis and Double Helix) create database files that can exchange information with each other. For example, you might have three interrelated files—*Order Entry*, *Customers* and ▐▐▐➡

Inventory. When you enter a customer's last name in the Order Entry file, the address and phone number are retrieved from the Customers file (if s/he's bought from you before) and automatically filled into the invoice you're preparing. At the same time, the information on the new purchase is added to the customer's record in the Customers file and the items purchased subtracted from the totals in the Inventory file.

If you don't need the power of a relational database, don't get one, because they're more expensive and much more difficult to set up. A real relational database is actually a specialized programming environment (some relational databases are easier, but they all require programming). It takes hours (and hours and hours) of designing and programming to get what you need. And that's not counting the days it will take just to learn how to use the program.

⚠ *important warning*

General database tips

🍎 *plan ahead*

There are two things to think about when designing a database—what information you need stored, and how to organize it. The first question is pretty straightforward but the second may require some thought.

As an obvious example, if you have a vast mailing list and want to print labels sorted by zip code, the zip code will have to be in a separate field, not part of a larger address field. Or, if you send form letters to clients, you'll want a separate field for a title, so the Mr.'s will get *Mr.*, the Ms.'s will get *Ms.* and the Dr.'s will get *Dr.* in front of their names.

Conversely, you don't need to put info in a separate field if it's never going to be used separately. For example, there's rarely any reason to keep apartment and suite numbers in their own field—it's faster and easier to just include them in the street address field.

very hot tip

⚫ *duplicate files before working on them*

It's good practice to keep at least two copies of any database file, and three of any active one. But if you're too lazy to do that, at least do yourself the favor of duplicating a database file before launching the application to work on it. Most databases keep their files on disk and constantly update them while you work. So the file you had on disk when you began to work is not the file you'll return to when you're done.

important warning

This constant, automatic saving to disk is a good feature, since it means that you don't have to worry about losing any appreciable amount of work if the system crashes. But if you make some changes you later want to discard, you're stuck—unless you made a copy of the file before you started, or are using a database like Panorama, which only saves when you tell it to.

FileMaker tips

⚫ *resizing in one direction*

To change an object's position or size in Layout in only one direction (just vertically or just horizontally), hold down ⧓Shift⧓ while you drag on the object or its handle.

⚫ *fast sizing & styling in layouts*

When you use the Text tool in Layout mode to type field labels or enter other text, you'll get the currently selected font, size and type style. Don't tediously reset these options; it's faster to just copy and paste an existing label that has the settings that you want and then edit it.

shortcut

Instead of cutting and pasting, you can also get a copy of any object on a layout by holding down ⧓Option⧓ and dragging it to another part of the layout. When you drag a field this way, you get a dialog box that lets you choose which field you want to appear in the new spot—it doesn't have to be the one you moved. This is an easy way to give several fields the same font and size.

shortcut

Spreadsheets

⌘ *spreadsheet basics*

A spreadsheet is a grid of *cells* (little boxes) that are arranged in (horizontal) *rows* and (vertical) *columns*. You put numbers in the cells and tell the spreadsheet to perform mathematical operations on them.

L et's say you create a column that represents your monthly budget, with the first cell for rent or mortgage, the next for utilities, the next for food, and so on. Then you put twelve of those columns next to each other, one for each month of the year. Such a spreadsheet can calculate your budget for each month (the total of each column) and how much you spent—or plan to spend—in any given category in the course of a year (the total of each row). You can also have a total calculated for all categories in the entire year, and averages for categories or months.

The great strength of spreadsheets is that if you change a number in one spot, every other number that depends on it is recalculated automatically. So if you change the utility cost for May (when your lover will be in Italy and you'll be making many long passionate international phone calls), the total for May will change, and so will the yearly total for utilities, the yearly total for all categories, the average monthly budget, and any other calculations you've set up.

very good feature

T hat's the key to the spreadsheet's *what-if* capability—you can change a number or two and see what effects it has. For example, you can figure out how large a mortgage you can afford at various rates of interest, or how much profit you'll make if you sell 1000, 5000 or 10,000 of a product.

Spreadsheets have other uses as well. Since you can put text as well as numbers in cells, spreadsheets provide an easy way to lay out complicated tables, even if you don't have them do any calculations. And most spreadsheets can also create charts, which can be very useful, since numbers are more easily understood when presented graphically.

(A *spreadsheet* is the document you create and a *spreadsheet program* is the software that creates it, but the program is also commonly called a *spreadsheet*—just as a database program is often simply called a *database*.)

As of this writing, Microsoft Excel is the most popular Mac spreadsheet program; others include Claris Resolve, Lotus 1-2-3 and MacCalc. Integrated programs like ClarisWorks and GreatWorks also include spreadsheet modules.

General spreadsheet tips

relative vs. absolute cell references

When you refer to a cell in a formula, the spreadsheet thinks of it *relatively*—that is, as the cell that's three columns to the left and two rows above the cell where the formula is. That's so the formula will still work if you copy it to a new cell (a sum, for example, will add up the cells above it, rather than the cells above the cell where the formula was copied from).

Sometimes, though, you don't want cell references to change when you move a formula—you want them to be identified by their actual, *absolute* locations (*A1, 4F* or whatever). To do that, put dollar signs before both the column and the row—for example, *4F.* You can also make just the column, or just the row, absolute—for example, *A$2* or *$B14.*

very hot tip

You can type the dollar signs in yourself, but most programs also have a command that does it. In Excel, for example, it's the *Reference* command in the Formula menu.

selecting the whole spreadsheet

To select all the cells in most spreadsheets, click in the box in the extreme upper left corner—that is, above the number *1* and to the left of the letter *A.*

shortcut

Excel tips

These tips work with Excel 4, 3 and 2.2.

⌘ *previews of printouts*

One of Excel's nice features is the ability to preview on the screen what printouts will look like on paper (by choosing *Print Preview* from the File menu or by clicking the *Print Preview* checkbox in the Print dialog box).

If the text in the Preview window is too small to read, you can zoom in on any part of it by clicking with the magnifying-glass pointer. You can move around while zoomed in by using the scroll bars. Click again and you're back at the overall view of the page.

very good feature

Unfortunately, this doesn't work on big screens. If Excel thinks it's showing you the whole page actual size, it won't let you zoom in on it to see details.

⌘ *outlining cells*

Although it's right there in the Border dialog box (on the

very good feature

Format menu), many Excel users don't realize that they can outline a cell they've selected simply by clicking on *Outline*. This is a lot easier than clicking on *Left*, *Top*, *Right* and *Bottom* all the time.

If you're working with a group of selected cells, *Outline* borders the group as a whole, not each individual cell within it. There's even a keyboard command for outlining a cell or group: Option ⌃⌘ `0` (zero).

◉ *escaping from cells with invalid formulas*

Excel won't let you exit a cell until the formula in it makes sense (you'll keep getting the *Error in formula* message). This can be maddening when you're working on a complex formula and can't seem to get it right.

T he way out is easy—just remove the equal sign at the beginning of the formula. Excel will now treat the entry as text and won't analyze it for correctness. After a while away from the troublesome formula, you may be able to go back to it and spot your mistake.

very hot tip

◉ *adjusting columns and rows*

When you put the pointer on, or slightly to the left of, the dividing line between column headings (A, B, etc.), it changes to a thick vertical line with arrows pointing right and left. Now you can drag the column to the left of this dividing line to make it wider or narrower.

W hen you put the pointer on, or slightly above, the dividing line between row headings (1, 2, etc.), it changes to a thick horizontal line with arrows pointing up and down. Now you can drag the row above this dividing line to make it wider or narrower.

When you've hidden a column or row (like D in the illustration below), put the pointer slightly to the right of, or slightly below, the dividing line between the visible column or row and the hidden one. Now dragging right or down will open up the hidden column or row, instead of widening the visible column or row.

Start dragging here…

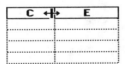

…and column C gets wider.

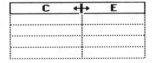

Start dragging here…

…to reveal hidden column D.

Integrated programs

🍎 *integrated programs*

Integrated programs combine a word processor with several other applications, most commonly a spreadsheet, database and communications program (each of which is called a ***module***), plus some drawing tools (or sometimes a whole drawing module). The features of these modules tend to be somewhat limited compared to those offered by stand-alone applications of the same type, but integrated programs save you money and give you the basic stuff you need.

For years, Microsoft Works was the only integrated program available, but now it's got competition from other "Works" programs, including Claris' ClarisWorks and Symantec's GreatWorks.

From the Visual Delights collection of Macintosh clip art. Copyright © 1991 by SunShine. All rights reserved.

Graphics overview

kinds of graphics programs

Graphics programs for the Mac fall into five basic categories:

☞ *Paint* programs create bit-mapped images—that is, ones that are made up of dots. The dot is their basic unit, so if you want to move a bit-mapped image, you have to surround all the dots that make it up and select them as a group. Claris' MacPaint, Electronic Arts' Studio/1 and Studio/32, Adobe's Photoshop, Fractal Design's Painter and Time Arts' Oasis all handle this type of graphic.

☞ *Draw* (or *drafting)* programs treat each item you draw as a discrete object. All you have to do to select a draw object is click on it. (On the down side, you can't fine-tune an object, removing a dot here and adding one there.) High-end draw programs go by the name of *CAD (computer-aided design)* and are sometimes specific to a particular profession. Claris' MacDraw and ClarisCAD, IDD's MacDraft, Autodesk's AutoCAD and Graphisoft's ArchiCAD are all draw programs.

☞ PostScript-based *illustration* programs create images that scale perfectly to all sizes. Aldus' FreeHand and Adobe's Illustrator are two popular illustration programs.

☞ *3D* graphics programs let you simulate a three-dimensional image on your two-dimensional computer screen. Infini-D, Sculpt 3D and MacRenderMan are all 3D graphics programs.

☞ *Combination* programs let you work with both bit-mapped and object-oriented images, placing them on different levels (which work like transparent overlays, so you can see everything that's on each level). SuperPaint and Canvas are both combination programs (Canvas provides paint, draw *and* PostScript tools).

In general, bit-mapped images are better suited for artistic tasks and object-oriented graphics for business applications like drafting and diagramming. PostScript images are hard-edged like object-oriented graphics but are capable of much greater sophistication and subtlety (they still don't have that bit-mapped look, though). This isn't an either/or proposition. If you do a fair amount of graphics work on the Mac, you'll want to have at least a paint/draw program (or separate paint and draw programs) and probably also a PostScript one.

A ny of these types of programs may or may not handle color. If they do, they're often used just for that, but some programs— Illustrator and FreeHand, for example—are commonly used for both color and monochrome work. The most basic color programs are 8-bit, which produce 256 colors. 24-bit color programs give you more than sixteen million colors, but working with 24-bit images requires faster hardware and more memory.

🍎 *graphics formats*

Each kind of Mac graphics program saves its files in its own, **native** format, which may or may not coincide with one of the basic file formats used to transfer images from one program to another (or even between Macs and other kinds of computers). Some programs give you a choice of several different formats to save files in, and some also recognize many different formats. Here are the most common ones:

☞ *Paint* files are 72-dpi, black-and-white-only, bit-mapped images; in addition, they're limited to an 8" x 10" page.

☞ Like paint files, *TIFF* files *(tagged image file format)* are bit-mapped, but they can be any size and have any resolution (number of dots per inch)—although 300 dpi is common. TIFF is generally used for images created by scanners. (Although it was intended to provide a high-resolution bit-mapped standard, everybody wanted to improve it—and did, in different ways—so the TIFF standard isn't exactly standard anymore. Some TIFF images are black-and-white only, most support grayscale information and a few do color—it all depends on the software that creates the image.)

☞ *PICT* files (from *picture*) are used to transfer the object-oriented graphics created by draw programs. PICT files use QuickDraw, which is also used to display things on the Mac's screen. ⫸

The original PICT only allowed for eight colors, but the current standard—PICT2, which is now used almost universally—allows for full 32-bit color, which is the most the Mac can produce.

☞ *EPS* files *(encapsulated PostScript)* are combinations of the PostScript code that tells the printer how to print the image and a PICT image that tells the screen how to display it. (You can just use the PostScript code—place it in PageMaker, for example—but you won't be able to see it on the screen, because the screen doesn't know how to display PostScript instructions. You'll get just a gray box instead.)

If you work with large, complex or 3D graphics or CAD software, you may also encounter files in the formats below:

☞ *DXF (drawing exchange format)* is the most common CAD format on personal computers, but some Mac programs can also handle *IGES* (initial graphics exchange specification), which is primarily used on minicomputers or CAD workstations.

☞ There's no industry-standard 3D format, but the closest so far is *RIB* *(RenderMan interface bytestream)*.

☞ Graphics files can be huge, and several compressed formats exist to reduce the size of them. Common ones are *RIFF (resource interchange file format)*, *JPEG (Joint Photographic Experts Group)* and *GIF (graphics interchange format)*.

Graphics software tips

🍎 [Shift] *key effects*

The [Shift] key usually acts as a ***constraint*** in paint programs, keeping a tool moving in a horizontal or vertical direction (depending on which way you move initially) or keeping shapes that you're drawing of equal length and width. For example:

very hot tip

[Shift] +	lets you:
🖌	paint straight horizontal or vertical lines
✏	make straight horizontal or vertical lines
✋	shift the window contents horizontally or vertically
🧽	erase in straight horizontal or vertical lines
▭	create squares
◯	create circles

🍎 *retaining the tool you're using*

In MacDraw, when you draw a shape or type text, the pointer normally reverts to the selection arrow as soon as you're done. If you want to retain the tool so you can use it again immediately, double-click on the tool in the palette to select it (instead of the usual single click).

very hot tip

Scanners

🍎 *scanners*

Scanners are devices that convert images—typically photographs or other artwork—into digital form so they can be stored and manipulated by computers. Mac-compatible scanners range in price from a few hundred dollars to a hundred *thousand* dollars. The ones under $10,000 are great for jobs that don't require precise detail or color reproduction, but they can't compete with high-end equipment when it comes to demanding jobs like color photographs in slick publications.

There are three major types of scanner:

☞ *Hand-held scanners* you literally roll across the artwork. They're small and relatively inexpensive, but they only scan in strips about four inches wide. Some come with software that lets you piece together multiple scans to build a larger image, but this process is annoying and imprecise. Also, images are often distorted, because it's impossible to roll a hand-held scanner without wavering or changing speed.

☞ ***Flatbed scanners*** operate like photocopiers; you place the artwork on a glass surface and a scan head and light source move across under the glass. Flatbeds can scan almost anything that has at least one flat side, even a slab of marble. Most of them can't scan transparencies and slides, but a growing number of manufacturers offer attachments for that purpose. All flatbeds will scan up to at least 8½" x 11", and some go up to 11" x 17".

☞ As their name suggests, ***transparency scanners*** scan transparent materials. (*Slide scanners* might be a more appropriate term, since units that can scan transparencies larger than 35mm tend to cost over $20,000.)

 OCR

OCR (for ***optical character recognition***) scanners go beyond merely scanning a page as a picture; with the help of software, they recognize the letters and store them as actual characters, editable in a word processing (or other text-handling) program. Make sure any one you buy lets you scan from within the OCR software you want to use;

important warning

otherwise you'll have to scan a page, save it as a graphic and then open it with your OCR software.

OCR really isn't worth getting involved with unless you're going to be digitizing lots of documents. And if you're going to be digitizing lots of documents, you'll want a scanner that's fast.

Some OCR scanners pull pages through a series of rollers. This means you can't scan books (or anything else that

you can't tear into single sheets) and the rollers have a tendency to mangle documents. Flatbeds are by far the best choice; the same problems that limit hand-held devices for image scanning make them a pain for reading documents.

very bad feature

Because most people expect OCR software to instantly and magically put text into their ▐▐▐▶

computers, they're often disappointed with the reality. OCR conversion takes time, and just as typists make mistakes, so do the programs. When you consider the cost of the hardware and software, you may be better off hiring a typist, unless you have hundreds or thousands of pages to scan into the Mac.

Page layout programs

⚫ what is page layout?

Whenever people prepare ads, newsletters, books or anything else for printing, someone has to figure out the layout—where the text, graphics, tables, photographs, etc. go on the page. Before 1985—when PageMaker, the first page layout program, appeared—layout artists sketched a design by hand and then fitted type into it after it came back from the typesetter.

A s the layout evolved, type might be reset repeatedly—sometimes at great expense. When the layout was finished, the columns of type were glued onto sheets of cardboard marked with the page dimensions— a laborious, time-consuming task.

Page layout programs completely revolutionized this process. Now designers (and editors, or anyone who learns how to use the programs) can arrange and rearrange text and graphics on a computer screen with an ease and flexibility completely unknown just ten years ago.

very good feature

L ayout changes can be done much faster, more easily and less expensively by using a laser printer to produce proofs (or even final pages). No more gluing paper strips, no more messing with wax or rubber cement and T-squares.

TimeWorks' Publish It! Easy and Aldus' Personal Press are two inexpensive, easy-to-use page layout programs; Quark's XPress (which most people just call *Quark)*, Aldus' PageMaker and Frame Technology's FrameMaker are more sophisticated professional-level programs.

General page layout tips

🍎 *seeing what you're moving*

When you drag something in PageMaker or Quark, what moves is an *outline* of the item; when you stop dragging, the item itself appears in the new position. But when you're trying to align something exactly (to a guide, say), the outline isn't good enough. So hold the mouse button down before dragging.

very hot tip

When PageMaker's pointer changes from an arrow to a cross with arrows at the end of each arm (how long that takes depends on how complex whatever you're dragging is), the Mac has loaded the object into memory and will show it to you in detail when you drag. When Quark's **item tool** (the four-directional arrow that's used for moving objects) turns into a clock, the object will be visible when it's dragged.

🍎 *the grabber hand*

You don't have to use the scroll bars to view different parts of the page you're on—there's a grabber hand you can use to slide the layout around in the window. In both PageMaker and Quark 3.1 (or with the FeaturesPlus XTension in Quark 3.0), you hold down Option and press (and hold) the mouse button. In Quark the hand appears as soon as Option is pressed, but in Pagemaker it only appears after the button is pressed.

shortcut

🍎 *copying tabs and indents*

To copy tabs and indents from the first paragraph in a selection to all the other paragraphs in PageMaker, select all the text and choose *Indents/tabs* from the Text menu. The tabs and indents in the first paragraph will be displayed in the dialog box. Now just click *OK* (don't do anything else). These settings will be applied to all the selected paragraphs.

very hot tip

To copy tabs and indents from one paragraph to paragraphs that *don't* follow it, copy part of the original paragraph and paste it at the top of the paragraphs you want to change. Select all the paragraphs, use the *Indents/tabs* trick and then delete the pasted paragraph (or piece of a paragraph).

I n Quark, you can copy only tabs in this way by choosing *Tabs...* from the Style menu. However, you can easily copy all of a paragraph's formatting whether the paragraphs are adjacent or not.

Place the insertion point in the paragraph you want to reformat, put the I-beam pointer over the paragraph with the desired formatting and Shift Option -click. This will only work between paragraphs in the same story; it doesn't change any character formatting.

🍎 *masking*

Every PageMaker expert we know uses *masking,* but many beginning users don't know about it. It couldn't be simpler—when there's something on the page that you don't want, it's often easier to cover it up than to try to remove it. To do that, you draw a rectangle (or some other shape, but rectangles usually work best) and place it over what you want to erase. Then go to the Element menu and select *Paper* under *Fill* and *None* under *Line.* The rectangle disappears, and so does what's behind it.

T his same technique also works in Quark. Boxes are frameless by default—you just have to make sure the background in the box specifications is either Black (0% shade), White or Registration. Either text or graphic boxes can be used to mask.

PageMaker tips

🍎 *shrinking PageMaker files*

PageMaker files get bigger as you work on them. That's because the program *appends* changes to the existing file when you save, rather than replacing it with the new, edited one. You can often cut the size of a PageMaker file in half (or more) by choosing *Save As...* instead of *Save.* When you *Save As...* with the same file

**very
hot
tip**

name, the old file is completed replaced by the current one, and all the appended changes are thrown away.

⚫ *slide shows*

To see a "slide show" of your document, hold Shift while you choose *Go To Page.* PageMaker will display each page (or spread if you're viewing facing pages) on the screen for about four seconds. To stop the show, just click anywhere with the mouse. To speed it up a bit, turn off the Rulers first—time won't be wasted redrawing them every time a new page is displayed.

*very
hot
tip*

⚫ *some useful keyboard shortcuts*

Here are a few of the more useful PageMaker shortcuts:

triple-click *(with I-beam pointer)*	select paragraph
Option ⌘ P *(with I-beam pointer)*	insert automatic page number
Shift *(while dragging on graphic handle)*	resize proportionately (rather than stretching)

shortcut

⚫ *rewriting the screen*

Sometimes when you move or resize objects on a page, they end up looking like they have chunks missing or are distorted. To fix this problem, use any of the size commands at the top of the Page menu (or their keyboard equivalents).

These commands make PageMaker redraw the screen, even if it was already showing the page at that size. If objects still look wrong after the screen redraws, make sure they're not overlapping objects in another layer.

Quark tips

🍎 fast moves

To drag a text or picture box without having to switch from the content tool to the item tool, hold down the ⌘ key. However, you don't have to select the box first. Simply ⌘-click and drag and the box will move immediately.

shortcut

🍎 pushing buttons

Almost every button in Quark's dialog boxes can be selected with a keyboard combination—usually ⌘ plus the first letter of the button's name. For example, if a dialog box has *Yes* and *No* buttons, you can select them by typing ⌘Y and ⌘N. Press ⌘. to select *Cancel* in any dialog box.

shortcut

🍎 Quark keyboard shortcuts

triple-click	selects line
quadruple-click	selects paragraph
quintuple-click	selects whole text block
Control-click	zooms in by 25% (or amount you define)
Option Control-click	zooms out by 25% (or amount you define)
Control-drag area with marquee	zooms to fill screen with area selected

shortcut

⌘ *palettes by keyboard*

You can also select items on the Tool or Measurements palettes with keyboard commands. To select the next tool down on the palette, hit ⌘Tab. To select the next tool up, type ⌘ShiftTab. If the Tool palette is closed, either command opens it. ⌘OptionM opens the Measurements palette (if it was closed) and selects the first item.

shortcut

⌘ *special characters in Quark*

Quark has lots of special characters especially for layout and typesetting purposes. Here are a few particularly useful ones:

☞ ⌘Spacebar is a nonbreaking space, useful for preventing two words from being separated with a line break or for forcing a word to the following line.

☞ ⌘= is a nonbreaking hyphen, useful for preventing a hyphenated word (name, phone number) from being separated with a line break.

☞ ShiftReturn is a *soft return;* it makes a line break without starting a new paragraph.

☞ ⌘Return is a discretionary return, similar to ⌘-, the discretionary hyphen. If Quark needs to break the word at the end of a line, it will do it where you insert the discretionary return, but will neither put in a hyphen nor make a new paragraph. This is useful for allowing a break after a slash in a compound word.

☞ ⌘\ is an "indent-here" character. It lets you create an instant hanging indent for a single paragraph without having to deal with margins and first-line indents. Wherever you insert the invisible character ⌘\, all following lines in the paragraph will indent to that point.

Chapter
13

Commun-
icating

Telecommunicating

● *telecommunicating on the Mac*

Telecommunications (transferring information between computers over telephone lines) has a reputation for being one of the least friendly areas of personal computing. That's because, all too often, it *is* one of the least friendly areas of personal computing. But telecommunicating can also be tremendously exciting, useful and fun. If you get the right software, it can even be easy to learn—especially on the Mac, where it tends to be easier than on other computers.

Y ou can telecommunicate directly with a friend's computer (it usually doesn't matter whether it's a Mac or PC, or even some other kind of computer) or indirectly, through a computer provided by an **online service** or **bulletin board** (both described below).

Sending a file to the distant computer is called **uploading**, and retrieving a file from the distant computer is called **downloading**. When you're connected to another computer on a phone line, you're said to be **online**, and *online* is also used to describe the things you find there—e.g. *online help, an online database*.

● *why "modem?"*

Modem is short for *modulator-demodulator*; on the sending end, it *modulates* (changes) your computer's digital information into sounds, which then travel over telephone wires; on the receiving end, it changes the sounds back into digital data again (*demodulates* them).

● *telecommunications basics*

To telecommunicate, you need a **modem** *(MOE-dum)*. This small piece of hardware lets you hook up your computer to a phone line and transmit data over it. Like hard disks, modems can be either external or internal (installed in expansion slots).   ‖➡

Hooking up an external modem is a cinch—there's a power cord to plug it in, a cable to connect it to the computer and a phone cord that connects it to the phone jack in the wall.

Since many people use a single phone line for both the modem and a phone, there's a second jack on the modem to hook the phone into. (But it's a real luxury to have two lines.)

In addition to a modem, you need **communications software**. Communications programs can be general-purpose or they can be adapted for a specific job, like the software that's designed to connect you with information services and is provided by them as part of their package. (These programs are designed to be easy to set up and use.)

Unfortunately, most general-purpose communications programs challenge you with a confusing array of options, labelled in unintelligible jargon. Even the bare-bones program FreeTerm has a dialog box like the one below.

Fortunately, with the exception of the **speed** setting, you can usually just leave the default settings suggested by your program and everything will be fine.

The speed setting determines the rate at which the modem sends and receives information, usually called the **baud rate** (after the communications pioneer Baudot) and expressed in bits per second **(bps)**. Most modems are capable of handling their own top speed as well as anything below that, so a 9600-bps modem, say, can transmit at 9600, 2400 and 1200 bps.

When two modems connect, they negotiate to determine the highest baud rate and **protocols** they share (protocols are sets of rules that control how information is transmitted— let your modem worry about them).

If you have trouble connecting with Ⅲ➡

Speed	○ 300	○ 1200	○ 2400
	○ 4800	◉ 9600	○ 19200
	○ 57600		
Data bits	◉ 8	○ 7	
Stop bits	◉ 1	○ 2	
Parity	◉ None	○ Even	○ Odd
Duplex	◉ Full	○ Half	
Port	◉ Modem	○ Printer	

☐ Prompt for port at startup

☐ BS -> DEL   ☐ LF after CR

☒ Xon/Xoff   ☒ CRC Xmodem

☒ MacBinary Xmodem ☐ Fast-Track Xmodem

[Make Default]   [OK]

another modem, compare notes with the person you're trying to connect to, and make sure all the settings are the same in both your communications programs. (If you really want to understand what these settings do, see *telecom terms* on the next page.)

Some communications programs include a basic programming or scripting language that lets you automate your telecommunications sessions. MicroPhone is a popular commercial telecommunications program; ZTerm and FreeTerm are shareware alternatives—the former is loaded with features and the latter is simple and easy-to-use.

what to do after you connect

You can telecommunicate in **real time**—which means that what you type appears on the other person's screen as you type it, and vice versa. (Most communications programs let you store everything you see on the screen to disk, so you can review it later.)

You can also communicate in real time with a bulletin board or online service, where there's no human on the other end but everything you send and receive still appears on the screen. But most telecommunications involves *file transfers*—something goes directly from your disk to the other computer, or from the other computer to your disk, and you don't see anything on the screen except a report as to the status of the transfer (how much time is left until it's finished, and/or how many bytes have been transmitted).

The most common protocol for transferring files with another personal computer (rather than with an online service) is **Xmodem**. **Ymodem** is essentially the same, but can send a group of files all at once; **Ymodem-G** is faster, but more precarious (any problems and the transfer gets cancelled); **Zmodem** is the best—both dependable and very fast.

disabling Call Waiting

Call Waiting—the phone company service that interrupts calls with signals when someone else is calling, and lets you switch between the two calls—disrupts data transmissions. But if your phone company uses electronic switching, you can temporarily disable Call Waiting for the duration of any outgoing call. Just precede the number you're dialing with *70, (on a tone line) or 1170, (on a pulse line). When the call is over, Call Waiting returns automatically.

very hot tip

To see whether you can do this on your phone, just try putting the appropriate code in front of a number you're dialing. If the service isn't available, you should get a recorded message that the call can't be completed as dialed.

If you're using an AT-compatible modem, add *70, to whatever number it's set up to dial in your communications software. When you tell the modem to dial, it'll disable Call Waiting, pause for a second or two to allow the dial tone to return, then dial the phone number (the comma after *70 generates the pause). You can get the same result by typing ATDT*70, phone number into your software's command window (needless to say, substitute whatever number you're dialing for phone number).

🍎 telecom terms

Even when both computers are using the same baud rate, one or the other of them might receive information faster than it can handle (it might need to pause to write information to the disk, for example). This situation is controlled by establishing a **handshake** with the other computer.

A common handshaking protocol is called **Xon/Xoff**

(pronounced *ex-on ex-off*, not *zon zoff*), in which an *off* signal is sent to the other computer to temporarily stop the flow of information and an *on* signal is sent to resume it (the X stands for *transmit*).

Data bits and **stop bits** have to do with the chunks of information you send. Most programs expect every character (every

byte, in other words) to be eight bits long, but some use only seven bits. A stop bit marks the end of one byte and the beginning of another.

Parity is a way of checking that the other computer received exactly what you sent. Since there are better ways to check this, most telecommunications transmissions use no parity at all.

the denser, the faster

You can speed your file transfers by first compressing the file you plan to send. There are commercial and shareware compression programs to choose from, and AppleLink (Apple's online service) even has one built-in. (For details, see the section on compression utilities in Chapter 9.) File compression can also be useful for keeping your data intact—if, for example, you're sending Nisus files over America Online, which normally trashes them.

Modems and
fax modems

modem speeds, protocols and standards

When you buy a modem, make sure it's compatible with the industry-standard Hayes AT command set (with which your Mac controls the modem). A modem may also have its own protocols (in addition to the ones you set up in your communications software) which can enable you to send and receive data much faster and more accurately—provided the modem you're connecting to adheres to the same protocols.

S*tandards*, each of which may include more than one protocol, cover three aspects of transmission—speed, error-checking and data compression. Their names begin with *V.* followed by a number (and sometimes the word *bis* or *ter,* which are French for *second* and *third).* Here's a guide to speed standards:

speed	standard
2400 bps	V.22bis
9600 bps	V.32 compliant (just compatible isn't enough)
14,400 bps	V.32bis

V.42 isn't a speed standard but rather an error-correction standard, and comes in conjunction with speed standards. (V.42 includes the MNP 2, 3 and 4 and LAPM protocols.) For data compression, look for V.42bis—it compresses data by a factor of four, so a 2400-bps modem can transmit at the equivalent of 9600 bps, and a 14,400-bps modem at the equivalent of 57,600 bps. (Don't use compression utilities like StuffIt and Compact Pro on your file before transmitting with V.42bis; it's unnecessary and may even slow down the transmission.)

It's wise to pick a modem that also has the MNP 5 protocol; its compression ratio is only 2:1 but it's more common than V.42bis. (As with compression software, the actual amount of compression depends on the file type—text and some graphics files shrink the most.)

fax modems

More and more modems come with the ability to send—and often receive—faxes through your Mac. (The fax modem's software converts your Mac documents to fax format and sends them over the phone line, to either a fax machine or another fax modem.)

As long as your Mac and modem are on (and the fax modem software is installed), receiving a fax is automatic; incoming faxes are stored on disk, and software lets you know they're there.

Fax software usually comes in at least three parts: a Chooser driver for sending faxes, an extension or control panel for receiving them and an application for viewing faxes you receive, maintaining a phone directory, setting preferences and so on.

Online services and bulletin boards

online services

Online services operate large computers that you access with a modem over phone lines. Their computers store software, documents, messages and other electronic information that has been uploaded (**posted**) by computer companies, by the people who work for the online service and by other subscribers like yourself, so that it's available to be downloaded. In other words, an online service is like a warehouse and package delivery service for information in electronic form.

In addition, online services let you ***chat***—type back and forth in real time with other users, or use ***e-mail*** (for *electronic mail)* which lets you send and receive messages and/or files directly to other users' accounts. What you send by e-mail waits in the addressee's electronic mailbox until the next time they log on and retrieve it.

There are many commercial online services, but America Online, AppleLink and CompuServe are particularly valuable for Mac users. They have tons of public-domain Mac software and shareware, and software publishers often post minor upgrades on them (ones that fix bugs or improve compatibility).

GEnie is another online service that has a good library of Mac shareware, but its user interface is confusing and unMaclike. (Not surprisingly, services that were originally created for Macs, like AppleLink and America Online, are a *lot* easier to use than ones that were originally created for PCs, like CompuServe and GEnie.)

Online services provide ***conferences*** (where a number of users chat on a given topic) and ***forums*** (sections of the online service that include software, messages and conferences in a particular area of interest). In addition, online services often offer syndicated news stories from AP and Reuters, job listings, stock quotes and financial information for investors—usually at an extra charge. Some will even send faxes for you, for about what you'd pay at a service bureau.

Networks

⁕ *networking basics*

A computer ***network*** is two or more devices connected to share information (so, technically, a single Mac hooked to a LaserWriter is a network, although it's seldom called one). Among Mac users, ***network*** usually refers to a ***local area network***, or ***LAN***—one that's confined to a relatively small area, like an office. Connecting Macs and other

(continued on page 210)

bulletin boards

An electronic **bulletin board** (abbreviated BBS, for *bulletin board system)* is sort of a home-grown, low-rent online service. It's a lot like an electronic user group—you'll find plenty of people online who are willing and able to answer your questions. Most bulletin boards also have the latest versions of public-domain and shareware software available for downloading (the sections of online services that do that are also sometimes called *bulletin boards).*

Best of all, many BBSs are *bargain* free. (But with a commercial online service—unlike a BBS—you virtually never get a busy signal. If you need information or software right away, that may be worth some money to you.)

The person who runs a bulletin board is called a **sysop** *(SISS-ahp,* for *system operator).* On small bulletin boards, the sysop does everything—takes care of the hardware, decides what's available for downloading, controls who's allowed to leave and retrieve messages, and so on. On bigger boards (and on online services), sysops control sections that are dedicated to specific kinds of information.

A complete list of every active Mac BBS in the country would take up many pages of this book and would probably be out of date by the time you read it. Here are four we can recommend, along with their fees, if any, and the maximum baud rate they can handle.

☞ **4th Dimension.** Cambridge MA, 617 494 0565. No access fee. 14,400 bps. Sysop: Zeff Wheelock.

☞ **Laserboard New York.** Queens NY, 718 639 8826. $18 a year. 14,400 bps. Sysop: Adam Wildavsky.

☞ **MacInfo.** Newark CA, 510 795 8862. No access fee. 9600 bps. Sysop: Norm Goodger.

☞ **SoftArc Online.** Scarborough, Ontario, 416 609 2250. No access fee. 9600 bps.

Some BBSs offer gateways to other bulletin boards (that is, you can call one board and access others through it—post and pick up messages, for example—without having to make another call). Thousands of individual BBSs around the world have linked together to form FidoNet *[after the founder's dog?—AN].*

devices into a network lets people share printers, send each other messages and access files on other networked Macs.

E very device on a network (whether a computer, a printer or whatever) is called a **node**. Each node on a Mac network automatically gets a unique ID number (called an **address**) when you turn it on, which identifies it to the other nodes on the network.

This automatic process means you don't have to shut down the network to hook up additional nodes, and that makes Mac networks a cinch to set up. (PCs and most other computers need special, additional software to network, and on networks made up of them, ID numbers aren't assigned when you turn the node on. The Mac's capabilities are more advanced because it's had networking software built in since the beginning—even back when 128K was a lot of RAM and virtually nobody had a hard drive.)

very good feature

On Mac networks, you also give each node a name—using the Sharing Setup control panel on System 7 Macs, the Chooser on System 6 Macs, and the setup programs that come with other devices. This name shows up in the Chooser on other Macs when they're picking the Mac whose files they want to share, the printer they want to use, etc.

P rotocols tell each node what to do with the information flowing through the network. Most Mac networks use the AppleTalk protocol, because that's the software that's built into all Macs. Other protocols—sometimes used by Macs but mostly used by other machines—include DECnet, TCP/IP and Token-Ring.

Large networks are often subdivided into smaller areas called **zones** (which show up in the Chooser) so that users can narrow down their Chooser selections to, say, the Macs and printers in their own office's zone, rather than having to select from every device in the building. Separate networks can be connected by **bridges**, **routers** or **gateways** (in order of increasing intelligence).

🍎 *basic networking hardware*

Apple's system of cabling and connectors for LANs is called **LocalTalk**. Not long after it was introduced, a small company named Farallon introduced an alternative to LocalTalk hardware called **PhoneNet**. It has several major advantages (and, as a result, Farallon is no longer small).

☞ **PhoneNet uses regular phone wire,** which costs about a third as much as LocalTalk cabling. You save even more if you use the two unused (yellow and black) wires in existing phone lines that probably already run where you want your network lines to go.

bargain

☞ **PhoneNet connectors are also somewhat cheaper** than LocalTalk ones.

☞ **PhoneNet allows networks to run up to 3000 feet** (LocalTalk limits you to 1000 feet).

☞ **PhoneNet's connectors are like the standard modular plugs on phone cords** (LocalTalk connectors have a tendency to pull out).

very good feature

☞ **It lets you use daisy-chain, backbone or star configurations** (LocalTalk restricts you to the daisy-chain).

If you have a network of any size, PhoneNet hardware can save you a lot of money, and imitations of it can save you even more. (If you already have LocalTalk cabling, just switch over to PhoneNet-type hardware for any additional needs. Farallon makes an adaptor

bargain

🍎 *network configurations*

There are three basic network configurations (ways of connecting the nodes) commonly used on the Mac. **Daisy-chain** (also called *series)* networks connect devices one after the other, in a chain. (The problem with this configuration is that if one node is disconnected, so is everything beyond it.)

A **backbone** configuration is an improvement, because each node has its own little branch off the main cable (like rooms off a hall); if one node is disconnected, it doesn't affect the others. A **star** configuration has a central node to which all the other nodes are connected.

There are two main cabling systems for hooking up a Mac network—**LocalTalk** and **Ethernet**. (See the entries above and below.)

for connecting LocalTalk to PhoneNet systems, so you won't lose whatever you have invested.)

Ethernet

Ethernet is one of the fastest networking systems available. A LocalTalk network can transmit data at 230 kilobits (about 5000 average-sized words) a second, while an Ethernet network can go as high as 10 megabits (over 200,000 words) a second—more than 43 times as fast! (But be aware that most hardware can't keep up with that speed.)

Each Mac in an Ethernet network needs EtherTalk software, an interface card, and special cabling. (The card and cabling are called **Ethernet**, the software and communications protocols are called **EtherTalk**—or, sometimes, **AppleTalk over Ethernet.**) Traditional Ethernet cabling resembles the coaxial cables that connect VCRs to TVs, but now most Ethernet installations use twisted-pair wiring, which looks like telephone wires and requires an Ethernet hub like Farallon's StarController EN. Several companies—including Apple, Asanté, Cayman, Dove, Farallon, Novell, NRC and 3Com—manufacture Ethernet cards.

file sharing

System 7's **file sharing** allows Macs on a network to access each others' files. It's a great way to copy files from one Mac to another—much easier and faster than carrying floppies back and forth. You can also work on a file on another Mac without copying it to your own, but that generally slows down both Macs.

shortcut

Your files are private until you turn on file sharing by clicking the *Start* button in the Sharing Setup control panel. Then you select a disk, folder or file you want to share and choose the *Sharing...* command from the File menu. In the dialog box that appears, you can set up **access privileges** for other users on your network, which determine whether they'll only be able to look at your files, or to make changes, rename, move or delete them.

If you want to assign different degrees of access to different users, you'll have to register each user's name (and give them passwords if

⌘ *file sharing tips*

Here are a few tips for getting the most out of file sharing with the fewest negative side effects:

☞ You can bypass most of the procedure for getting a shared item onto 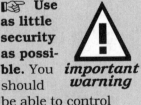 *shortcut* your desktop by **making an alias** of it once you get it there the first time. The next time, just double-click the alias and click *OK* in the dialog box that appears.

☞ You can share up to ten separate items, but unless you're setting up different access privileges for each of them, it's much easier to **gather everything you're** sharing into one folder and share *it.*

☞ The fewer people you share files with, the less time your Mac will spend responding to their requests instead of your own. Ask the people you share with to disconnect from your Mac as soon as they've copied the files they need, to free your Mac up.

☞ **Share as few files as possible.** The fewer files you share, the fewer opportunities there will be for someone else to accidentally delete or rename your files—or see something they shouldn't.

☞ **Use as little security as possible.** You should be able to control

⚠️ *important warning*

access to your sensitive files by being careful which folders you share. As soon as you start creating users and groups and setting privileges for them, you'll find yourself tangled in a web of security that you'll constantly be asked to change. A lot of people will forget their passwords, and there's no place to look them up—you can only change them to new ones.

☞ **If you do register users, make sure all owners of file-sharing Macs on the network register users with the same names.** If someone named Margaret were registered as Meg on one Mac, Peggy on another and Maggie on a third, she'd have to remember which Mac had her set up under which name.

you want) in the Users & Groups control panel. You can also organize users into *Groups,* so you can set access privileges for several of them at once. The File Sharing Monitor control panel lets you keep track of who's using which of your shared items.

To access shared files on someone else's Mac, you open the Chooser, click on the AppleShare icon, select the Mac's name in the box on the right, and click *OK*. In the next couple of dialog boxes, you'll be asked to enter the name you were registered under and your password (if any), and to select the shared item you want to use. When you've clicked *OK* in the last dialog box, the shared item's icon shows up on your desktop, just like another disk.

In the same way, you can access your own Mac's hard disk—its complete contents, without restriction—from another networked Mac; just enter your owner's name and password (you entered them in the Sharing Setup control panel when you turned file sharing on).

Although only System 7 Macs can share their files, Macs running System 6 can access files on other Macs—all they need is the AppleShare workstation software, which comes on System 6 installation disks since version 6.0.4. To share files from a System 6 Mac, you need Claris' Public Folder or Sitka's TOPS.

● *file servers and AppleShare*

A *file server* is a computer on a network that everyone can access and get applications and documents from. Some file servers are *dedicated* machines; they might also take care of print spooling and e-mail for the network, but you can't sit down in front of them and use them as workstations.

AppleShare is Apple's file-server software, which can turn any Mac on a network into a dedicated file server. With AppleShare running, the file server's hard disk appears to everyone on the network as another icon on the desktop, with its own window, folders and files. AppleShare predates file sharing (described above) and has some similar security features; each file or folder can have an *owner* and only someone with appropriate access privileges can get at it. A *network administrator* can set up work groups with various levels of access privileges.

PCs can be connected to AppleShare with the PhoneNet Card/Local-Talk from Farallon. To the PCs, the server looks like another disk drive, and they can access the documents on it (not the applications, but what could they do with them anyway?).

PC to Mac and back

🍎 from the sublime to the ridiculous

If you use a personal computer at work, there's a frighteningly high probability that it isn't a Mac. Yes, the ugly reality is that most personal computers are IBM PCs or clones thereof—known generically as **PCs** or, if they use the MS DOS or PC DOS operating system, as **DOS** (pronounced *dahss*) **machines** (although *dross machines* might be a more appropriate name).

A lthough there's no way around the wrenching feeling in your gut you have to endure every morning when you travel back into the pre-Mac Stone Age of computing (or, if you're running Windows, into the pseudo-Mac Gilded Age, where everything is just slightly out of focus), you can at least transfer data back and forth between the office machine and your Mac at home. The tips below tell you how.

🍎 what gets lost in the translation

Some popular programs—like Word, WordPerfect, Excel and PageMaker—come in both Mac and PC versions. Documents created by either version are readable by both computers. Most major word processors and integrated ("Works") programs also include translators that let you import files from other programs and other computers. The XTND translators, developed by Claris but widely used by other manufacturers, allow programs like MacWrite and Nisus to open files created by the PC versions of Word and WordPerfect, or even WriteNow files from NeXT computers or AppleWorks files from the Apple II.

very good feature

I f you need to use a PC file from a program that has no Mac counterpart, find out if the file can be saved in or converted to a format the XTND translators can handle. If it can't, you'll have to save it as a text *(ASCII)* file and all your formatting will be lost.

Spreadsheet users are in good shape, thanks to some standards in the industry and to the flexibility of Excel, the most popular spreadsheet on the Mac, which can read files from 1-2-3 on the PC (that com-

⌘ reading PC disks

very good feature

Apple's **Super-Drive** floppy disk drive can transfer files onto and off of DOS-formatted 3½" (hard-case) disks. (SuperDrives are built into every new Mac; if your old Mac doesn't have one, you can buy one, but it may require an upgrade to your Mac's ROM.)

PC disks don't show up as icons on the desktop, so you have to access their contents from within the **Apple File Exchange** (AFE) software that comes on your Mac software disks. Of course, just because you can *transfer* the files doesn't mean the Mac can *read* them— they generally have to either be text files or specially formatted by a PC program—but read on for some exceptions.

Three other utilities—Apple's **Macintosh PC Exchange**, Dayna's **DOS Mounter** and Insignia's **AccessPC**— create disk, folder and file icons for PC disks. DOS Mounter even generates the correct icon for the application, based on the PC files' extensions. For example, it can add a PageMaker icon to all PC files with PM extensions. AccessPC allows you to mount PC-formatted SyQuest cartridges on your desktop.

Apple and Dayna both make external floppy disk drives that read 5¼" PC disks (the ones that are soft and actually floppy). But as with the Super-Drive, the disks don't mount on your desktop unless you use one of the programs described above.

puter's most popular spreadsheet) directly. You can also save Excel files in 1-2-3 format. The main limitation is that macros written in one product won't work with the other.

Database files also transfer fairly easily if the PC program uses the Mac standard format of Tab between fields and Return between records. Several Mac databases (FileMaker and FoxBase, for example) can read files from the popular PC database program dBase (but they feel debased afterwards).

Fonts often have different names on the PC and Mac, in which case you have to rename them or get printouts in Courier (which is what PostScript printers substitute for fonts they can't find). PageMaker comes with a translation table that can convert some, but not all, fonts.

Chapter

14

Other software

Personal and business management

🍎 *address book programs*

Address book programs give you a specially-designed file where you can keep names, addresses and phone numbers. Most of them come both as applications and as DA's and can print your addresses out in an alphabetized booklet or onto address labels, Rolodex cards or envelopes. Power Up's Address Book Plus and Portfolio's Dynodex are two commercial programs; there's also an excellent shareware program called Address Book by Jim Leitch.

🍎 *project managers*

These programs are designed to help you manage large projects involving many concurrent tasks. At minimum, they let you build Gantt charts, which use bars to chart tasks along a timeline. The sample below is from Varcon's Great Gantt!, a program that specializes in this type of chart. Claris' MacProject also includes Gantt charting capability among its many features.

Creation of the World

Name	Description	Days	Planned Start	Planned End
create heavens and earth	formless, dark		01	01
create light			01	01
name light and darkness	day and night		01	01
create firmament	heavens		02	02
gather waters together			03	03
dry lands appear			03	03
name waters and land	seas and earth		03	03
create plant-life			03	03
create great light	sun		04	04
create lesser light	moon		04	04
create lights in heavens	stars		04	04
create animals			05	05
create humans			06	06
rest			07	07

⬤ schedule managers

There are various programs available to help you keep track of your schedule:

☞ **The shareware Calendar DA** shows a monthly calendar on the screen and displays each day's schedule when you click on it.

☞ **Amaze's Far Side Computer Calendar** shows you a different Gary Larson cartoon daily, and lets you view or print your calendar in day, week, month or year formats.

☞ **Pastel Development's DayMaker** is a calendar and alarm program that keeps to-do lists, maintains project schedules, serves as a basic address book and lets you take notes.

☞ **Attain's In Control** gives to-do lists the flexible row and column setup of a spreadsheet, the expandability/contractibility of an outliner, and the sorting and entry shortcut features of a database.

☞ **Group schedulers** like the ones built into WordPerfect Office and Microsoft Mail let you set up meeting times with others on a Mac network. On Technology's Meeting Maker does the same, but with more features.

⬤ personal accounting programs

Programs like Intuit's Quicken, Survivor's MacMoney and Meca's Managing Your Money help you keep track of all your accounts—checking, savings, credit cards and cash. They provide reports on your cash flow, net worth, and expenses, as well as business reports like balance sheets and profit and loss statements. But if you're choosing one for your business, be careful—they don't all adhere to accepted accounting practices.

⚠️

important warning

⬤ small business accounting software

Keeping a good set of books can sometimes make the difference between survival and failure for a small business. Too often, the boss thinks the problem is solved by buying an accounting package, forgetting that the staff is already working full time on other things. How are they

rant

going to learn to use the software, set it up and begin using it, while still being responsible for all their other tasks? And what's the use of entering all that data if no one uses the reports from the accounting package to make informed management decisions?

W hen you've found a program you like, ask the manufacturer for a demo disk so you can try it out. And be sure to buy the software somewhere that offers at least a 30-day money-back guarantee, so you can really put it to the test before committing the time necessary for training and setup.

very hot tip

   Peachtree Accounting for the Macintosh and Teleware's M.Y.O.B. are two basic, inexpensive packages for small businesses (M.Y.O.B. costs a bit more, but offers different levels of accounting for different needs). For accountants, CheckMark's MultiLedger is straightforward and elemental, but the rest of us may feel at a loss. Softsync/BLOC's Accountant, Inc. is more full-blown, with over 100 built-in reports, but is still priced within a small-business budget.

⌘ *high-end accounting programs*

A high-end accounting system makes sense only for those with industrial-strength needs—a networked environment, thousands of transactions a month, two or more full-time employees working on the books and so on. Don't try to install a high-end system without a qualified installer whose references you've checked out *[thoroughly—AN]*. Plan on four months or more to get the system up and running *[if you're lucky—AN]*. And be aware that the first year's bill for consulting, training, software and tech support for a high-end accounting program like Great Plains may run over $10,000.

important warning

G reat Plains offers more than most other Mac accounting systems, but it was developed for the PC, and still looks and acts like a MS-DOS program. SBT's Database Accounting Library was also developed on the PC, but you can buy the source code and hire an SBT-trained programmer to modify it to suit you. And you can use the FoxBase database manager to design any report you want.

very good feature

Canada's HoneyBee Accounting makes an impressive package called 4th Power—written in the 4th Dimension database language—that's making its way into the US market. 4th Dimension gives 4th Power a flexibility similar to SBT's, but unlike SBT, 4th Power was designed for the Mac from the start, and looks it.

very good feature

[I'm told there's a saying in business accounting circles that no one is ever happy with their accounting package. Although I didn't appreciate hearing that from the people who had just customized and installed ours (as a response to the blizzard of problems that ensued), it certainly was my experience. If you need to find something now, all I can say is, do plenty of research, and don't be surprised to find that your accounting package is dictating how you run your business.—AN]

order-processing software

Accounting programs tend to be cumbersome (at best) to use for the daily transactions of a retail business. For point-of-sale businesses, ShopKeeper Plus can connect a Mac to a cash drawer and a bar code reader, giving

very good feature

wills, living trusts and record-keeping

Nolo Press, publisher of scores of extremely useful self-help law books and crusader against the ruling shysterocracy, offers several useful programs:

☞ **WillMaker** is a terrific program that helps you write your will. *[Dying without a will is really a mistake.*

The legal and judicial buzzards will feed off your financial corpse, greatly reducing what your friends and family get. After all, do you really want your Mac sold to pay the predatory fee of some troll at the courthouse?—AN]

☞ **Living Trust** helps you create a living trust, which lets you will property to people without it having to go through probate.

☞ **Personal RecordKeeper** helps you organize all your personal, financial and legal records so you can find them when you need them.

you a smart cash register that prints receipts, keeps track of inventory, and can export data to other accounting packages. For mail-order businesses, National TelePress' SuperMOM simplifies order entry and manages everything from accounts receivable to inventory, sales tax and telemarketing.

Sound on the Mac

🍎 *the Mac's built-in sound*

Unlike most other computers, the Mac was designed with the ability to play back sounds over its built-in speaker. You can choose any of several sounds to be used as the Mac's system alert, and some Macs have built-in recording capability (see the entry called *Sound settings* in Chapter 7).

very good feature

There are also plenty of colorful, bizarre and silly sounds available from user groups, electronic bulletin boards and on-line information services, as well as in commercial packages like the two-volume Star Trek Collection from Sound Source Unlimited.

Sounds come in various formats, the most convenient of which is System 7's resource format (it lets you copy sounds directly into System 7's System file, and when you double-click their icons, the Mac plays them over the speaker). In System 6, you have to install sounds with a utility like Sound Mover (it's shareware, available from online services and user groups).

Music

🍎 *MIDI*

In addition to recording sound via sampling, Macs can record and recreate musical performances on synthesizers or other electronic musical instruments that use the **MIDI** (*musical instrument digital*

🍎 digital sound

The Mac records and stores sound digitally. Digital recording is like making a movie, but instead of taking a series of photos that become frames in a moving picture, you're taking **samples** (audio snapshots) of a sound wave at regular intervals and translating them into numbers for storage on the computer. When you play them back at the same rate, they reproduce the original sound.

The number of samples taken per second is called the **sampling rate**; the higher the sampling rate, the greater the accuracy of the recording, and the better it'll sound when played back. (Recordings made in this way are often called **samples** too.)

The Mac's built-in 8-bit sound can record or play back up to 22,254 samples per second (usually abbreviated as 22 kHz),

which yields sound quality comparable to an AM radio. A Mac with a 16-bit audio card (like the one in Digidesign's Audiomedia package) can handle sampling at up to 44 kHz, which preserves the live sound's pitch and dynamic range (loudness) much better and virtually eliminates distortion, producing CD-quality recordings.

very good feature

interface) standard. A MIDI file contains the instructions needed to play a piece of music, rather than the actual sound produced by such a performance. It's like the roll of paper that tells a player piano what to play, as opposed to an audio tape you play back on a stereo.

To use MIDI software, all you need is a Mac, a MIDI-compatible instrument and a MIDI interface box (which translates between the instrument and the Mac). Some problems have been reported using MIDI with PowerBooks—check with the software's manufacturer if you're a PowerBook user.

bug

MIDI is very popular among composers and musicians because it lets them compose and edit performances in special programs called **sequencers**. You can play a piece of music on a synthesizer, then go in the sequencer and change the pitch, stress or duration of any note, align notes to beats automatically, copy and paste sections, increase or decrease the tempo of the piece, or transpose it to another key. Unlike digital sound editors, where you have to work with a picture of a sound wave, a sequencer displays actual notes and/or measures, so you can work with them directly.

Once you've created a track of music in this way, you can have the sequencer play it back on the synthesizer and record another track on top of the first one. You can then edit the second track in the same way, and continue layering tracks until you've recorded an entire composition. Most sequencers will let you save a composition as a standard MIDI file that any MIDI program can read.

Entry-level sequencers include Opcode's EZ Vision and Passport's Trax; the pro-level versions are Vision and Master Tracks Pro. There's also an inexpensive program called Band-in-a-Box that simulates a backup band, creating sequences that you can play along with on another instrument.

🍎 scoring programs

Sequencers let you compose music, but to print out a composition as sheet music, you need a **scoring** (or **notation**) program. With it you can compose directly onto a standard music staff, import MIDI files created with a sequencer, or enter music by playing it on your MIDI instrument (in real time or note-by-note). You can then edit your composition using standard music notation, and print out a professional-quality score.

Finale, from Coda Music Systems, and Encore, from Passport Designs, are two fairly sophisticated scoring programs; Coda's MusicProse is more basic and less expensive.

Video

🍎 QuickTime

Imagine getting a letter on disk from a friend. *[Suspend your disbelief for a moment, gentle reader, and don't ask why you're getting a letter on disk rather than on paper.—AN]* When you double-click the file, you see a color picture of her new baby pasted into the letter. Then you click a little button beneath the picture and it suddenly comes to life—the kid cries and drools, and your friend walks into the frame to say hello. *[After many years of drooling over letters, at last I can get letters that drool back at me! Isn't progress wonderful?—AN]*

Apple's **QuickTime** data format has made this kind of home-video-in-a-letter possible by letting you paste dynamic data (anything you can play back over time) into documents the same way you'd paste in text or graphics. You can combine sounds, video and/or animation into one QuickTime file (called a *movie*). The latest versions of many word processing, database and presentation programs support QuickTime, and Apple expects it to eventually become as universally supported as the PICT graphic format.

Since the animation, video and graphics data in a QuickTime movie can take up a lot of disk space, the QuickTime extension (that's how it comes, as an extension) has built-in image compressors you can access from within applications. These can reduce file sizes by as much as twenty times, often with little effect on image quality, and they work on still images like PICT files as well as QuickTime files.

The QuickTime extension is available from Apple dealers and user groups. To use it, you need a color-capable Mac (one with a 68020 chip or better), at least four megs of RAM and System 6.0.7 or higher.

To get a feel for what you can do with QuickTime, consider getting Apple's QuickTime Starter Kit. It includes the QuickTime extension, a collection of utilities for viewing and editing QuickTime movies and sample QuickTime movies and images.

Animation and presentation programs

🍎 *traditional vs. computer animation*

Animation creates the illusion of motion by displaying, in rapid succession, a series of pictures (called *frames*) in which an image's position changes incrementally from one frame to the next.

Traditionally, a chief animator draws **key frames** that define the images, style and motion occurring in a scene, and assistants draw the intervening frames (a process known as **in-betweening**, or just **tweening**). A computer can often handle the tweening (in fact, major animation studios have used computers to do this for some time).

Path-based animation relies even more on the computer—the animator creates an initial scene and maps out paths for the objects to move along, and the computer then draws the frames along those paths. Path-based animation provides more precise control over an object's motion than key frames do, but it has its own limitations.

bargain

Some scenes are better suited to key-frame animation, others to path-based. Animation software should let you choose the best approach for any given situation. Animation programs include Macromedia's FilmMaker and Director programs, Gold Disk's inexpensive Animation Works, and for 3-D animation, Macromedia's Three-D and Specular's Infini-D.

🍎 *presentation software*

Presentation programs are basically tools for producing electronic slide shows, usually to accompany talks. You can create the slides from scratch using the program's own text and graphics tools, or import them from other sources.

When you display a presentation on a Mac monitor, each slide fills the screen, covering the usual menu bar, windows and icons, regardless of your monitor size. You can also print the slides onto transparencies for an overhead projector, have a service bureau make them into actual photographic slides or put the presentation onto videotape (with video-out cards made by RasterOps, Truevision, Generation Systems and Mass Microsystems).

Popular presentation programs include Aldus' Persuasion, Microsoft's PowerPoint and Symantec's More—or, for the ultimate in multimedia capability, Macromedia's Director. Director, and less expensive programs like Claris' HyperCard and Aldus' SuperCard, combine sound, animation, etc. and can produce **interactive presentations**, in which the viewer selects choices from the screen that affect what happens in the presentation.

Games and learning

🍎 *educational, shmeducational*

Why do we insist that computer games for children be "educational"? Unless kids are crippled by bad teaching or physical or emotional blocks, they can't *not* learn from anything they do. So don't rationalize that they're learning hand-eye coordination (even though they are); just tell yourself they're having fun. That's what counts in

rant

games (and educational programs generally). When they aren't fun, kids don't play them and therefore don't learn from them.

🍎 *free (and cheap) games*

For a long time, one of the complaints about the Mac was that there weren't any good games for it. Well, now there are plenty of good games for the Mac—many of them adapted straight from great arcade games. What's more, lots of them are either very low-cost shareware or free (you can get them from bulletin boards and user groups).

🍎 *games are fussy*

Games—and educational programs, which are usually disguised as games—sometimes make unusual demands on your system (and on you). For example, while few business products are copy-protected, many games are; you may need to insert the master disk (the one you bought), or supply arcane information you look up in the instruction booklet.

Games also tend to use some pretty fancy programming tricks to squeeze top performance out of your Mac. Specific software may need to be in just the right spot, or the game may need to use a specific area of memory another program is occupying. If you have trouble, remove any unnecessary extensions and close any other open programs. If you still run into problems, boot from the floppy and run the game from there, instead of from your hard disk.

Some games run only on compact Macs (ones with 9" or 10" screens), some run only in color, and many don't run if another program is loaded into memory. If you upgrade your system, you may have to leave some of your favorite playthings behind.

⚠️ *important warning*

Before you buy a game, find out which Mac models it works with. If you have problems, call the product's tech support; a newer version of the program might help.

Programming on the Mac

🍎 *basic programming terms*

The first thing to understand is the difference between a ***programmer*** and a ***user****.* Programmers use ***programming languages*** to write programs; when bugs turn up in the programs, they fix them, and when new features are needed, they add them. Users simply use the programs; the programming language is invisible to them (or should be).

It's like the difference between an automobile mechanic and a driver. Just as you don't need to know how a carburetor works to be an expert driver, you don't need to know anything about programming to be an expert Macintosh *user*.

T he actual statements or instructions in a program are called *code.* Code is normally broken into *lines*. A relatively small piece of code, which does a specific task, is called a *routine*. Put a bunch of routines together and you have a *program*.

which language to learn

Many people who use a Macintosh want to learn to program. This desire is often inspired by an anguished "I can write something better than *this!*" when a program doesn't do what they want. Unfortunately, writing programs for the Mac isn't nearly as easy as using one (in programming, as in so many other areas, easy is hard). You need to know fundamental programming concepts and at least one programming language. It can take years to become an expert.

If you want to take the time, you have three avenues to choose from: **HyperCard** (or one of its competitors, like SuperCard), **C** (the most popular language for professional programmers) or a *graphical programming language* like Prograph.

H yperCard—designed for amateurs—is much easier to learn than C because it has a simpler structure and fewer hard-and-fast rules (it's like the difference between learning Spanish and Latin). A novice programmer can get more done more quickly with HyperCard—and without even having to learn about the Mac Toolbox. On the other hand, you can't go nearly as far with HyperCard as you can with C, which is why most sophisticated HyperCard applications include add-on programming modules created in C or Pascal.

A graphic language like Prograph takes more time than HyperCard to learn, but you can get results a lot faster in it than you can in C.

From the Visual Delights collection of Macintosh clip art. Copyright © 1991 by SunShine. All rights reserved.

Chapter
15

Software buying tips

This chapter was written by Arthur Naiman.

against stupidity, the gods themselves struggle in vain

When Schiller wrote that line (in his play *The Maid of Orleans* in 1801), he probably wasn't thinking specifically of software companies. But he might as well have been. Most of them don't have the brains God gave a slice of French toast.

rant

For example, almost all of them have installed computerized call routing. You call up—hoping against hope to speak to a human being (what the hell, you've always been a crazy optimist) and a canned voice tells you to press 1 if you have a touch-tone phone.

Don't do it! It's almost always better just to sit there on the line until the computer stops blathering at you and connects you to a real person. (Soon, no doubt, there will be a way they can tell whether you actually have a touch-tone phone, and you'll run the risk of being arrested by the Federal Communications Police for fraudulent rotary phone impersonation. But for the time being, you're safe.)

things to come

If you do fall into the trap of telling them you have a touch-tone phone, you're stepped through a multiple-choice maze: *If you're calling about DorkMaster on the PC, press 1. If you're calling about DorkMaster on the Mac, press 2. If you've ever known lust in your heart, press 3.* And on it goes, each question more petty and irrelevant than the last.

Computerized call routing is sometimes called *voice mail*, but that's a base slander. Voice mail is actually a wonderful system that lets you leave a message for someone in your own voice, instead of having to tediously dictate it to some third party—which isn't very efficient, as we all know from the childhood game of *telephone* (where you whisper messages around a circle).

Not that voice mail can't be made irritating too. I particularly hate it when, just as the person you're calling finishes asking you to leave a message, the computer comes on to say, "Please leave your message now." *That's exactly what I was <u>about</u> to do before you intruded.* "When you are finished leaving your message," the computer continues, just as if you hadn't spoken, "press 5 for more options." *Oh, great! Just what I wanted—options.*

Voice mail systems throw in all that crap simply to justify their high price tags. After all, since all callers really want to do is leave messages, there's no reason not to simply buy a bunch of inexpensive answering machines. It's fear of that obvious, logical alternative that makes the voice-mail vendors promote a bunch of unwanted "features."

In any case, whether it's called voice mail or something else, computerized call routing is basically a form of automated passive aggression, designed to discourage every telephone call that isn't an order (you notice how rare these systems are in the *sales* departments). Some MBA who's never produced anything anyone wants to buy (and who doesn't have a clue about how to do that) looked at how much time and money the company was wasting actually talking to its customers and decided that that was the perfect place to cut costs.

You'd think even MBAs would know better, with the example of WordPerfect staring them right in the face. I've never used it myself, but I'm told that WordPerfect for the PC is relatively clumsy, counterintuitive and hard to learn. How, then, did they make it the best-selling word processor in the world? By always putting customer support first. By hiring hundreds of employees whose only job it is to answer the phone. By caring about the people who use their product.

Now consider Aldus. This is the company that literally invented the term *desktop publishing*. Their pioneering program PageMaker dominated the field from the start. But Aldus coasted on PageMaker's early lead and didn't improve PageMaker as needed (see *we fear change* below); now Quark has passed them by—in quality, if not yet in sales.

So how does Aldus deal with this dire situation? By setting up a maze of recorded messages that offers, as one of its options, *nothing* but synthesized voices to respond to the keys you press. In other words, it's not just that you have to negotiate a labyrinth of computerized messages, each alive with ersatz cheerfulness and sham warmth, in order to talk to a human being—no, if your problem is one of the common ones, the synthesized voices are *all* you get!

very bad feature

(Actually, a lot of companies are now "offering" these automated help line systems.)

Quark's support line is better now, but it used to be just as bad. Instead of computerized call routing, you'd get put on hold forever. This is the old-fashioned, brutal-ist approach, but the subtext is the same: "Our lines are *rant* busy. They'll be busy forever. Isn't it obvious that we don't want to talk to you? If we *did* want to talk to you, we'd hire enough people to answer our phones. Can't you take a hint?"

Naturally, the people who use the infinite-hold approach don't come out and say that. No, they say just the opposite, interrupting your reverie of a romantic idyll with, say, Laura San Giacomo—which you've drifted into as a subconscious defense against catatonia, as you sit there with the phone pasted to your ear—with a synthesized voice that says things like "your call is very important to us." Yes, it's important to us—it's cutting into our profits. So hang up and stop bothering us.

Another line that really annoys me is, "due to an unusual volume of calls...." There should be a law requiring any such message to also state what *percentage* of the time it plays. If it's more than 50%, the message should be required to say, "due to our *usual* volume of calls...."

When I was in high school, we called people we considered phonies *pseudos*. Yes, I realize that *pseudo* isn't a noun—or even a whole word—but we didn't know that then. We didn't know much, with the three pounds of grease on our crew cuts compressing our brains. Those were benighted times. I like to say that I experienced one of the great ironies of world history—growing up in Chicago in the '50s being told how the *Russians* brain-washed people.

Anyway, a pseudo was someone who had any vision beyond our own rigidly constricted one. Pseudos said *DRAH-muh* instead of *DRAM-uh*, weren't Bears fans, had *feelings*. You know the type.

My views on who's a pseudo have evolved since then. Now I think of them as people who program computers to say things like, "your call is very important to us." Not only are they as phony as a televangelist asking for "seed money," they're also so dumb that they actually think *you're* so dumb that this recorded reassurance, played over and over again, will make you forget that you've been on hold since the Norman invasion.

Why am I ranting on about the fatuousness of companies that can't even answer their own phones (aside from how much fun it is)? To lead up to a simple point: if the gods themselves struggle in vain against stupidity, why should you waste your time doing it? Before you buy a product, call the company's support line and see how long it takes to talk to an actual, knowledgeable human being. If it's longer than you like, choose another product.

very hot tip

♦ *we fear change*

Remember in Wayne's World when Benjamin suggests a change in the show and Garth says, "We fear change" and starts pounding on a mechanical hand with that deranged look on his face? Well, there are companies who should adopt that as their motto. Can't you just see their title card on PBS?

One of the ways this shows up most often is when a company has a winning product and is so astounded by the fact (and/or so short-

> **TechnoDynoTronics**
> The Sexy Buzzword Corporation
> *We fear change.*

sightedly greedy) that they stop developing and improving it. The problem with this *if it ain't broke, don't fix it* philosophy is that if everybody followed it, we'd all still be driving Model Ts and listening to Rudy Vallee. As technology progresses, standards (and users' expectations) rise. Things don't have to break to be superceded.

So no matter how much you like a program, and how comfortable you are with it, keep an eye on the competition. There may come a time when you'd be foolish *not* to switch over.

♦ *ease of use is your birthright—insist on it*

A lot of software—with its impenetrable manuals, commands reminiscent of Shriners' initiation rites and what Michael Ward calls "unpleasant surprises"—isn't worth the trouble it takes to learn it. One of the major reasons people buy the Mac is to avoid all that intimidating, user-hostile gobbledygook.

Fortunately, most companies that publish Mac software seem to realize that. But not all. Some let their programmers' bizarre thinking mold the final product and others let dollar-crazed marketing executives make the decisions.

You shouldn't have to put up with any of that, so *don't*—not even for a second. The Mac is an inherently easy-to-use machine. If you find yourself having a lot of trouble learning to use a program, stop wasting your time and find another program that doesn't give you the same trouble.

very hot tip

🍎 *look for a logical hierarchy of commands*

For software to be easy to use, it should be hierarchically organized. This means that most basic operations are simple and central to how the program works and the more advanced operations are off to the side, so you don't even know about them until you need them.

🍎 *Mac software should be Maclike*

Aside from being easy-to-use, the Mac's interface has another major virtue: you don't have to learn a new set of commands and procedures for each program. At least you *shouldn't* have to.

Some Mac programs, however, use nonstandard commands, or cripple the standard commands so they don't do what you expect them to. Whether you like one of these programs or not depends on whether you find the features it offers spiffy enough to justify switching gears between it and other Mac programs (and hitting a lot of wrong keys in the process).

very hot tip

🍎 *if it is broke, you should be able to fix it*

Although the commands in Mac software are much more standardized between programs than those on the PC, they're still nowhere near as standardized as they should be. One thing that really irks me is the lack of consistency around the commands for boldface, italics and plain text.

On many programs (including the ones I learned on), you get italics with ⌘I and boldface with ⌘B. But in PageMaker and other programs, you have to hit ⌘ Shift I and ⌘ Shift B (this was true for a long time in Word too). Even worse is the command for plain text (that is, stripping out italics, boldface and all other type styles). In the original MacWrite, it was ⌘P; in MacWrite II and Nisus, it's ⌘T; in Word, it's ⌘ Shift Z; and in PageMaker, it's ⌘ Shift Spacebar.

Does this lead to frustrating typing mistakes? Is the Pope Catholic? Do presidents lie? Does the bear sit in the woods?

Y ou can use QuicKeys or Tempo to customize most programs, but some are structured so you can't change all their commands. For example, in PageMaker, you can't change the command for plain text, because there's another command with the same name *(Normal)* on an earlier menu.

Since there are lots of people who are now very used to lots of different commands, true Macintosh consistency is a lost cause. What you can get instead (and which is almost as good) is the ability to change a program's commands to what you want them to be.

very hot tip

🍎 *if you can, deal with the best*

The best program isn't always the most expensive, although it usually isn't the cheapest (if it is, jump on it). And, of course, it often isn't easy to know which program is the best. But if you have a pretty good idea, don't tell yourself, "Well, I really can't afford that," or "I can get by with less."

T his is almost always a false economy, as we all know from our experience of buying junky products that soon fall apart. You end up not only having to pay to replace the defective product (or program), but you also lose the time you've invested installing (or learning to use) the first one. So bite the bullet and get the best to start with—if you can figure out which it is.

🍎 *speed counts*

As many people have learned to their sorrow, ease of use isn't everything. How fast a program runs can be even more important. Unfortunately, that's seldom mentioned in ads or by salesclerks and it's one of the hardest things to evaluate in an in-store tryout.

(continued on page 239)

⌘ *no program is an Iland, intire of it selfe*

When you buy a program, you don't know if you're going to want to always use it for everything. Even if you do, you're going to need to convert files created in other programs.

So the most elementary logic tells you that if you hope to succeed selling a Mac program, it needs to *import* documents from other Mac programs and *export* documents to them. And this is particularly true if you're hoping to break into a market dominated by a competing product.

If there was ever a category of software dominated by one product, it was (and is) Mac spreadsheets. Excel had 85–90% of the market when a slick new spreadsheet

called Wingz tried to challenge it. Wingz' publisher lavished (what looked like) millions of dollars promoting the product before it came out, with a trade-show booth that looked like a space ship had landed, free jackets with their name on it, etc. etc.

I couldn't wait to see what Wingz' powerful graphics capabilities could do for my tired old Excel spreadsheets. So as soon as I got Wingz, I tore open the package, flipped the manual open to the index and looked up *import* (or *importing*, or *importing data)*. No entry. So I looked up *data, importing*. No entry. So I looked up *Excel*. No entry. So I looked up *foreign files*. No entry.

So I looked up to the sky, shook my head, thought about how many Excel spreadsheets I used in an ongoing way and

am not about to redo, and tossed Wingz back into the box.

By the way, it wasn't just the index. Wingz had no way to directly import Excel files (although you could, of course, do it if you jumped through hoops). As a result of this (and no doubt other bad planning), Wingz is no longer a Mac product.

This would be pathetic if it were merely the story of one publisher. But it's the story of dozens.

They act as if their product is the only one around, the only one their potential customers have ever—or will ever—come in contact with. They treat connecting with other software almost as if it were treason or something. It's sort of like xenophobia, but what I really think it is, is stupidophilia.

But delays of even a few seconds can be very annoying if you keep running into them. Because of that, speed is one of the prime things to look for in a program. Many computer novices tend to ignore this consideration—since doing something on a computer is always so much faster than doing it by hand. But, believe me now or believe me later, if you buy a slow program, you'll live to regret it. (Steve Michel says no one *ever* realizes this; they just go for the power.)

⚠
important warning

❖ *you want a great manual you don't need*

No matter how great a program is, it doesn't do you any good unless you know how to use it. Mac software should be so clear, its menu commands so understandable, that you don't even need a manual. If you *do* need a manual, at least it should be a good one.

I ronically (but predictably), the easiest programs to learn tend to have the best manuals and the hardest programs to learn tend to have the worst manuals.

❖ *a manual should have an index,*
not an imitation of one

I don't know about you, but I'd rather have all my teeth removed without anesthetic than follow the tutorial in most manuals. They're the equivalent of being strapped into a chair and forced to listen to scales for three months, then *Three Blind Mice*, then *Twinkle, Twinkle, Little Star*, then Lawrence Welk—all under the guise of teaching you music appreciation.

rant

(I once saw a sign in an old New York elevator that read: *To actuate elevator mechanism, press button corresponding to floor desired.* Now try to imagine someone who could read and understand that message but who didn't know how to press a button in an elevator. Most tutorials take the same approach.)

A ll I want from a manual is a good index, so I can look up what I need to and get out of there. Unfortunately, the only purpose most indexes serve is to allow the company whose manual it is to say, "Look!

Look! An index!" And it's true—they do *look* like indexes. Why should I spoil the illusion by pointing out that you can never *find* anything in them?

As far as I'm concerned, if the index is worthless, so is the manual. And if the manual is useless, so—usually—is the program (the exception being those programs that are so intuitive, so easy to use, that you don't need the manual at all).

shareware is worth trying

To be absolutely sure you're going to want a program before you buy it, you need to use it for some reasonable period of time. The best way to do that is *shareware*—software you're allowed to copy freely and only pay for if you like it and continue to use it. As you'll discover from reading this book, some of the best Mac programs are shareware.

bargain

In order to encourage this proconsumer approach to software distribution, always give shareware a try before spending money for a commercial program that does the same thing, and *always* pay for any shareware you end up keeping and using.

If you don't, the people who write it will have to find some other way to make a living and will no longer be able to update their programs or create new ones. In the short run, you'll save a little money; in the long run, you'll lose a lot, as you end up paying more for programs you're not even sure you'll use, because no good shareware alternatives are available.

in-store tryouts

Any decent computer store will let you sit and play with software for hours at a time, as long as no one else wants to use the machine (unfortunately, someone almost always will). Trying a program in a store will often (but not always) give you enough of a feeling for it to decide if you want to buy it.

money-back guarantees

If you're buying a program mail-order and sight unseen, try to get a money-back guarantee. Remember—a lot of software isn't worth using, no matter how good it sounds.

■ public-domain software

Lots of programs are available absolutely free, thanks to the generosity of their authors. You can get

bargain

this software from good computer stores (if you've done business with them), user groups or bulletin boards.

You often have to put up with skimpy documentation, or none at all, and early versions of most programs have bugs. But there's a lot of terrific public-domain software, some of it better than commercial programs.

(You can get a sampling of great Mac shareware and public-domain software on *The Macintosh Bible Software Disks,* which have a money-back guarantee. See the order form at the back of this book or call Peachpit Press at 800 283 9444.)

■ support, support and support

There's a saying in real estate that the three most important things to consider when buying property are *location, location* and *location.* Likewise, the three most important things to consider when buying a computer product are *support, support* and *support.* (Support is the availability of someone to answer your questions, usually on the phone, and to fix things if they go wrong.)

very hot tip

Support is the reason it often makes sense to pay a little more to buy from a vendor whose staff knows something (whether it's a local store or a mail-order distributor). Don't imagine you can depend on the publisher's telephone support line. As mentioned above, most of them are so understaffed that you might as well just play a tape recording of a busy signal and not tie up your phone.

Fortunately, there are some exceptions. Microsoft, once one of the worst offenders, has gotten impressively good lately—I've had short (or no!) waits and reached knowledgeable techies. Claris also has generally good support, and so do most small companies.

very good feature

❡ *don't use a bazooka to kill a fly*

You should use a computer to do things you can't do more easily in some other way (with pencil and paper, for example). The Mac can't make you organized or creative (although it can certainly help you organize and create).

A long these lines, check out integrated "Works" programs (mentioned in Chapter 11). For many people, who don't really need a full-powered word processor and a full-powered spreadsheet and a full-powered database (and so on), they offer the best value.

❡ *thou shalt not steal*

In the case of some programs, there are more illegal copies in existence than legal ones. (Not that this is always bad for the publisher. WordStar became an industry-standard word processing program at least partly because so many people had bootleg copies of it.)

⚠️

important warning

M ost of the problem is that people give copies to their friends; few computer hackers are despicable enough to steal someone else's work and then *sell* it. Still, the average program represents many person-years of labor, and you can't blame a publisher for wanting to protect that investment.

As a result, most Mac software used to be *copy-protected*. (There are many ways to make it difficult to copy a disk and no way to make it impossible, so it becomes a question of percentages: "How many hackers can we outsmart?")

C opy-protection was a real drag and virtually all Mac software publishers have stopped doing it. This puts the burden on us. If people can't make money developing software because everyone is stealing their software instead of buying it, soon there won't be any good programs at all. (I know I'm repeating myself. This bears repeating.)

❡ *beware of vaporware*

So much software has been promised that never saw the light of day (or saw it on a day many months after it was supposed to) that there's even a name for it—*vaporware*.

So when some salesclerk (or ad, or friend) tells you that a new product will be along "real soon now," don't depend on it. Few computer products come out on time, and a significant number end up being nothing more than vaporware.

🍎 don't pay to be a beta tester

When software publishers get a product to a certain stage, they hand out copies to people on the outside and ask them to test it. This work, called **beta testing**, is almost always unpaid; the testers are motivated by the advantage (or prestige) of being the first to know about something.

That's all fine, but don't *pay* to beta-test a product that's already been released. Vaporware is bad enough, but it's much worse to spend your good money on a product that's full of bugs.

So wait a while when a new product comes out. Go to a user group meeting or two and see if anyone's having problems with it. If you telecommunicate, ask about it on a bulletin board. Remember: feeling impatient is a lot less painful than feeling victimized.

🍎 trust good publishers

Since movie reviewers spend most of their time telling you the plot (and usually can't even do that with any accuracy), one of the best ways to decide if a movie is worth seeing is to find out who directed it. Similarly, one of the best ways to tell if a program is worth buying is to judge by the company that publishes it.

🍎 take reviews (including ours)
with a grain of salt

One problem with reviews is that most reviewers aren't like most users. They tend to have much more experience with Mac programs and to be much more interested in exploring the Mac as an activity in itself. (I call this tendency *expertosis*; it also causes a problem with manuals.)

very hot tip

Another problem is that reviewers are seldom given enough time to really get to know the ins and outs of the software they're evaluating. Lots of programs are complicated enough that you don't really get a feeling for their strengths and weaknesses until you've used them fairly heavily for a couple of months.

A third problem is that magazines are supported by advertising revenues, and while I'm always surprised by how tough they're willing to be in spite of that fact, no magazine's reviews are going to be, on the average, 75% or even 50% negative. Still, reviews are a great place to learn about products. Just be sure to take them with a grain of salt.

There's a scene in an episode of *The Big Valley* (one of those rare moments when we're not looking at Barbara Stanwyck and thinking, "Boy she looks good! How old is she anyway?"—which, as near as I can figure, is the main point of the show). Someone has just finished destroying some lame-brained idea of Heath's (he's the dumb one, remember). There's no argument Heath can make in

gossip/ trivia

response; his viewpoint is utterly without merit. So he snarls, "You've got all the answers, don't you?" (How can you respond to that?)

Well, we don't have all the answers, and neither does anyone else, and you shouldn't expect anyone to. It's obvious when stated that baldly, but in practice, it's regularly ignored. People are always asking me what products to buy. All too often, they don't want to learn about what's available, they don't want to think about their needs—they just want me to *tell* them what to buy. I ask them, "Would you buy a car that way?"

There's a Yiddish saying that sums up perfectly the approach you should take: *frayg an aytsa yaynem, un hob dayn saykhel bei dir*— ask for advice, then use your own head.

Part Four

Reference

Appendix

A

What to do when trouble strikes

Trouble on the Mac

what can go wrong

Zillions of things can go wrong while you're using the Mac, but aside from hard disk failures, almost nothing short of physical abuse can permanently damage the Mac's hardware. Generally, the most you have to lose is any work you haven't backed up and whatever time it takes to solve the problem (and, sometimes, whatever you pay someone else to solve it for you).

W hen something goes wrong, the Mac usually lets you know by beeping and/or displaying a message on the screen. It may be that nothing's actually wrong with the computer—you've just asked it to do something it can't, and the message will tell you that (e.g. a file can't be opened because it's already in use, or a printer can't be found). The message stays on the screen until you click the *OK* button, which allows you to fix the problem (for example, maybe the printer wasn't turned on) and go on with your work.

very good feature

You get a similar message when there's a problem with the Mac's hardware or software. For example, if your hard disk's directory file is corrupted, you may get a message that says *disk error; unable to read file.* Again, you simply click the *OK* button and continue working (although if you need the file that the Mac couldn't read, you may have to run a repair utility on the disk).

I n a *hang* (or *freeze*), no message appears, but the Mac ignores everything you do with the mouse and/or keyboard. Nevertheless, you can sometimes escape from a hang unscathed (see *if your Mac hangs* in the *Other problems* section below).

Crashes are problems that stop the Mac in its tracks, usually requiring you to restart your computer. Some crashes fill the screen with dots, strange patterns or garbage characters; sometimes the Mac makes a noise like a muted machine gun. (If you're really lucky, you get both together.) But usually it's not that dramatic—typically, the Mac will simply freeze and present you with a message like the one on the next page:

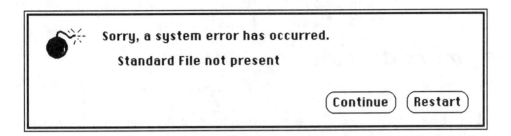

Sorry, a system error has occurred.

Standard File not present

(Continue) (Restart)

This type of crash (called a **system bomb, system error** or **system crash**) looks like it's giving you the option to *Continue* or *Restart*. In reality, clicking the *Continue* button rarely does anything, and often the *Restart* button won't work either; instead, restart your Mac using the reset button on your Mac's case (see *the best way to restart your Mac* below). Unfortunately, this means losing any changes you'd made but hadn't saved in your open documents.

very hot tip

⌘ *what causes trouble*

Most problems are software-related. Common causes include *insufficient memory, incompatibilities, file corruption* and *bugs* (described below) and *viruses* (described in their own entry below).

☞ **Memory-related** problems occur when either the Mac doesn't have enough RAM installed to do what you've asked, or the RAM that it has isn't allocated properly (you can adjust this—see *setting an application's memory allocation* in the *Tune-up techniques* section below).

☞ An **incompatibility** is when two programs make conflicting demands on the Mac, or one program conflicts with some aspect of the system software.

☞ For various reasons, files can become **corrupted**. If it's an ordinary document that gets corrupted, this may be no big deal—you just replace the corrupted file with the backup copy. But if it's a file that performs vital functions, like one of the invisibile directory files for your hard disk, you may lose some or all of what's on your hard disk. That's where disk repair and recovery utilities come in (they're described in the *Advanced troubleshooting* section below).

☞ A **bug** is a mistake in how a program was written. The mistake can have various consequences, from causing the Mac to crash or hang to simply preventing a feature from working. Bugs can only be fixed by rewriting part of the program (which is called *patching* it).

how to diagnose a problem

Most symptoms (bombs, hangs, etc.) can stem from a variety of problems, so to determine which is causing your trouble, you have to isolate the possibilities. If a symptom suddenly appears after you've made a change to your system (installing a new control panel, say) try undoing it (see *extension and control panel conflicts* in the *Advanced troubleshooting* section below).

You narrow down the source of the trouble by a process of elimination. For example, if you're having a problem with a document, try working with a different document from the same application. If it works, something in the original document is probably the culprit. If not, try using another application. If *that* works, it could be the application. If not, maybe it's the system software or the hard disk (try using a different startup disk). Keep trying to isolate each possible cause so you can test it. Start with the most likely cause, or with the one that's easiest to test. It's all a question of logically eliminating possibilities—and not panicking. *[Remember—computers aren't smart enough to be illogical.—AN]*

Unfortunately, many more problems can strike your Mac than we can cover in this Appendix—whole books have been written on the subject, and even they don't cover everything. Two that are worth checking out are The *"What Do I Do Now?"Book* and *The Dead Mac Scrolls* from Peachpit Press.

viruses

A **virus** is a program that functions on your computer without your consent. A benign virus may do nothing more than duplicate itself—although even that can screw things up if it gets out of hand. Some viruses, however, are *meant* to destroy data—anything from a single file to an entire network. Luckily, few of the known Mac viruses so far have been designed to purposely destroy data.

[Unlike (most) viruses that infect human beings, computer viruses are always created by some emotionally stunted little nerd whose interper-

🍎 the happy idiot's troubleshooting tip (JK)

My first approach to many mysterious crashes and error messages is to simply retry whatever it was that seemed to cause the problem in the first place. Fairly often, it works fine the second time, and I go merrily (or drearily) on with my work.

Sometimes, the problem happens again. In the absence of any new clue as to its cause, I then shut down the Mac, turn off all the periph- erals, *very hot tip* wait ten seconds, and turn them back on again in reverse order (i.e. the Mac last, after everything else is warmed up). That cures another signifi- cant number of problems.

Among other things, shutting down flushes out the Mac's memory, which can get *fragmented* (disorganized) as you use the Mac—a diffi- cult condition for pro- grams to operate in. But shutting down also solves problems that aren't memory- related, so it's worth a try in just about any situation. You may never learn the source of the trouble, but if it doesn't come back, who cares?

sonal skills are so weak that he (I can't prove it, but I bet it's almost always a he) thinks it's amusing to cause other people pain—just to prove he can do it. There's really only a difference of degree between creating computer viruses and creating biological ones, and no doubt little difference in personality between the puerile misfits who make computer viruses and the moral zeros who engage in biological warfare. (It is, of course, possible to create computer viruses for moral pur- poses, but even if you're on the side of the angels, this sort of sabotage does virtually nothing to sway public opinion, which is ultimately what you have to do if you want the changes you're seeking to last.)—AN]

rant

You get a virus by using an infected program or disk—that is, one that already has the virus on it—sometimes over a network, from an infected network server. Symptoms of infection vary widely—your Mac may just slow down, or you may get unexplained beeping, lots of crashes, or files that disappear or become corrupted (although all of these symptoms are caused by other things more often than they're caused by viruses).

⬤ *antivirus software*

Antivirus programs work as detectors (letting you know you're infected), eradicators (getting rid of viruses) and/or as preventers (screening inserted disks for viruses and ejecting them if they contain any). Just as in the world of medicine, it's a game of leapfrog—the viruses evolve to outwit the cures and the cures get more sophisticated to handle the new viruses.

Disinfectant is a terrific program generously made available for free by its author, John Norstad (and/or his employer, Northwestern University; we're not sure exactly who to thank, since some of the program was a collaborative effort). It's widely available from user groups and online services and it's updated promptly as new viruses are discovered.

very good feature

Other shareware virus programs include Chris Johnson's Gatekeeper and Jeffrey Shulman's VirusDetective. Symantec's SAM and Microseeds' Rival are more sophisticated, commercial antivirus programs that can, for example, prevent unauthorized users from turning them off or changing their level of protection, but that's more than the typical user needs.

Some people use more than one antivirus program, but that's rarely beneficial, takes up extra memory and slows down startup. What's more, the programs can get in each other's way. So pick one program and use only that.

very hot tip

Remember, you can only control viruses if you update your software frequently. To find out about current viruses, check *Macworld* magazine's monthly update in its *News* section. If you learn there's a new virus making the rounds, get an update to your antivirus software and run it on all your disks. (Often you can download the update from an online service or bulletin board, or get a copy from a user group.)

very hot tip

Avoiding (and preparing for) trouble

🍎 avoiding hardware trouble

For tips on how to set up your Mac to avoid the slings and arrows of outrageous fortune, see the section of Chapter 3 called *Protecting your Mac (and yourself)*.

🍎 habits to make second nature

Here are some good habits to get into; they'll spare you lots of problems:

☞ **Use the *Save* command frequently during your work on a document** (except in programs like FileMaker that save automatically). If the application you're using unexpectedly quits, or your Mac hangs or crashes, you'll only be able to recover the file as of the last time you saved it—whatever changes you'd made since then will be lost.

important warning

☞ **Keep at least one current backup of every file you've got.** *[I make at least two backups, so when I'm working on a document, I have four copies of it— the one in memory, the one that's automatically saved (every ten minutes or 200 keystrokes) to my main hard disk, and two copies that I saved to other disks at the end of the last work session. You may think that's overkill, but it only takes a few seconds and can save you many hours of work. Disks go bad, files get corrupted, and one backup is sometimes not enough, especially if you decide you want to go back to an earlier version of a document.—AN]*

☞ **Always shut down by selecting *Shut Down* from the Special menu in the Finder;** this gives the Mac a chance to tidy up and save important information. You may think you're saving time by turning the power off without shutting down, but that just makes the Mac take even more time when it starts up.

☞ **Always leave a little extra space on every disk.** Your Mac may need it when updating the disk's directories (lists of where everything is), and if it doesn't find any, the disk may crash. Some applications also need space for invisible files. (To find

very hot tip

out how much space is left on a disk, see the entry *measuring RAM, disk capacity and file size* near the beginning of Chapter 4).

---

be discriminating

Many fun and useful programs are either extensions or control panels, but the more of them you install, the more likely one of them will be incompatible with other programs. An incompatibility may show up as a feature that won't work or a system crash when you're using another application. Some extensions, like virus protection software, are essential, but be selective about the other ones you use. If you load up on all the latest extensions, sooner or later you may spend a lot of time troubleshooting (see *extension and control panel conflicts* below).

Security programs, which require you to enter a password to open files, can cause more trouble than they're worth. If you forget your password, or someone accidentally (or maliciously) changes it, you may lose access to your important files. Security software also makes it more difficult—if not impossible—to recover data if your disk drive ever crashes.

important warning

---

a hard disk first-aid kit

What happens if your hard disk fails and the only tools you have for fixing it are on the damaged disk itself? To avoid such a predicament, keep nearby:

☞ **the complete set of system installation floppies** (or CD-ROM disk) that came with your Mac (the Mac can start up off the CD ROM or the Disk Tools floppy, which also contain disk-repair software)

☞ **a copy of the Disk Tools disk** that has SCSI Probe or SCSI Tools (shareware control panels) in its System Folder

☞ **a floppy containing the formatting software for your hard disk** (for the drive that came with your Mac, it's the disk with HD SC Setup on it)

☞ **floppies containing any other repair or recovery utilities you own**

Remember to lock all those disks so they can't be accidentally erased or damaged by a floppy drive that isn't working right (the entry *locking disks and files* in Chapter 4 tells how).

Consider buying at least one recovery package before anything goes wrong. Installing a program like FileSaver (part of Norton Utilities) or Mirror (MacTools Deluxe) in advance makes it easier to salvage data from a damaged disk or to retrieve files that have been erased accidentally.

very hot tip

Problems at startup

⚫ the healthy startup sequence

When you turn on your Mac, here's what should happen:

☞ you hear a chime

☞ the screen turns gray

☞ you hear the drives being accessed

☞ you see a happy (smiling) Mac on the screen

☞ *Welcome to Macintosh* appears on the screen

☞ icons of extensions and control panels (if you've added any to those that came with the Mac) appear across the bottom of the screen

☞ the desktop appears, with the icons and windows where you left them when you last shut down

If your Mac doesn't make it all the way through this sequence, see the appropriate entry below.

⚫ no startup chime

If the Mac doesn't chime at startup (so there's no startup sequence at all):

☞ Make sure the Mac isn't already on, with the screen turned down.

☞ If you're starting from the keyboard, make sure its cable is plugged in at both ends.

☞ Check that the Mac's power cord is plugged in securely at both ends and that the outlet or power strip is also on (some outlets are controlled by light switches and can be accidentally turned off).

☞ Try a different outlet or a different power cable.

☞ If you have a surge protector, tap the reset button.

⌘ *screen stays black*

If you hear the chime and the sound of the hard drive spinning but the screen stays black:

☞ Make sure the monitor's brightness knob is turned up (if it's got one).

☞ With an external monitor, be sure it's plugged in and turned on. If so, turn off both it and the Mac. Then turn the monitor back on first, followed by the Mac. If the monitor is attached to a video card in your Mac, make sure the card is set snugly in place. If you can, try a different monitor with the Mac, and/or a different Mac with the monitor, to determine which is the source of the problem.

☞ With compact Macs, tap lightly on the side of the Mac's case (if this brings the display back, have your Mac checked out by a repair person).

☞ If you have a compact Mac and see a vertical line across the black screen, turn your Mac off *immediately* and leave it off until it's been repaired.

important warning

⌘ *the question-mark floppy*

If the screen turns gray but then shows a blinking floppy disk icon with a question mark, it means that the Mac can't find a startup volume—a disk with a System Folder on it. If you get this icon, try the following steps until one of them solves the problem.

☞ Turn off everything, wait a few seconds and turn on all your external devices; after another fifteen seconds or so, turn the Mac back on.

☞ If your Mac has an internal hard drive and one or more SCSI devices attached, and the previous step didn't help, try turning everything off, unhooking the SCSI cable from the back of the Mac, and restarting the Mac. If that works, go to the Startup Disk control panel and select your Mac's internal drive. Then reconnect the SCSI cable and restart.

☞ Try zapping your Mac's PRAM, as described below.

☞ Reinstall the system software with the installation floppies or CD ROM that came with your Mac.

☞ If none of the above suggestions works, see *hard disk problems* below.

🍎 *the sad Mac*

The Mac performs a series of tests on itself while starting up. If it passes all of them, it displays the happy Mac icon; if it fails any, it displays the sad Mac accompanied by a series of tones and a code that describes the problem.

Here are two common sad Mac codes:

can't load System file into RAM

0000000F
00000064

on the Mac Plus and earlier machines:

0F0064

can't load Finder into RAM

0000000F
00000065

on the Mac Plus and earlier machines:

0F0065

I f you get either of those codes, turn off your Mac and any devices hooked up 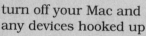 *very hot tip*

to it. Then reinstall system software using the installation floppies (or CD ROM) that came with your Mac. If that doesn't work, see *hard disk problems* below.

If your error code isn't exactly the same as the codes above, but has an F in the same position as they do, it's probably a disk problem. See the *hard disk problems* entry below. If your error code is completely different, take your Mac to a repair shop.

☀ *hangs or crashes during startup*

If your system hangs or crashes:

☞   during or directly after the happy Mac, the cause is generally either software or the hard disk. It's more likely to be a disk problem, so that's where to start looking (see *hard disk problems* below).

☞   while *Welcome to Macintosh* is on the screen, suspect a damaged System file and reinstall your system software.

☞   after *Welcome to Macintosh* disappears (you may see extension and control panel icons appear across the bottom of the screen) see *extension and control panels conflicts* below.

☞   when startup is almost finished (you may even see the desktop briefly), rebuild the desktop (as described below) before you try anything else. If you haven't upgraded your virus detector recently (or if you—horrors—haven't ever installed one), it could be a virus. Get the newest version of Disinfectant or another program and scan your disk for infection.

Other problems

☀ *if your Mac hangs*

In a *hang* (or *freeze)*, the screen looks OK but the pointer won't move (or disappears entirely), or input from the keyboard is ignored, or both. Despite the Mac's apparent indifference to keyboard input, you may be able to save the document you were working on by hitting ⌘S.

very
hot
tip

The next step is to try forcing the application to quit by holding down ⌥⌘ and pressing Esc (this only works in System 7). You should get a dialog box that says *Force [application name] to quit? Unsaved changes will be lost.* Click the *Force quit* button and the application should close and return control of the Mac to you.

If you don't get the dialog box, or nothing happens when you click the *Force quit* button, or you can't click the *Force quit* button because the pointer won't move or has disappeared, you'll have to restart your Mac (see the next entry).

the best way to restart your Mac

If your Mac gets a system error, or hangs and the suggestion in the previous entry doesn't help, you'll have to restart your Mac. But don't switch the power off and on again—press the reset button instead. The *reset* and *interrupt* buttons on the Mac's case are identified by symbols (a left-facing arrow for reset, a circle for the interrupt button, which is mostly for programmers).

They're located on the front of some Macs (like the Centris 650 and the Quadra 800), on the side of others (like the Classic II and older modular and compact Macs, where they come on a piece of plasic you have to install yourself), and on the back panel of others (like the PowerBooks).

Other Macs (like the Color Classic, the LC family and the si) don't have reset or interrupt buttons at all—on these models, hold down `Control` `⌃⌘` and hit the `Option` key (the one at the top of the keyboard you use to start up the Mac).

The PowerBook's buttons are recessed into small holes—poke a pen or paper clip in there to press the switch. If your Mac's buttons are in front, and it has to stay in a place where curious or careless people could accidentally press them while you work, consider taping a matchbox over the buttons to protect them.

important warning

problems with an application

Many of the problems that occur when you're working in an application can be fixed by allocating more memory to the program (see *setting an application's memory allocation* in the next section). Here are some potential symptoms of insufficient memory:

☞ Files suddenly vanish from the screen and are replaced by the message *The application [application name] has unexpectedly quit.*

☞ The Mac gets really slow when you're working with large documents or several documents at once.

☞ You're getting hangs or system bombs.

O ther circumstances can also cause hangs and system bombs, like having multiple System Folders or System files on your startup disk, or running certain older applications while 32-bit addressing or virtual memory is turned on in the Memory control panel. If turning off virtual memory or 32-bit addressing solves the problem, call the program's manufacturer and ask for a version that's compatible with these memory features.

Here are some more general tips for problems with applications:

☞ If you've recently added a new extension or control panel, it may be incompatible with the application. Try removing it and see if that fixes the problem.

☞ If the application used to work, and you haven't made any changes in your System, the problem can often be fixed by throwing away the application (including its preferences file) and replacing it with a fresh copy from the master disks the application came on. With some applications, simply throwing away its preferences file may be enough.

☞ If you've recently upgraded your system software to a new version, call the application's publisher to find out which System versions the program is compatible with and whether you need to upgrade it too.

🍎 *problems with printing*

☞ If you get a message like *The printer [printer name] could not be found*, most likely you've forgotten to turn the printer on, or you haven't selected its icon in the Chooser, or its cables aren't firmly plugged in at both ends. (Remember that when you select the LaserWriter icon in the Chooser, you also have to select the printer's name in the list box on the right.)

☞ If you get a message in the middle of a print job that there's been a PostScript error, select all the text in your document (don't forget headers and footers), change it to a different font, and try printing again. If several pages print before the print job stops and the error message appears, check what's different about the first page that didn't print. Try changing it to a different font. If there was a graphic on a page that wouldn't print, remove the graphic and try the page again.

☞ If the problem was a font, remove it from your system and install a fresh copy from a backup disk. If the problem was a graphic, you may have to recreate it (unless the graphic contains type, in which case try reinstalling whatever font the type is in).

Next try reinstalling the printer driver, using the installation disk that came with the printer (if it's an Apple printer, run the Installer program on the system software installation disks—choose the *Customize* option, select your printer's name from the scrolling list, and click the *Install* button).

☞ If your printer starts madly spitting out random numbers and letters, try zapping your Mac's PRAM (as described in the next section).

☞ If none of the above helps, contact the printer's manufacturer to find out about any known incompatibilities between its driver and other software you're running.

¿ when the Mac rejects a floppy

Eventually it happens—you put a floppy disk with important data on it into your Mac and get one of those dreaded messages: *This is not a Macintosh disk: Do you want to initialize it?* or *This disk is damaged: Do you want to initialize it?* (The answer is no, unless you want to lose all the data on the disk.) When you click *No*, the Mac ejects the disk. Lock it immediately; a misaligned drive or some types of directory damage may cause the Mac to write over your data on an unlocked disk, permanently erasing it.

Here are some things to check out:

☞ **If it's a high-density (1.4MB) floppy, make sure the drive is a SuperDrive** (the drives in early Macs like the Plus and some Mac II's and SE's can only read 800K disks). If the drive you're using is a SuperDrive but there's a chance the disk was initialized in an 800K drive, cover both sides of the hole in the floppy's upper-left corner with tape and try it again. If your Mac reads it, copy the data off of it and throw the floppy away. (See the entry *1.4MB disks initialized as 800K* in Chapter 4 for more information).

☞ **Try the disk in another drive.** Floppy drives reject disks when they get full of dust or out of alignment, and need to be cleaned or realigned. If changing drives works, try the disk in a third drive. If it works there, bring the first drive in to the repair shop. If it doesn't, the second drive may be misaligned and therefore the only drive that can read the floppy, so *it* should go to the shop—*after* you've copied the data off the floppy.

☞ **Wait and try again later.** If a disk is too cold or too warm, it might not be read correctly. You can try leaving a cold disk on top of the Mac to warm up for a few minutes.

If none of the above helps, and you don't have a backup, try to recover the data on it using a disk-repair program like the ones in Norton Utilities, 911 Utilities or MacTools Deluxe.

Floppies don't turn up bad every day—or at least they shouldn't. If you think your floppy drive is bad, copy the important data from your floppies to a hard disk, and take the floppy drive to a shop (in particular, some early PowerBook 140s and 170s had bad floppy drives).

ejecting stubborn floppies

If the normal methods of ejecting a floppy disk (dragging it to the Trash or choosing *Eject Disk, Restart* or *Shut Down* from the Special menu) don't work, you can physically force it out by poking a straightened paper clip into the little round hole next to the opening for the disk. Turn the Mac off first, though.

---

a jumpy pointer

If your mouse feels rough when it rolls or your pointer moves erratically around the screen, the rollers inside the mouse probably need to be cleaned. See *cleanlimouse is next to smoothlimouse* in Chapter 3.

very hot tip

A jerky pointer can also result from a loose mouse cable. To check that out, shut down your Mac and make sure that both ends of the cable from the mouse to the keyboard (or to the Mac, if yours is attached there) as well as the cable from the keyboard to the Mac, are all attached securely.

There's also an extension that makes the pointer jerk around (some jerk apparently wrote it as an homage to jerkiness), so if a silly friend has messed with your Mac recently, check the System Folder for extensions you don't recognize.

---

recovering deleted files

When you empty the Trash, files don't actually get erased from the disk—their names just get erased from the directory, and the disk space they occupy is made available for other documents. So until you copy or save other files, or create new ones, it's likely you can retrieve files you've trashed (obviously, the sooner you try, the better).

As soon as you realize you need something you've deleted, run a utility like UnErase (which is part of Norton Utilities). (You can make it easier to get files back the next time by installing a utility like Norton's FileSaver or MacTools' Mirror in advance.)

Tune-up techniques

🍎 *fixing desktop problems*

The Mac keeps track of the files and folders on your desktop by creating invisible **desktop** files on each disk you use. (Don't confuse these with the Desktop Folder that sometimes shows up when you connect to a shared Mac via file sharing.) Desktop files keep track of deleted items as well as current ones, so they keep getting bigger as you use your Mac. A bloated or corrupted desktop file can cause many different symptoms:

☞ Icons may turn into the generic document icon (an empty page with the corner turned down).

☞ When you double-click on a document, you may be informed that *the application program that created it couldn't be found* (even though you know the program is on an attached disk).

☞ Folders open lazily or not at all.

☞ There's less space available on a disk than you'd expect (especially on floppy disks).

☞ External disks take a long time to appear on the desktop.

You rebuild the desktop to return it to normal. You do that on a hard disk by restarting while holding down ⌥⌘. For a floppy, hold down ⌥⌘ and insert the disk. In both cases, click *Yes* when asked if you want to rebuild the desktop. Under System 7, the floppy must contain something—an empty folder will do—before you can rebuild the desktop.

When you rebuild the desktop, you lose any comments you typed in Get Info boxes, but everything else will be fine. (A number of shareware programs are available that preserve your Get Info comments when rebuilding the desktop; your local user group or bulletin board should know about them.)

setting an application's memory allocation

When you start an application under System 7 (or Multi-Finder in System 6), the Mac sets aside a certain amount of RAM for the program and any documents you open with it.

Under some circumstances (if you're using very large files, for example) that amount may not be enough, causing the program to respond very slowly to your commands or suddenly quit without allowing you to save your work.

To set aside more memory, quit the application,

select its icon on the desktop and hit ⌘I. The Memory section of the window that appears will list a Suggested size and a Current size (called Application Memory Size in System 6).

All you have to do is make the current size

larger (as shown above) by clicking inside the Current size box and typing a new number. Try adding 256K to the existing number at first—if that's not enough, add more later.

Later, when you're trying to squeeze more applications into memory, you may want to reduce it again. But never go below the suggested size, because that's the minimum for safe operation.

The dialog box you see when you go to the menu and choose *About this Macintosh...* (or *About the Finder...* in System 6) ‖▮➡

Microsoft Word Info

Microsoft Word
Microsoft Word 4.0

Kind: application program
Size: 704K on disk (717,464 bytes used)

Where: Macintosh HD : Applications :

Created: Mon, Apr 10, 1989, 5:00 PM
Modified: Wed, Feb 12, 1992, 9:37 AM
Version: 4.0, © 1987-1989 Microsoft Corporation
Comments:

☐ **Locked**

Memory
Suggested size : 512   K
Current size : 1024   K

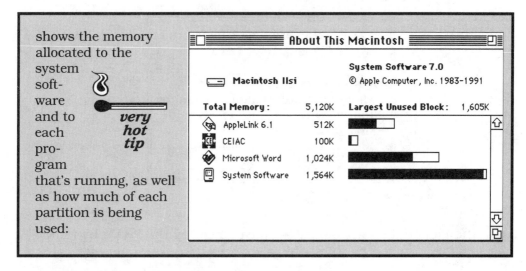

shows the memory allocated to the system software and to each program that's running, as well as how much of each partition is being used:

very hot tip

🍎 zapping the PRAM

When you shut down the Mac, you cut off power to its RAM, flushing out the information that gets stored there while the computer is on. But the Mac needs to hold onto control panel settings like the date, time and normal startup disk, so it keeps this information in a separate type of RAM called *parameter RAM*, or *PRAM* (pronounced *PEE-ram)* that's powered by a built-in battery. If the PRAM becomes corrupted, your Mac may not start up normally, or will have other problems, often related to disk drives.

You can fix corrupted PRAM by "zapping" it, which resets most of your control panel settings—sound selection and volume, rate of insertion point blinking, etc.—to their defaults (date and time settings stay current). Under System 7, start your Mac and immediately press the Option ⌘ P R keys together. Hold them down while your Mac begins its startup sequence; when it chimes a second time and starts over, release the keys to let your Mac start up normally.

Under earlier system software, select *Control Panel* from the 🍎 menu while holding down Shift Control ⌘. You'll get a dialog box that looks like the one at the top of the next page:

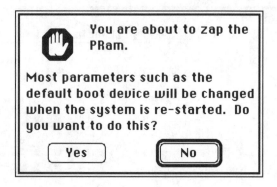

Click *Yes*.

On the Plus and earlier models, you can also zap the PRAM by removing the battery for ten minutes (this also loses date and time settings).

Advanced troubleshooting

⌘ *extension and control panel conflicts*

If you get a lot of hangs or crashes—especially during startup—you may have a conflict among your extensions and/or control panels; for the purposes of this entry, we'll call both types of files *extensions*. To check out this possibility under System 7, disable all your extensions by restarting with the ⬚Shift⬚ key held down.

shortcut

(Under System 6, restart your Mac with a floppy startup disk—like the System Tools or System Startup disk that came with your Mac—in the floppy drive. Then create a new folder and move the System and Finder files from your regular startup disk's System Folder into it. Then restart. If you still can't start from the drive, reinstall your system software using the disks that came with your Mac.)

I f the problem disappears when you restart this way, you've got an extension conflict. (If you're running System 6, move the System and

Finder back into the System Folder.) If you've recently added an extension, remove it from the System Folder and restart. If that doesn't solve the problem, read on.

To figure out which file is causing the trouble, move all your System Folder's control panels and extensions (except your favorites, if they've been reliable) into a separate folder on your hard disk. (Under System 6, they're called *control panel* and *startup* documents in the Kind column.) One at a time, add them back into your System Folder, restarting your Mac after each one. When the problem reappears, you'll know that the last file you added is the culprit. Call its manufacturer and ask for advice.

If you can't reach the manufacturer immediately, here's another tip that may help: extensions load alphabetically. Sometimes you can get around incompatibilities by renaming the troublemaker, to make it load before or after the other files.

very hot tip

🍎 *hard disk problems*

If you're having trouble with a hard drive but its icon shows up on the desktop, skip to *hard disk repair and recovery* below. (But first back up the data on it; you may never get another chance.)

If the drive doesn't mount (i.e. its icon doesn't show up on the desktop) shut down everything. If it's an external drive, make sure that all cables are plugged in at both ends. Turn it on (and any other devices connected to it), wait fifteen seconds, and then turn the Mac on. If that doesn't help, try using a utility like SCSI Probe to mount the drive.

If the drive still won't mount, try the following steps (shut down your Mac before making any changes, and see the *SCSI devices* section of Chapter 4 for an explanation of any terms that aren't clear to you):

☞ Make sure every device in the SCSI chain has a unique ID number.

☞ Try using a different SCSI cable, if you've got one.

☞ Make sure the SCSI chain is terminated properly (see *SCSI termination problems* below).

☞ If you've recently turned on virtual memory, turn it off. If the problems go away, leave virtual memory off and contact the drive's manufacturer for advice.

If you just upgraded to System 7, or if you've hooked up an old hard drive to a new Mac, the driver on your hard disk may not be compatible with your new system. Contact the drive's manufacturer for advice.

If none of the above solves your problems, or if you get a message indicating that *This disk is not initialized* or *This is not a Macintosh disk* or *This disk is damaged* (plus, in each case, *Do you want to initialize it?*) see the next entry.

🍎 *hard disk repair and recovery*

Using a damaged disk can produce a number of symptoms—like files that disappear or unexplained bombs that occur when you try to access the disk. If you can still access your files, often the best solution is to back up everything on your hard disk, reformat the disk using the software that came with it, and then copy all your data back onto it. If you don't have your data backed up, you have two options: **repair** and **recovery**.

Repair utilities try to reconstruct lost information from invisible directory files on the disk. (If you've installed a utility that records directory changes—like Norton's FileSaver—you have a better chance

🍎 *SCSI termination problems*

Theoretically, the first and last devices in a SCSI chain—and only those two—must be terminated. In practice, though, the best way to troubleshoot a SCSI chain is to test each device by itself in turn, with and without termination. (You may need to boot from a floppy if your startup drive is disconnected.) If all the devices work alone but not together, you probably have a termination problem.

You solve termination problems largely by trial and error. Try adding and removing terminators, keeping in mind that some SCSI devices have internal termination. If you can't figure out a termination scheme that works, try rearranging the order of the SCSI devices. Very long SCSI cables can also act like terminators, so try using shorter ones. On the other hand, if you're using a short cable, try a longer one. (For a discussion of SCSI basics, see the *SCSI devices* section of Chapter 4.)

of getting your files back.) Successfully repairing a volume may save all your data, but often only some of it survives.

If a disk can't be repaired, you may still be able to get some or all of your data safely off of it with a **recovery utility**, which tries to copy files from it to an undamaged disk.

Here's a series of steps to follow when you have a damaged disk, beginning with the least powerful—and least dangerous—repair utilities, then proceeding to the bigger guns. (If it's a floppy that's damaged, first see the next entry.)

☞ Start repairs with Disk First Aid, which comes free with your system software. Disk First Aid isn't very powerful, but it can fix many common problems, and it almost never creates new ones.

☞ If Disk First Aid fails, try a more powerful repair utility, like the ones in Norton Utilities, 911 Utilities or MacTools Deluxe.

☞ If a repair utility doesn't fix everything the first time, run it several times; sometimes it will fix more damage with each pass. Or use a different repair utility. Sometimes one program will restore some of your lost files, and pave the way for another to restore the rest.

very hot tip

As soon as you can access any files, back them up. Doing further repairs may lose them again.

☞ If you can't repair a volume, try a recovery utility like those in the latest version of Norton Utilities (the one in an earlier version isn't nearly as good) and MacTools Deluxe.

important warning

If none of these programs helps, there are companies that specialize in rescuing drives (like DriveSavers, which advertises in the back pages of Mac magazines). This may cost you more than it would to replace the drive, though, so don't do it unless it's critical that you recover your lost data.

🍎 *floppy disk repair and recovery*

Some utilities, like FastCopy, which comes with MacTools Deluxe, can make exact copies of damaged or unreadable floppies; before you attempt any repair, make a copy with one of them, so if something goes wrong with the repair process, you can try again on a fresh copy. (If a disk is badly damaged, these utilities may not work.)

very hot tip

Sometimes the copy of the damaged a floppy will work just fine, or be easier to repair, so work with it, rather than the original. Once you've repaired, recovered or given up on a damaged floppy, it may be possible to reformat and reuse it, but it's safer to throw it away and use a fresh disk instead.

From the Visual Delights collection of Macintosh clip art. Copyright © 1991 by SunShine. All rights reserved.

What all those little things on the back of the Mac are for

The back panels of most Macs have an array of sockets (or ***ports***) for plugging in ***peripherals***—external devices controlled by the Mac. The table below identifies what type of peripheral plugs into which port.

this icon:	*appears above this port:*	*which is where you attach:*
	sound input	a microphone or other sound input plug
	sound output	headphones or speakers
	modem	a modem or other serial device[1]
	printer	a printer, LocalTalk network cable or serial device[1]
	SCSI *(scuzzy)*	external hard disks, CD-ROM or cartridge drives, scanners or other SCSI devices[2]
	Ethernet	Ethernet network cabling
	video	a monitor (one that your Mac is designed to support)
	floppy drive	an external floppy drive
	ADB	a keyboard, mouse, trackball, or other ADB device
	power	the power cord

1. **Serial devices** *include modems and most non-PostScript printers, like the DeskWriter, StyleWriter, ImageWriter, Personal LaserWriter LS and LaserWriter Select 300. Most laser printers are PostScript devices, which must be connected to the printer port (or to network cabling that connects to the printer port). Some modems, like Global Village's Teleport series, attach to the ADB port instead of the modem port.*

2. *Some PowerBooks have a square-shaped 30-pin SCSI port instead of the flat, 25-pin port on most Macs. SCSI cables are normally designed to fit the 25-pin ports, so you'll have to get a special cable or adapter to attach a SCSI device to one of these PowerBooks.*

Amid all the ports, you may also notice a button with this icon above it: ①. This button turns the Mac's power on or off. You have to use it to turn on non-Duo PowerBooks, but on other Macs, you should use the keyboard's power-on button (◁) and the Special menu's *Shut Down* command instead.

Where to find good information and inexpensive software

Books & magazines

🍎 *magazines and newsletters*

The three major Mac magazines are *Macworld, MacUser* and *MacWeek* (listed in chronological order of when they were founded, to avoid even the slightest hint of favoritism). They're all jam-packed with useful information and, although they're written for readers who have a fair amount of technical knowledge, this book should take you to the point where you can follow pretty much whatever they talk about.

very good feature

MacWeek—subtitled *The Newsweekly for Macintosh Managers*—is the most technical, filled with breaking news for people who have to stay on top of the latest developments. *MacUser* and *Macworld* are more for regular users; they're great if you're considering a major hardware or software purchase, or just want to learn more about a particular topic than we've been able to tell you in this book. Pick up a copy or two and, for an investment of a few dollars, you'll know all you need to know about them.

The Cobb Group (800 223 8720) puts out several excellent monthly newsletters for Mac users, including ones on Word, Excel and Microsoft Works, and a general one of Mac tips and tricks.

🍎 *books*

If we tell you about the *Macintosh Bible,* we sound conceited (and greedy). But if we don't, you miss out on a book that more than 800,000 readers have described as "a godsend," "the most useful book I have ever purchased," "extremely helpful," "tremendously useful," "fantastic," "marvellous," "fabulous" and "better than sex" (among thousands of similar comments).

Reviewers have been equally enthusiastic, calling it "brilliant...the best" *(Macworld),* "the single most helpful book about the Mac" *(The New York Times)* and "far and away the best collection of Mac tips around" *(Computer Literacy).* The readers of *Publish* magazine voted it their favorite Mac book three years in a row, and it's the only book to ever have been nominated for *MacUser's* Editor's Choice award.

Most of the information in this book (the one you're reading, that is) was drawn from the *Macintosh Bible,* but there's *lots* more there—1241 pages of tips on every conceivable subject, tricks and shortcuts for every conceivable situation and jokes to offend every conceivable sensibility.

A nd while this book has tried to avoid evaluating specific programs, the *Macintosh Bible* contains hundreds of hard-hitting product reviews. It's got a 140-page index, a 70-page glossary and comes with three free 30-page updates that keep you informed about the latest hardware and software developments, bug fixes, etc.

very good feature

The *Macintosh Bible* is available in any bookstore that has its wits about it, as well as wholesale clubs, computer stores, etc. You can also order it directly from the publisher; just send in the order form at the back of this book, or call Peachpit Press at 800 283 9444. Shipping adds a little to the cost, but Peachpit offers an unconditional money-back guarantee on direct orders.

P eachpit also publishes two troubleshooting handbooks that are worth checking out—*The Macintosh Bible "What Do I Do Now?" Book* and *The Dead Mac Scrolls*—as well as several other *Macintosh Bible* guides (they're listed on the order form in the back of the book).

User groups

¢ *what user groups are*

User groups are clubs made up of people who are interested in computers in general, a particular kind of computer, a particular kind of software or even an individual program. They're typically nonprofit and independent of any manufacturer or publisher.

U ser groups are an excellent source of good informa-tion—which isn't surprising, since sharing informa-tion is their main purpose. Nowhere else are you likely to find so many dedicated people eager to help you solve your problems, none of whom would dream of charging

very good feature

you a nickel for it. (On the other hand, a lot of their opinions and recommendations have to be taken with a grain of salt.)

User group meetings are usually free and open to the public. Joining the group normally costs somewhere between $20 and $60 a year and gives you access to the group's library of public-domain (free) software and shareware (cheap). Large groups often feature guest speakers from the computer industry who describe new products at their meetings, and also have subgroups called *SIGs* (which stands for *special interest groups)* for members with particular interests or needs: beginners, developers, musicians, graphic artists, desktop publishers and so on.

bargain

Here's a description of what a typical (large) user group meeting is like. Before the meeting starts, people line up to buy disks and other items like modems that the group sells to members, usually at very low prices. The meeting begins with an open session where people can ask any question they have about any aspect of the Mac, and usually get a definitive answer from someone in the room. When the question-and-answer session is over, one or two guest speakers describe their products, using a Mac that projects onto a giant screen.

[I vividly remember the night the ebullient Andy Hertzfeld (who wrote much of the code in the original Finder, as well as the software Radius distributes with its monitors) debuted a program of his called Switcher at a local user group. (Switcher was eventually bought by Apple and became the basis for the part of the system software that lets you have two applications open at the same time.) When the display on the big screen switched from the first open application to the second, the audience literally leapt to its feet and cheered.—AN]

Unless you live in a very remote area, finding a local user group shouldn't be hard—especially if there's a college or university nearby. Either check with an Apple dealer (any good one will know all the local user groups) or call 800 538 9696, which is Apple's user group hot-line (you give them your zip code and they give you the names and numbers of up to three user groups in your area). If you can't find a group in your community, get together with some other Mac users and start one of your own.

Glossary
of basic
Mac terms

The definitions in this glossary only apply to the Mac. They may not be accurate if you try to apply them to other computers or—heaven forfend!—to the world outside comput- ers.Very basic terms (like mouse and keyboard) are omitted.

When a term that's defined below occurs in the definition of another term, we usually put it in italics—so you know you can look it up if you don't know what it means (but we don't do that for the most common terms, like file and folder). Italics are also used for sen- tences that show how the word is used. Words are alphabetized as if spaces and hyphens didn't exist; thus copying comes before copy protection and e-mail comes after ellipsis.

Although many people's suggestions have been incorporated into these definitions, the final wording is mine, and I'm to blame for any imprecision, confusion or bad jokes.—AN

---

access privileges

The ability to view or change a file or folder that's being shared over the network by an *AppleShare file server* or a Mac using System 7's *file shar- ing*. The privileges are assigned to other users on a *network* by the shared item's owner or by a network administrator.

access time

How long it takes for a *hard disk* (or similar device) to find data stored on it.

active window

The currently selected *window*, where the next command (or any- thing you type from the keyboard) will be applied. The active window is always on top of any overlapping windows, its title bar is high- lighted—that is, there are six hori- zontal lines on either side of the title—and its scroll bars are gray (when all its contents won't fit).

ADB *(pronounced as separate letters— needless to say)*

The *Apple Desktop Bus*—a standard for connecting peripheral devices like keyboards and mice to all Macs since the SE (as well as to the Apple IIGS). The connections are different from those on the Plus and earlier Macs.

alert box *(or simply* alert*)*

A *box* that appears unbidden on the screen, announced by one or more beeps, to give you information. Alert boxes don't require any information back from you (although you may have to click a button like *OK, Cancel* or *Restart)*. A bomb is one example. Also called a message box, although alert box is the correct name. Some people call them simply alerts.

alias

A small file (usually about 2K) that serves as a remote control for open- ing another file, folder or disk. You can put an alias anywhere—on the desktop, in a folder or on the menu—and it will find and open the original when double-clicked, selected from the menu, or opened in any other way.

alphanumeric

Letters and numbers. Punctuation and symbols are not alphanumeric characters.

Apple Events

A System 7 feature that lets you use the functions of one program on files created by others (in software that's designed to work that way). For example, you might use a spreadsheet program to make a chart out of the data in a database program.

menu

The Apple menu, which is available on the *desktop* (that is, in the *Finder)* and from within most applications; its title is an that appears at the extreme left end of the menu bar. Under System 7, you can make any file or folder appear on the menu by adding it to the *Apple Menu Items folder;* under System 6, the menu only gives you access to *desk accessories.* With either version, you also get information about the current application.

AppleShare

1. A *Chooser extension* that lets you access shared files on other networked Macs or AppleShare *file servers.*

2. Software that turns a Macintosh with a hard disk into a *file server,* allowing other Macs on the same *network* to access the files kept on it.

AppleTalk

The Mac's built-in networking software, and the *protocols* it uses. Networks using those protocols are also called AppleTalk. Originally, AppleTalk referred to the cabling as well, which is now called *LocalTalk.*

application

(or *application program)* Software that does relatively complex tasks and that lets you create and modify documents. Some common types of applications are word processors, spreadsheets, databases, graphics programs, page layout software and communications programs. All programs are called applications, except utilities and system software.

Application menu

In System 7, the menu at the extreme right end of the menu bar that lets you switch between programs (and lets you hide the windows, etc. of programs you're not using at the moment). The menu's icon changes to match whichever program is currently active.

arrow keys

On the standard ADB keyboard, four keys (indicated by ⬆, ⬅, ➡ and ⬇ in this book) that move the insertion point, move you through list boxes, etc.

arrow pointer

The basic shape the pointer takes—a left-leaning arrow that looks like this: ➤

ascender

The part of lowercase letters like *b, d* and *l* that extends above the x-height. Compare *descender*.

ASCII *(ASK-ee)*

The *American standard code* for *information interchange,* a system for referring to letters, numbers and common symbols by code numbers. The ASCII standard is widely used by small computers like Macs and PCs, and is useful for transferring files between them. On the Mac, ASCII files are usually referred to as text files.

A/UX *(pronounced as separate letters)*

A version of Unix designed for use on the Mac by Apple.

backbone

A type of network configuration in which each node has its own branch off a main cable (like rooms off a hall). Compare *daisy chain* and *star*.

background printing

A feature that allows you to keep using your Mac while it's sending a document to the printer. See also *print spooler*.

backup

A copy of a program or document that you can use if the original is destroyed. To back up is to make a copy.

Balloon Help

A feature of System 7 that automatically displays cartoon-like message balloons that explain items on the screen when you point to them with the mouse. (You turn it on or off from the Help menu.)

baseline

The imaginary line on which the letters of a font sit (only descenders extend below it).

BASIC

A *high-level programming language* that's relatively easy to learn but is also relatively lacking in power and sophistication. The name is short for beginner's all-purpose symbolic instruction set.

baud rate

A measure of how fast data is transmitted—by a *modem*, for example—usually expressed in bits per second (bps). (In some circumstances, there's a difference between *bits* per second and the baud rate, but for all practical purposes you can consider them to be the same.) The most common baud rates are 1200, 2400, 9600 and 14,400 bps. The term comes from the name of a communications pioneer, Baudot.

BBS

Short for *bulletin board system*.

benchmark

A test (or set of tests) used to compare hardware or software speed.

beta tester

A person, not employed by the company developing a product, who tries to discover bugs in it. Beta testers are almost never paid; they do it for the fun of being in on the development of the product and/or because their work requires that they know what's going on before the product is released.

beta version

A version of a program at the point at which it's in beta test. Usually there are several beta versions. Compare *release version.*

Bezier curves *(BEZ-yay)*

Mathematically generated lines that can display nonuniform curvatures (as opposed to curves with uniform curvature, which are called *arcs)*. Named after Pierre Bezier, they're defined by four control points. It's relatively easy to make Bezier curves assume complex shapes and to join their endpoints smoothly, which makes them particularly useful for creating the shapes of letters and other complex graphics.

binary numbers

The base-2 numbering system that almost all computers are based on, as opposed to the base-10, decimal numbers people use. The number 1 is the same in both binary and decimal, but 2 in decimal = 10 in binary, 3 in decimal = 11 in binary, 4 in decimal = 100 in binary, and so on.

bit

The smallest possible unit of information. It can represent only one of two things: yes or no, on or off, or—as it's expressed in the binary numbers used in computers—0 or 1. Short for binary digit. Also see *byte.*

bit map

An image made up of dots.

bit-mapped font

A font that's made up of a pattern (map) of dots, and requires different maps to look right in different sizes. Also called a fixed-size font by Apple (and by nobody else). Compare *outline font* and *screen font.*

bit-mapped graphic

A picture or other graphic made up of dots rather than of objects. Typically produced by paint programs. Compare *object-oriented graphic.*

block move

Cutting and *pasting* a large block of text.

board

A piece of fiberglass or pressboard on which chips are mounted. Also called a circuit board. The connections between the chips are normally printed with metallic ink—in which case it's a *printed circuit* (or *PC*) board. The main board in a computer device is called the *logic board* or *motherboard*. A board made to plug into a slot is called a *card*.

bomb

A *message box* with a picture of a bomb in it. It appears unbidden on the screen to let you know that a serious problem has occurred with the *system software* (in other words, that you've *crashed*). Bombs usually force you to restart the system. Compare *hang*.

booting

Starting up a computer by loading an operating system—in the case of the Mac, the System and either the Finder or a Finder substitute—into its memory. The more common Mac term is *starting up* or simply *starting*. (The name *boot* comes from the idea that the operating system pulls itself up by its own bootstraps— since it's a program that tells a computer how to load other programs, but loads itself.)

box

1. An enclosed area on the Mac's screen that doesn't have a title bar (and thus can't be dragged around). *Dialog boxes* and *alert boxes* are two examples. Certain kinds of boxes, like *list boxes* and *text boxes,* appear inside other boxes (in this case, inside dialog boxes). Compare *window*.

2. Any of various rectangular icons that control windows—like *close*

boxes, scroll boxes, size boxes and *zoom boxes.*

3. A rectangular button, like a *checkbox.*

bridge

The most basic sort of connection between networks. Compare *gateway* and *router.*

buffer

An area of *memory*—or a physically separate memory *cache*—that holds information until it's needed. Buffers are used to speed up printing, redrawing the screen, etc. by providing a reservoir of information that's readily accessible to the printer or monitor, rather than allowing a bottleneck to develop between it and the Mac.

bug

A mistake, or unexpected occurrence, in a piece of software (or, less commonly, a piece of hardware). Bugs are distinguished from design flaws, which are intentional (that is, the programmer put them there).

Most computer programs are so complex that no programmer can test out (or even conceive of) all the possible situations they can generate. Thus most bugs aren't quite errors, but are rather untested paths, unanticipated contingencies. They're discovered when a user breaks new ground— for example, by using a particular series of commands in a particular order that no one has tried before (or in a particular set of circumstances that no one has been in before).

Bug is an old electronics and phone company term. It comes from the fact that bugs eating the insulation off wires was actually a common cause of problems in early telephone systems, until they figured out how to coat wires with stuff bugs don't like the taste of. (But they haven't figured out how to turn off pack rats. If you leave your car sitting outside for several weeks in the desert—on the outskirts of Tucson, say—pack rats will eat the insulation off the wiring.)

bulletin board (or bulletin board system)

A computer dedicated to maintaining messages and software and making them available over phone lines at little or no charge. People *upload* (contribute) and *download* (gather) messages and files by calling the bulletin board from their own computers. Abbreviated *BBS*.

bus

A path over which electronic impulses travel between various computer devices. Examples include the *Apple Desktop Bus (ADB)*, which connects keyboards and mice to the Mac, and the *SCSI* bus, which connects hard drives and other *peripherals* to the Mac.

button

1. On the Mac's screen, an outlined area in a *dialog box* that you click on to choose, confirm or cancel a command. For example, when you quit from most applications, you get a dialog box that asks if you want to save the current document, and it gives you three buttons to choose from: *Yes, No* and *Cancel*. A button with a heavy border, which is activated when you hit Return or Enter, is called the default button. Also see *radio buttons.*

2. The switch on top of the mouse you use for clicking. When there's a danger of confusion with the first meaning of button, this one is called the *mouse button.*

byte

Eight *bits*. Bytes are typically used to represent characters (letters, numbers, punctuation marks and other symbols) in text.

cache (cash)

A place where you keep additional information. See *disk cache* and *buffer.*

CAD (pronounced as a word, not separate letters)

Computer-aided design, usually in areas of engineering, product design and architecture (CAD can refer to either hardware or software).

CAD/CAM *(CAD-cam)*

For *CAD*, see the previous entry. The *CAM* half stands for computer-aided *m*anufacturing—computers and programs that run manufacturing machinery or even entire factories. (You seldom see the word CAM alone; it's usually combined with CAD.)

card

A kind of board that plugs directly into a *slot*. Cards have connectors right on their edges, rather than at the ends of a cable.

cartridge drive

A drive that uses a removable hard disk called a cartridge. (SyQuest is the most common brand.)

CD ROM *(SEE-dee RAHM)*

A compact disk read-only memory—a kind of optical storage device (or medium) used on the Mac and other computers. Hyphenated when used as an adjective.

cdev *(SEE-dev)*

In System 6, a utility program that, like an init, must be placed in the System Folder to work. Unlike an init, it then displays an icon on the left side of the Control Panel, along with Apple's General, Keyboard and Mouse cdevs. Cdev is short for Control Panel device. In System 7, they're called control panels.

character

The generic name for a number, letter or symbol. Included are "invisible" characters like Tab and Return.

character key

Any key that generates a character. Compare *modifier key.*

checkboxes

A group of boxes that work as *toggles*—that is, when you click on an empty checkbox, an X appears inside it, turning the option on; when you click on a checkbox with an X in it, the X disappears, and the option is turned off. Unlike *radio buttons*, any or all of a group of checkboxes can be on at one time.

chip

Silicon is a chemical element found in sand, clay, glass, pottery, concrete, brick, etc. A tiny piece of silicon (or *germanium*), usually about the size of a baby's fingernail, is impregnated with impurities in a pattern that creates different sorts of miniaturized computer circuits. This is a chip.

Chips are primarily used as CPUs or memory and are normally mounted in DIPs or SIMMs, or on boards.

chip family

A group of related *chips*, each of which (except, of course, the first) evolved from an earlier one. The *CPU chips* used in most Macs are members of Motorola's 68000 family.

Chooser

A *desk accessory* primarily used to tell the Mac which printer you want to use, what *port* it's connected to, whether *background printing* is turned on and whether *AppleTalk* is active or inactive. You also use it to gain access to a file server or another Mac's shared files.

Chooser extension

When you place one of these inside your System Folder, it displays an icon in the Chooser window. Chooser extensions normally control external devices like printers, or emulate them. Some examples are: the ImageWriter, StyleWriter and LaserWriter drivers that come with the Mac; FaxSTF's FaxPrint file, which lets you send a fax over a fax modem; and AppleShare, which lets you access other volumes on a local area network.

circuit board

See *board*.

clicking

Pressing and immediately releasing the *mouse button.* To click on something is to position the *pointer* on it and then click.

Clipboard

The area of the Mac's *memory* that holds what you last *cut* or *copied.* (If there's not enough room in memory for what you cut or copy, some of it is put on disk.) *Pasting* inserts the contents of the Clipboard into a document.

clock rate (or clock speed)

A computer's *CPU* is synchronized to a quartz crystal that pulses millions of times each second. These pulses determine things like how often the screen is redrawn and how quickly the CPU accesses *RAM* or a hard disk. The frequency of the pulses—how often they occur—is measured in *megahertz* (millions of cycles per second) and is called the clock rate or clock speed. (When comparing Macs, the clock speed usually discussed is the CPU's, which is half the crystal's.)

clone

A machine that's compatible with the IBM Personal Computer but that isn't made by IBM.

close box

A small box at the left end of the active window's title bar. Clicking on it closes the window. Compare *size box* and *zoom box.*

closing

On the *desktop,* closing a window means collapsing it back into an icon. Within an application, closing a document means flushing it out of the computer's memory (at which point, you have to save the document to a disk or lose any changes you made to it since you opened it).

code

The actual statements or instructions in a program; what programmers produce. *Clean,* or *elegant,* code is well-written; *spaghetti code* is not.

Color Wheel

A segmented circle containing many colors that's used to specify the color of the desktop, highlighted text, etc. You get to the Color Wheel via System 7's Color and General control panels or the Color section of System 6's Control Panel.

command

The generic name for anything you tell a computer program to do. On the Mac, commands are usually listed on menus, or are generated by holding down the ⌘ (command) key while hitting one or more other keys. To choose a command from a menu, you drag down the menu until the command you want is highlighted, then release the mouse button.

commercial

Said of computer products that are sold for profit through normal distribution channels, with the purchaser paying before taking possession of the product. Compare *shareware* and *public-domain.*

communicating

Transferring data between computers, either over phone lines *(telecommunicating)* or on a *local area network.*

compact Mac

A Mac (like the Classics or the Plus) with a small monitor built into the same box as the CPU. Compare *modular Mac* and *portable Mac.*

compression

Reducing the size of files so they'll take less time to transmit via a *modem,* or so that more of them can fit on a disk.

configuration

1. The components that make up a particular computer system (i.e. which model of Mac and what *peripherals).*

2. The actual physical arrangement of those components (i.e. what's placed where).

3. The physical arrangement of nodes on a network (see *backbone, daisy-chain* and *star).*

4. The software settings that tell computer devices how to communicate with each other (as in configuring your modem software).

control key

A *modifier key* on ADB keyboards (but not on earlier Mac keyboards). Widely used in the world of the IBM PC, Control can be used on Macs as part of keyboard commands for menu commands or for macros.

control panel, Control Panel, Control Panels

In System 7, a *control panel* (small letters) is a *utility* that lets you set things like how loud the beeps (and other sounds the Mac makes) are, how fast the *insertion point* blinks, how fast you have to click in succession for the Mac to recognize it as a doubleclick, and so on. Control panels are kept in a folder called *Control Panels* (initial caps); one way to open it is by selecting *Control Panels* from the menu.

In System 6, control panels are called *cdevs*, and they're accessed through the *Control Panel* (capitalized, singular) command on the menu.

coprocessor

A *chip* that specializes in math, graphics, or some other specific kind of computation. When the *CPU* is given the kind of job the coprocessor specializes in, it hands the job off to it. The most common coprocessor chips used in Macs so far (the 68881 and 68882) both specialize in mathematical computation.

copying

1. Creating a duplicate of a file or folder from one disk on another disk.

2. Putting a duplicate of text or graphics material onto the Clipboard. To do that, you select what you want to copy and then choose *Copy* from the Edit menu or hit ⌘C. Also see *cutting* and *pasting*.

copy protection

Any of many various schemes for preventing the unauthorized copying of software. They're all a pain

(although to varying degrees) and are seldom used any more.

CP/M *(pronounced as separate letters— needless to say)*

An early *operating system* for personal computers on which MS DOS was modeled. (The name stands for *control program for microprocessors.*)

cps

Characters per second (used to describe printer speed).

CPU *(pronounced as separate letters— needless to say)*

The *central processing unit*—the central part of a computer (or other computer device). It includes the circuitry—built around the *CPU chip* and mounted on the *motherboard*—that actually performs the computer's calculations, and the box in which that circuitry is housed. (Sometimes just the CPU chip itself is called the CPU.)

CPU chip

The brain of a computer (or other computer device); the main *processor chip* that actually does the computing. The CPU chip is the primary determinant of what software will run on that particular computer and, with the *clock rate*, determines how fast the computer will run.

crash

A noun and verb, both of which mean that your system has suddenly and unexpectedly stopped working, or is working wrong. You normally have to restart. Also see *bomb* and *hang*.

CRT *(pronounced as separate letters— needless to say)*
A *cathode ray tube*—the display technology used on virtually all desktop computer monitors and television sets. On portable Macs, the most common technology is the *LCD*.

curly quotes (and curly apostrophes)
Ones that look like this: " " ', rather than like this: " ' .

cursor
Unlike more primitive computers, the Mac has nothing called a *cursor* (although Mac *programmers* use the term; see the next paragraph). This clumsy and imprecise term is sometimes used to replace the more accurate terms *pointer* and *insertion point*. (Cursor is a Latin word that means runner or messenger.)

Mac programmers call the pointer the cursor—which doesn't make any sense at all, since the insertion point, not the pointer, is the equivalent of what's called the cursor on other computers. But, hey, that's why you use the Mac—so that all that nerdy computerese will be invisible to you.

cutting
Removing something from a document by selecting it and then choos-

ing *Cut* from the Edit menu or hitting ⌘X. What you cut is placed in the Clipboard. Also see *copying* and *pasting*.

DA *(pronounced as separate letters)*
The common name for a *desk accessory*.

daisy chain
A type of *network configuration* in which *nodes* are connected to one another in a chain (so that information has to pass through each node to get to the next). Compare *backbone* and *star*.

data
Data is the generic name for anything you input to a computer, or anything it outputs to you (except for *garbage*).

debug
To search out *bugs* in a piece of software and eliminate them.

dedicated
Used for a specified purpose only. For example, your computer might be on a dedicated electrical circuit that's used only for the computer (no lamps, refrigerators or other electric appliances would be on it), or you might dedicate a phone line to your modem and/or fax.

default
What you get if you don't specify something different. Often used to

refer to default settings (for example, the margins in a word processing program, or Speaker Volume on the Sound control panel).

default button

A button with a heavy border, which is activated when you hit [Return] or [Enter].

delimiter

A character used to separate chunks of information—particularly when exporting and importing database files, where delimiters are used to separate information into *fields* and *records*.

descender

The part of lowercase letters like g, y and q that extends below the *baseline.* Compare *ascender.*

deselecting

See *selecting.*

desk accessories

Small programs that are normally accessed from the menu (in System 7, they can be kept anywhere). Desk accessories can usually only open one document at a time, and quit automatically when you close the document. Commonly called *DAs.*

(the) desktop

Apple's official definition for this term is: *Macintosh's working environment—the menu bar and the gray area on the screen.* But in common usage, it refers only to the *Finder's* desktop—that is, what the Mac's screen displays when you're in the Finder.

desktop file(s)

Invisible file(s) on every Mac disk that record information like the size, shape and locations of windows. There's one desktop file in System 6, two in System 7. Compare *directory.*

Desktop Folder

An invisible folder, containing all the files and folders stored on the Finder's desktop, that's automatically created on every disk by System 7. If you connect to a shared Mac under *file sharing,* its Desktop Folder becomes visible, and you have to open it to see the files and folders that are on its *desktop.* The same thing happens to a System 7 Mac's disk when you restart under System 6.

destination

What you call the folder into which (or the disk onto which) a file gets copied, moved, installed or received over a *modem.* Compare *source.*

device

A piece of computer hardware.

dialog box

A *box* on the screen requesting information, or a decision, from you. In some dialog boxes, the only possible response is to click on the *OK* button.

Since this hardly constitutes a dialog, those are more often called *message boxes* or *alert boxes*.

dimmed

When something is *dimmed* (gray) on the Mac's screen, it means that you can't currently access it. For example, commands you can't choose (in a given context) appear dimmed on the menu. When you eject a disk, its icon is dimmed, as are all windows and icons associated with it. Also called *grayed* or *disabled*.

directory

An invisible file that keeps track of where various files are stored on a disk. Compare *desktop file(s)*.

disabled

Another word for *dimmed*.

disk

A round platter with a coating similar to that on recording tape, on which computer information is stored magnetically (except for optical disks, which store information optically). Although the disk itself is always circular, the case it comes in is usually rectangular. The two main types are *floppy disks* and *hard disks*.

disk cache

An area of *memory* set aside to hold information recently read in from disk—so that if the information is needed again, it can be gotten from memory (a much faster process than getting it from disk). The size of the disk cache can be adjusted in the Memory control panel. (In System 6, it's called the *RAM cache,* and can be adjusted in the Control Panel's General *cdev.)*

disk capacity

The maximum amount of data a disk can hold. It's measured in *kilobytes (K), megabytes (MB)* or *gigabytes.*

disk drive

A device that reads information from, and writes information onto, disks. The two main types are *floppy disk drives* and *hard disk drives.*

disk window

The window that opens when you double-click on a disk's icon. Also called the *root directory.*

display

Another name for a *monitor.*

document

What you create and modify with an *application*—a collection of information, grouped together and called by one name, and saved as a file on a disk or treated as one in *memory.* Some examples are a letter, a drawing or a mailing list.

documentation

This term includes manuals, online tutorials and help files, reference cards, instructional audio cassettes and videotapes, and so on.

dogcow

A picture of a dog that appears in the LaserWriter's page setup option *dialog box* (it looks a bit like a cow as well). The dogcow demonstrates what certain options do by acting them out as you select them.

DOS *(dahss)*

Short for *PC DOS* or *MS DOS*—the *operating system* used on IBM Personal Computers and compatible machines. (The D stands for *disk*.)

dot

Another name for a *pixel*, or for the smallest unit that makes up a bit-mapped character or graphic.

dot-matrix printer

A printer that forms characters out of a pattern of dots, the way the Mac forms images on the screen. Usually each dot is made by a separate pin pushing an inked ribbon against the paper. Apple's ImageWriter is one example.

dots per inch

A measure of screen or printer *resolution*; the number of dots in a line one inch long. Abbreviated *dpi*.

dots per square inch

A measure of screen or printer *resolution*; the number of dots in a one-inch square. Abbreviated *dpsi* or *dpi²*.

double-clicking

Positioning the pointer and then quickly pressing and releasing the mouse button twice without moving the mouse. Double-clicking is used to open applications and documents (when the pointer is an arrow) and to select whole words (when the pointer is an I-beam).

double-sided disks

Floppy disks that store information on both surfaces—top and bottom. There are two types currently in use: *double-density* floppies, which hold 800K, and *high-density ones*, which hold 1.4MB. Compare *single-sided disks*.

downloading

1. Retrieving a file from a distant computer and storing it on your own. Opposite of *uploading*.

2. Sending a font file or PostScript program to a laser printer.

dpi

An abbreviation for *dots per inch*.

dpsi, dpi²

Abbreviations for *dots per square inch*.

dragging

Placing the pointer, holding down the mouse button, moving the mouse and then releasing the button. If you place the pointer on an object, dragging moves the object. If you place the pointer where there is no object, dragging often generates the *selection rectangle* (in the Finder and in graphics programs, for example). If you place the pointer on a menu title, dragging moves you down the menu (and releasing the button when a command is highlighted chooses it).

draw program

A graphics program that generates *object-oriented graphics*, which are treated as units, rather than a series of dots. Compare *paint program.*

draw/paint program

A graphics program that combines the features of draw programs and paint programs, usually by putting *object-oriented graphics* and *bit-mapped graphics* on different layers.

drive

See *disk drive.*

driver

A piece of software that tells a computer how to run an outside device—typically a printer—or that emulates doing that (for example, it might tell the computer how to print a file to disk as if it were sending it to a printer).

eight-bit color

Said of images where each *pixel* has eight *bits* of memory assigned to it. Eight-bit color can produce a palette of 256 colors (or shades of gray). Compare *24-bit color.*

ELF

Extremely low frequency radiation, between 60Hz and 75Hz, which is generated by computer monitors

and other devices that produce electric and magnetic fields. Compare *VLF.*

ellipsis

A symbol composed of three dots (...). When it appears after a menu item, it means that selecting the item won't immediately execute a command; you'll either get a *dialog box* asking for more information or a *message box* telling you something.

e-mail

Electronic *mail;* messages sent from computer to computer over phone lines (or over a local area network).

encapsulated PostScript

See *EPS.*

enhanced resolution

Any of several printer technologies that give the appearance of higher-resolution output by smoothing *jaggies* and/or sharpening gray-scale images.

`Enter`

A key on the Mac's keyboard that doesn't generate a character and is used for different purposes by various applications. In dialog boxes and on the desktop, the `Enter` key usually has the same effect as the `Return` key.

error message

A message that tells you of a programming or communication error. It usually appears in an *alert box* and is accompanied by a sound.

EPS *(pronounced as separate letters)*
Encapsulated PostScript, a standard graphics format that consists of the

PostScript code that tells the printer how to print the image and a PICT image that tells the screen how to display it. Compare *paint, PICT* and *TIFF.*

Ethernet

A very fast LAN cabling system developed by Xerox. Many companies now manufacture Ethernet components, and some Macs come with Ethernet support built in (other Macs require special Ethernet cards or SCSI devices).

EtherTalk

The AppleTalk networking protocol, as implemented for Ethernet networks.

expansion card

See *card.*

expansion slot

A place in a computer where you can install a card. (Its name comes from the fact that it allows you to expand the computer's capabilities.) Also called simply a slot.

expertosis *(eks-per-TOE-sis)*

The tendency of experts in a field to lose sight of the needs, concerns and limitations of people who aren't experts in that field. On the Mac, expertosis most often manifests itself in unintelligible manuals, abstruse features and strange, uncommunicative names for things.

[This is my bid to insert a word into the English language, after years of envying Paul Krassner for yippie, *Alice Kahn for* yuppie, *Jack Mingo for* couch potato *and Denise Caruso for* interCapped. *It does, after all, describe a common phenomenon, and one that there's no other word for. Won't you help me in my quest by using* expertosis *whenever possible? I'll be eternally grateful.—AN]*

extension

A file that loads automatically when the Mac starts up and that "adds functionality" to the *system software.* Also called a *system extension.* Called an *init* under System 6.

false alarms

Correctly spelled words a spelling checker flags as possible errors because it doesn't recognize them.

fax modem

A type of *modem* that can send (and, in many cases, receive) faxes to and from fax machines or other fax modems. Unlike regular fax machines, fax modems can't (by themselves) fax paper documents—only disk files.

field

1. In *databases,* a specific portion of a *record.* For example, if the record is in a mailing list file, there will be—at least—a name field, an address field, a

city field, a state field and field for the zip code.

2. *In the field* means anywhere but the factory where a computer—or any piece of hardware—is manufactured. *We've designed this system so just about any repair can be made in the field.*

file

A collection of information on a disk, usually either a *document* or a *program*. Although the information in a file is normally cohesive—that is, about one thing—it doesn't actually have to be; what makes it a file is simply that it's lumped together and called by one name.

file compression

See *compression*.

file server

A computer on a *network* that others on the network can access and get applications and documents from.

file sharing

A feature of System 7 that allows *networked* Macs to share each other's files across the network.

Finder

The basic program that generates the *desktop* and lets you access and manage files and disks. Together with the System file and the Mac's *ROM*, it comprises what—on other computers—is called the *operating system*. There are also Finder substitutes, which perform the same basic tasks as the Finder (and usually give you other capabilities as well).

fixed-size font

Apple's name for a *bit-mapped font*. Compare *outline font* and *scalable font*.

flicker

Rapid pulsation of the image on a screen, visible to some people, as the result of the *refresh rate* being too slow.

floppy disk

A removable disk that's flexible (although the case in which the actual magnetic medium is housed may be hard, as it is on the 3.5" floppies used by the Mac). Compare *hard disk*. Also see *disk*.

floppy disk drive

A device for reading data from, and writing data to, *floppy disks*.

folder

A grouping of files and/or other folders that's represented by a folder-shaped icon on the desktop. (The equivalent on MS-DOS machines is called a *subdirectory*.)

font

A collection of letters, numbers, punctuation marks and symbols with an identifiable and consistent look; a Macintosh typeface in all its sizes and styles.

Font/DA Mover

A *utility* program used for installing, removing and moving fonts and desk accessories to and from *suitcase files* and the System file itself.

font family

A term that's sometimes used to refer to all the styles and weights (bold, semibold, bold italic, and so on) of a particular font.

footer

A piece of text automatically printed at the bottom of several pages (although the text may vary from page to page—as it would if it contained page numbers, for example).

footprint

The amount of space a device takes up on the surface where it sits (and the shape of that space).

format

The file structure that a particular document is saved in (e.g. *ASCII, PICT, EPS, TIFF*). Most applications can save documents in one or more standard formats as well their native format.

formatting

1. All the characteristics of text other than the actual characters that make it up. Formatting includes things like italics, bold-facing, type size, margins, line spacing, justification and so on.

2. Another term for initializing a disk.

freeware

See *public-domain software.*

freeze

Another term for a *hang.*

function keys

Special keys on some extended key-boards (both from Apple and other manufacturers) that are labelled F1, F2, etc. You can assign commands of your own choosing to them.

garbage

Bizarre and/or meaningless charac-ters. When garbage appears on the screen, it means something has gone wrong somewhere.

gateway

One of the most intelligent connec-tions between networks (it translates between different network *protocols).* Compare *bridge* and *router.*

Get Info window

The window that appears when you choose *Get Info* from the File menu (or hit ⌘I). It tells you the size of the selected file, folder or disk, when it was created and last modi-fied, and where it resides. There's also a space for entering com-ments, and, in the case of a file or a disk, a box for locking and unlocking it.

Other options may also be avail-able, depending on what you're Getting Info on. Get Info is used for changing how much memory is allo-cated for an application, changing the icon that's used to represent the file, turning off the Trash's warning message, and finding the original from which an alias was made.

gig

An abbreviation for *gigabyte.*

gigabyte

A measure of computer memory, disk space and the like that's equal to 1024 *megabytes* (1,073,741,824 *bytes),* or about 179 million words. Sometimes a gigabyte is treated as an even billion bytes but, as you can see, that's almost 74 million bytes short. Sometimes abbreviated *gig* (more often in speech than in writing). Compare *kilobyte* and *megabyte.*

GIGO *(GUY-go)*

Garbage in, garbage out. In other words, you're not going to get good information out of your computer if you put junk information into it. (Unfortunately, the opposite isn't always true. Sometimes you put good information into a computer and still get garbage out.)

glitch

Although sometimes used as a synonym for *bug,* glitch strictly means a sudden voltage surge or electromagnetic pulse that causes a piece of hardware to malfunction. More generally, glitch means a design flaw in hardware, or any suddenly occurring problem or interruption. It's not usually applied to software,

but when it is, it means a design flaw and not a bug. (See *bug* for more on the distinction.) Glitch comes from the Yiddish *glitshen,* which means to slip.

glossary, Glossary

1. In English, uncapitalized, a glossary is a list of definitions like this one.

2. Capitalized, in Microsoft Word (and some other applications), a Glossary is a set of abbreviations you've linked to longer text entries. You type ⌃⌘Delete, followed by the abbreviation—*wds,* say—and Word automatically inserts the longer phrase—in this case, *wine-dark sea.* (You didn't know Homer wrote *The Odyssey* on a Mac, did you? Yes, it was the very early ½K Macedonia. Plato later perfected the mechanism that projected forms onto the screen.)

gradient

A smooth and even shift from one color or shade to another, through a continuum of intervening shades or colors.

grayed

Another term for *dimmed.*

grayscale

Said of images that contain shades of gray as well as black and white, and of *monochrome* monitors that can display grays, rather than just black and white.

group

In *file sharing*, a collection of *users* on a *network* who share the same *access privileges*.

guest

In *file sharing*, someone who logs on to a *shared item*, but not as a *registered user*, and therefore gets the same level of *access privileges* available to everyone on the *network*.

hacker

Someone who enjoys fooling around with computers in a technical way, programming them and/or doing sophisticated things to the hardware. See usage note at *nerd*.

halftone

A way of rendering a *grayscale* image (a photograph, say) as a pattern of black and white dots.

handshake

What computers do when communicating, in order to establish a connection and agree on protocols for the transmission of data.

hang

A kind of *crash* where the Mac ignores input from the mouse and the keyboard, usually requiring you to restart the system. Also called a *freeze*. Compare *bomb*.

hanging indent

Paragraph formatting in which the body of the paragraph is indented further than the first line.

hard copy

A printed version of something from your computer.

hard disk (or hard disk drive or hard drive)

A rigid, usually nonremovable disk, and/or the disk drive that houses it. Hard disks store much more data and access it much more quickly than *floppy disks*. Also see *disk*.

hard hyphen

A hyphen that holds the words on either side of it together when it falls at the end of a line, rather than allowing the second word to drop down to the beginning of the next line. Often generated by pressing Option-.

hard space

A space that holds the words on either side of it together when it falls at the end of a line, rather than allowing the second word to drop down to the beginning of the next line. Often generated by pressing Option Spacebar.

hardware

The physical components of a computer system. Compare *software*.

header

A piece of text automatically printed at the top of several pages (although the text may vary from page to page—as it would if it contained page numbers, for example).

Help menu

A menu that lets you turn Balloon

Help on and off; with some programs, you can also use it to access other information. The menu's title is a question mark inside a balloon, and it appears near the right end of the menu bar.

hertz

One cycle, occurrence, alteration or pulse per second. Abbreviated *Hz*. The regular electrical current that comes out of a (US) wall socket is 60 Hz—that is, it alternates sixty times a second. Named after the great German physicist, Heinrich Rudolph Hertz (1857–94). Compare *megahertz* and *kilohertz*.

high-density disks

Floppy disks that hold 1.4MB. Also see *double-sided disks*.

high-level programming language

A *programming language* whose instructions are relatively close to English, rather than to the machine language the computer understands.

highlighting

Making something stand out from its background in order to show that it's selected, chosen or active. On the Mac, highlighting is usually achieved by reversing—that is, by substituting black for white and vice versa, or by reversing colors.

hot spot

The actual part of the pointer that has to be positioned over an object in order for a click to select the object (or have some other effect on it). The hot spot of the arrow pointer is its tip, and the hot spot of the crosshairs pointer is its center (where the two lines cross).

Hz

An abbreviation for *hertz*.

I-beam

The shape (⌶) the pointer normally takes when it's dealing with text. Also called the *text tool*.

icon

A graphic symbol, usually representing a file, folder, disk or tool.

imagesetter

A high-resolution digital phototypesetting machine that's capable of producing graphic images as well as type. Many imagesetters are PostScript-compatible and can therefore serve as output devices for Macs.

ImageWriter

A *dot-matrix* printer made by Apple. Also see *LaserWriter* and *StyleWriter*.

init (in-IT)

What System 7 calls an *extension*. It's short for *initialization program*.

initializing

Preparing a disk for use on the Macintosh. Initializing checks the disk to make sure the media is OK, divides it into tracks and sectors and sets up a directory, desktop file and the like. If a disk contains information, initializing will remove it. Disks can be initialized again and again. Also called *formatting*.

inkjet printer

A printer that forms characters and images with tiny jets of ink.

insertion point

The place in a document where the next keystroke will add or delete text. The insertion point is represented by a blinking vertical line and is placed by clicking with the I-beam pointer.

interCapped

Denise Caruso's wonderfully useful term for words that are capitalized in the middle (like *SuperPaint*).

interface

See *user interface*.

interrupt button

One of the two buttons on the programmer's switch. It accesses debugging software. Compare *reset button*.

invisible files

Files that don't normally show up on the screen (they can be accessed with utilities like DiskTop and ResEdit).

item

A generic name for anything that can be represented by an icon in the Finder, like a disk, file, folder or the Trash.

jaggies

If we put even one picture in the glossary, it would be like opening the floodgates. So I'm not going to give in to temptation. But jaggies are so easy to illustrate and so hard to define. Well, here goes: When you enlarge bit-mapped characters, they lose their smooth curves (or what look like smooth curves when they're small) and instead display jagged rectilinear staircasing...you know, why don't you just look at the picture on page 155.

K

See *kilobyte*.

kerning

Closing up the space between certain letter pairs—like *AV* or *To*—to make them look better. Increasing the space between the letters is usually called *letterspacing*.

keyboard command

A combination of keystrokes (almost always involving ⌘ and often Shift, Option, Control and/or Caps Lock as well) that executes a command without your having to go up to a menu and choose it. Also called a *key combination* or *keyboard equivalent*. Compare *menu command*.

key combination

Another name for a *keyboard command*.

kilobyte

A measure of computer *memory*, disk

space and the like that's equal to 1024 characters, or about 170 words. Abbreviated *K*. Compare *megabyte* and *gigabyte*. Also see *mini-K*.

label

In System 7, one of seven descriptive names that you can attach to files or folders using the Label menu. List-view windows can be sorted by label (to group related files and folders together). On color systems, labels also assign a user-defined color to a file's icon.

LAN *(pronounced as a word, not separate letters)*

An abbreviation for *local area network*.

landscape

Printing sideways on a page, so that the longer sides are at the top and bottom. Compare *portrait*.

laser printer

A computer printer that creates images by drawing them on a metal drum with a laser. The image is then made visible by electrostatically attracting dry ink powder to it, as in a photocopying machine.

LaserWriter

A line of *laser printers* made by Apple. Also see *ImageWriter* and *StyleWriter*.

launching

Opening (an application)—i.e. loading it into *memory* from disk.

LCD

Liquid crystal display—the display technology used on the screens of PowerBooks and the Mac Portable (as well as digital wristwatches and tiny-screen TVs). Compare *CRT*.

leading *(LEHD-ing)*

The amount of space from the *baseline* of one line of type to the *baseline* of the next. Usually measured in *points*.

line spacing

See *leading*.

list box

A box with *scroll bars* that appears within a dialog box or other window and lists things—files, fonts or whatever.

local area network

A network of computers and related devices that's confined to a relatively small area, like one office or one building. Abbreviated *LAN*. More often simply called a *network*. Compare *wide area network*.

LocalTalk

Apple's cabling hardware for *AppleTalk networks*. Compare *PhoneNet*.

logging on

Connecting to a *bulletin board, online service, file server* or *shared item* (usually by entering a user name and password).

logic board

The main *board* in a computer (or other computer device); it holds the *CPU chip*, the *ROM* and the *RAM* (or some of it).

machine language

The actual instructions a computer obeys. Compare *high-level programming language*.

macro

A command that incorporates two or more other commands or actions. (The name comes from the idea that macro commands incorporate "micro" commands.)

macro program

Software that creates macros by recording your *keystrokes* and mouse clicks or by giving you a sort of pseudo programming language to write them in.

magnetic media

See *media*.

mail merge

The merging of database information like names and addresses into a letter template, in order to create personalized letters.

marquee

The rectangle of moving dots that surrounds a selection in some programs. So called for its resemblance to a movie marquee.

MB

An abbreviation for *megabyte*.

media

The generic name for floppy disks, hard disks (the disks themselves, not the devices that record on them), tapes and any other substances that store computer data, usually magnetically.

meg

An abbreviation for *megabyte*.

megabyte

A measure of computer *memory*, disk space and the like that's equal to 1024K (1,048,576 characters) or about 175,000 words. Abbreviated *MB* or *meg*. Some companies try to make a megabyte equal to an even million characters, to make their machines seem more powerful. [*I call this smaller "meg" a min-imeg.—AN*]

megahertz

A million cycles, occurrences, alterations or pulses per second. Used to describe the speed of computers' *clock rates*. Abbreviated *MHz*. Also see *hertz*.

memory

The retention of information electronically, on chips. Compare *storage*. (For more on the distinction, see the beginning of Chapter 4.) There are two main types of memory: *RAM*, which is used for the short-term retention of information (that is, until the power is turned off), and *ROM*, which is used to store programs that are seldom if ever changed.

menu

A list of commands. Compare *palette*. Also see *pop-down menu, pop-up menu, submenu* and *tear-off menu*.

menu bar

The horizontal area across the top of the screen that contains the menu titles.

menu box

A menu title or a command in a drop-shadowed box that you click on to display the rest of a pop-up menu.

menu command

A command you choose from a menu with the pointer, as opposed to a *keyboard command*. (They might both do the same thing—the difference is simply in how you invoke the command.)

menu title

Both the name by which a menu is called and the way you access it. Menu titles are arranged across the top of the screen in the menu bar; when you point to one and hold down the mouse button, the menu pops down.

message box

See *alert box*.

MHz

An abbreviation for *megahertz*.

microprocessor

See *processor*.

mini-K

Arthur's name for *"kilobytes"* that are figured at an even one thousand characters instead of the standard 1024.

minimegs

Arthur's name for *"megabytes"* that are figured at an even one million characters instead of the standard 1,048,576 characters (1024K).

mnemonic *(nuh-MAHN-ik)*

Aiding memory. ⌘S is a mnemonic command, since the S stands for Save, but ⌘V (for Paste) isn't. Don't confuse mnemonic with *Naimonic* (irritable, perfectionistic).

modem *(MOE-dum)*

A device that lets computers talk to each other over phone lines (you also need a communications program). The name is short for *modulator-demodulator*.

modem port

One of the two serial ports on the Mac's back panel, where you can attach modems and other serial devices.

modifier key

A key that modifies the effect of the character key being pressed. The standard ADB keyboard has five modifier keys: Shift, Option, ⌘, Caps Lock and Control.

modular Mac

A Mac (like the various Quadras and Mac IIs) whose monitor isn't built into the same box as the *CPU.* Compare *compact Mac* and *portable Mac.*

monitor

The screen on which a computer displays things so you can read them. (Usually it's a CRT like those used in TVs, but sometimes it's an *LCD.)* Also called a *display,* or simply a *screen.*

monochrome

A monitor that displays variations of one color only. It can be either black-and-white or grayscale.

monospaced

Said of fonts where all the characters occupy the same amount of horizontal space. Two such fonts on the Mac are Courier and Monaco. Compare *proportionally spaced.*

motherboard

See *logic board.*

(to) mount

To make a disk icon available in the Finder.

mouse button

The button on top of the mouse (using the word *mouse* helps distinguish it from a button in a *dialog box).*

movie

The QuickTime file *format,* which lets you cut and paste sound, video or animation data as if it were text or graphics.

MS DOS

The original, and still the most popular, *operating system* used on IBM PCs and compatible computers. (The name stands for *Microsoft disk operating system.)*

MUG *(pronounced as a word, not as separate letters)*

Frequently appended to the names of user groups, it stands for *Macintosh user group.*

MultiFinder

An Apple program that allows several applications, including the Finder, to be open at the same time under System 6. (System 7 doesn't need this separate program, since the capability is built in.)

multimedia

Presenting information via a variety of media, including sound, animation, video, text and graphics.

multitasking

Said of software or hardware that lets you do more than one thing at once.

multiuser

Said of software or hardware that supports use by more than one person at one time.

nanosecond

A billionth of a second. Used to

measure the speed of memory chips, among other things. Abbreviated *NS*.

native format

The *format* an application normally saves files in.

nerd

Someone who's involved in computers to the exclusion of various social and sartorial skills. The archetypical nerd wears a plastic pocket protector full of pens and is profoundly uneasy conversing with people about anything other than computers. The term is generally used affectionately and many people apply it to themselves in mild and/or humorous self-deprecation. The adjective is *nerdy*.

Usage note: Nerd isn't synonymous with *hacker*. Although both terms connote passionate enthusiasm about, and involvement with, computers, *hacker* focuses on the technical sophistication and power that such involvement often produces, while *nerd* focuses on the social price at which such power and sophistication are often bought. Not all nerds are hackers, and not all hackers are nerds (although, of course, many are).

nesting

1. Putting folders inside folders (or anything inside anything).

2. Staying home and watching videotapes or working on your computer instead of venturing out into the dreaded "real world."

network

Two or more computers (and/or other computer-related devices) connected to share information. Usually the term refers to a *local area network*. Also see *AppleTalk*.

network administrator

The person responsible for setting up, maintaining and troubleshooting a *network*.

node

Any one of the computers or other devices connected to a *network*.

NS

The abbreviation for *nanosecond*.

NuBus

A high-speed bus used by the expansion slots in the Quadras and the Mac II family.

numeric keypad

A grouping of number keys (and other, associated keys) arranged in a rectangle and separate from the regular keys. It can be part of or separate from the regular keyboard.

object-oriented graphic

A picture or other graphic where each object, rather than being made up of separate dots (as in a bit-mapped graphic) is treated as a unit, as they are in draw programs.

So if you have a bit-mapped rectangle, you can erase a corner of it (say). But you also have to lasso (or somehow group) all the dots to select it as a unit (in order to move it, for example). An object-oriented rectangle can be selected simply by clicking on it, but you can't cut off a corner of it—it has to remain a square (or at least a four-sided polygon of some kind).

OCR *(pronounced as separate letters) Optical character recognition*—the ability of software and/or hardware to read text from paper. Unlike a regular scanner that reads text (and everything else) as a series of dots, OCR scanners and software recognize the characters and thus generate editable text, as if someone had typed the characters in.

OEM *(pronounced as separate letters)* The *original equipment manufacturer*—the actual producer of the basic equipment incorporated into a product and sold under another name. For example, Quantum is an OEM that makes many of the hard disks that come inside Macs.

OEM is also used as an adjective to describe products that are incorporated into products by other companies and marketed by them. So someone might say: *We're thinking of expanding out of the OEM market and selling some products under our own name.*

offline *(or off-line)*
Said of things done while you're not actively connected to a computer or a network. For example, you might work on a message offline, then log onto an electronic mail system to send it. Opposite of *online*.

online *(or on-line)*
On, or actively connected to, a computer or computer network. For example, online documentation appears on the screen rather than in a manual. Opposite of *offline*.

online service
A large commercial timesharing computer, accessible from a Mac via a modem, that gives users access to a wide variety of information and capabilities. AppleLink and America Online are examples.

opening
1. Expanding an icon, or a name in a list box, to a window—usually by double-clicking on it. With disk icons and folders, this happens on the desktop. With document icons, the application that created the icon is launched first, then the document is opened within it.

2. Launching a program (i.e. telling it to load into memory from disk).

operating system
The basic software that controls a computer's operation. On the Mac, it consists of the System file, the ROM, the Finder (or a Finder substitute) and related software.

optical disk

A storage medium in which the data is read by, and written with, a laser.

outline font

A *font* that's made up of an outline of the shape of each letter and that can be scaled to any size without degradation of quality. Sometimes called a *scalable font*. Also see *PostScript font* and compare *bit-mapped font*.

outline view

What you get when you click on the triangle next to a folder in the list-view windows of System 7's Finder: the folder's contents appear indented below it, in the same window.

paged memory management unit

See *PMMU*.

paint

A standard graphics format for low-resolution (72-dpi) *bit-mapped* images (sometimes abbreviated in writing as *PNTG*). Compare *EPS*, *PICT* and *TIFF*.

paint program

A graphics program that generates *bit-mapped* graphics (collections of dots) rather than *objects*. Compare *draw program*.

palette

A collection of small symbols, usually enclosed by rectangles, that rep-resent tools available in a graphics program. When you click on a box in the palette, the pointer changes to that tool. Compare *menu*.

paragraph widow

See *widow*.

parameter RAM

A small portion of the Mac's RAM that's used to store control panel settings and other basic, ongoing information. It's powered by a battery so the settings aren't lost when the computer is turned off (but they are lost if you pull the battery). Also called *PRAM*.

password

A word or group of characters a user has to enter to log onto an *online service* or to gain access to password-protected files.

pasteboard

In page layout programs, a storage and work area outside the page, the contents of which don't print out.

pasting

Inserting something into a document from the Clipboard by choosing *Paste* from the Edit menu or hitting ⌘V. Also see *copying* and *cutting*.

PC

1. Some people who are relatively new to computers (or unsophisti-cated about them) call any personal computer a PC; in their

usage, even a Mac is a PC (what a thought!). But people who've been around for a while know that the term PC originated as a nickname for the IBM Personal Computer, which was introduced in 1981, and its various clones. They refer to other kinds of personal computers simply as—brace yourself—*computers,* or by their specific names (Macs, Apple IIs, etc.) That's the usage followed in this book.

2. An abbreviation for printed circuit, as in *PC board.*

PDS
See *Processor Direct Slot.*

peripheral
Any electronic device connected to a computer (e.g. a printer, hard disk, scanner, CD-ROM reader, etc.). Usually *peripheral* only refers to something that's either sold by a third party or that clearly isn't an integral part of the original system. For example, you wouldn't normally think of a keyboard sold with a machine as a peripheral, but you might consider a third-party keyboard a peripheral.

PhoneNet
Farallon Computing's cabling hardware for AppleTalk networks. Compare *LocalTalk.*

phosphor
The coating on the inside of CRTs (the cathode ray tubes used in many computer monitors and television sets). When a beam of electrons hits it, the phosphor glows, creating the image on the screen.

pica
A typesetting measure equal (for all practical purposes) to ⅙ of an inch—and exactly equal to 12 points.

PICS *(pronounced as a word, not separate letters)*
A standard format for animation files.

PICT *(pronounced as a word, not separate letters)*
A standard format for *object-oriented* graphics. (The name is an abbreviation of *picture.)* Compare *EPS, paint, PICS* and *TIFF.*

piracy
See *software piracy.*

pixel
One of the little dots of light that make up the picture on a computer (or TV) screen. (The name is short for *picture element.)* The more pixels there are in a given area—that is, the smaller and closer together they are—the higher the *resolution.* Often, pixels are simply called *dots.*

platter
In a hard disk drive, the rigid substrate (that is, the physical foundation) to which the information-bearing magnetic coating is applied.

PMMU

The *paged memory management unit* that makes virtual memory possible on the Mac (along with the appropriate software, of course). Called the 68851, it's part of the 68030 chip and can be added to the 68020.

PMS

1. The *Pantone Matching System*, an international standard coding system for colors that lets you specify and match them by number.

2. Premenstrual stress. *[I only put this in so I could tell you Roberta Cairney's line about it. She says the reason men are so crazy is that they're <u>always</u> premenstrual.—AN]*

point

A typesetting measure equal (for all practical purposes) to ½ of an inch. The size of fonts and the amount of *leading* is typically measured in points. Compare *pica*.

pointer

What moves on the screen when you move the mouse. Its most common shapes are the arrow ( ), the I-beam ( ) and the wristwatch ( ).

pop down

What the Mac's regular menus actually do. Compare *pull down*.

pop-down menu

The Mac's standard kind of menu (usually—but inaccurately—called a *pull-down menu*). It pops down when you click on the menu title; to keep it extended, you hold down the mouse button. Dragging down the menu highlights each command in turn (except the dimmed ones). Compare *pop-up menu*. Also see *submenu* and *tear-off menu*.

pop-up menu

A Mac menu whose title doesn't appear in the menu bar and which, as its name implies, pops up (or out) rather than down. Pop-up menus appear when you click and hold the mouse button on a box that generates them (which is indicated by a drop shadow around the box). Compare *pop-down menu*. Also see *submenu* and *tear-off menu*.

port

Computerese for a jack where you plug in the cables that connect computers and other devices together. Most Macs have a SCSI port, two serial ports (marked for the printer and modem) and others.

portable Mac

A Mac (like the PowerBooks or the Portable) that includes the CPU, monitor and keyboard in a single, fold-up unit designed for portability. Compare *compact Mac* and *modular Mac*.

portrait

The normal way pages are printed, with the shorter sides at the top and bottom. Compare *landscape*.

PostScript

A *programming language* developed by Adobe that's specifically designed to handle text and graphics and their placement on a page. Used primarily in laser printers and imagesetters. Compare *QuickDraw*.

PostScript font

An *outline font* that works with PostScript (although PostScript also makes its own versions of bit-mapped fonts when you send them to a PostScript printer).

power supply

The part of a computer or computer peripheral that converts the 115-volt AC electricity from your wall socket to DC electricity of the voltage the device needs. The name is a little confusing, since power supplies don't supply power, but merely modify it.

power user

Someone who uses and understands advanced features of a computer. Compare *nerd* and *hacker*.

PRAM *(pronounced PEE-ram or, less accurately, as one word)*

See *parameter RAM*.

preferences

User-adjustable features of software. Many programs create separate files to keep track of preferences, and store them in the System Folder.

presentation program

A type of program that's basically a

tool for producing electronic slide shows, usually to accompany spoken presentations.

printed circuit board

A *board* on which the electrical connections between the *chips* are made by printed metallic ink. Also called a *PC board*. There's one in every Mac.

printer driver

A file that tells the Mac how to send information to a particular kind of printer.

printer font

An *outline font* designed to be used by printers (not on the screen). Printer fonts are normally represented on the screen by *bit-mapped* screen fonts. For example, PostScript printer fonts always come with screen fonts.

printer port

A *serial port* on the computer's back panel where you attach a printer or connect to Apple Talk.

print spooler

A piece of software that intercepts a print file on its way to the printer and reroutes it to the disk, where it's held until the printer is ready for it. This allows you to continue working on other things while the printing takes place. Compare *print buffer*.

processor

A *chip* that carries out the actual

computing tasks in computers (and in smart peripherals). Macs often contain two processors—the *CPU chip* and a *coprocessor* for math calculations. Also called a *microprocessor*.

Processor Direct Slot (or PDS)

An *expansion slot* that connects to the *CPU* directly, rather than via a bus like *NuBus*.

program

A group of instructions that tells a computer what to do. Also called *software* and—by members of the Department of Redundancy Department—a *software program*.

programmer

Someone who writes programs, fixes bugs in them, adds new features to them, etc. As opposed to a *user*, who simply uses programs and to whom the programming is invisible (or should be).

programmer's switch

A small piece of plastic containing the *reset button* (which lets you restart your Mac in virtually any situation) and the *interrupt button* (which is used by programmers to debug software and by ordinary users to escape from some situations without having to take the more drastic step of restarting). On some Macs it comes installed; on others, you have to install it.

programming language

An artifical language for writing

instructions that tell a computer what to do (as opposed to the natural languages, like English, with which people communicate with each other). A group of such instructions is called a *program*. Also see *high-level programming language* and *machine language*.

proportionally spaced

Said of *fonts* whose characters occupy different amounts of horizontal space, depending on their size. Proportional spacing makes fonts much easier to read. Virtually all Macintosh fonts are proportionally spaced. Compare *monospaced*.

protocols

A set of standard procedures that control how information is transmitted between computers.

public-domain

Said of products you have the right to copy, use and give away without having to pay any money for the right. Things come into the public domain either because the copyright on them has expired or—as is the case with computer programs—because the copyright holder (usually the author) puts them there. Abbreviated *PD*.

Technically, you can do whatever you want with things that are in the public domain, including modify them and sell them, so many authors who don't charge for their software call their programs *freeware* and explicitly prohibit their alteration or sale. Many people aren't aware of this distinction and use the terms public-domain software and freeware interchangeably, but it's an important distinction nonetheless. Compare *shareware* and *commercial.*

publish and subscribe

Twin features supported by System 7 that let you link data in two files (or two places in one file) so that when you change it in one place, it automatically changes in the other.

pull down

What most people—including Apple—say the Mac's standard menus do. But it's not true—they pop down. For more on this earth-shattering distinction, see the rant on page 25.

QuickDraw

Bill Atkinson's brilliant programming routines that enable the Mac to display graphic elements on the screen with great speed and agility. QuickDraw is also used for outputting text and images to certain (non-PostScript) printers. Compare *PostScript.*

QuickTime

An *extension* that lets you cut and paste animations (or still pictures), with or without sounds.

quitting

Leaving an *application* (flushing it out of the computer's *memory).*

radio buttons

A group of *buttons* only one of which can be on at a time (like the presets on a car radio). If you select one radio button, any other that's selected automatically deselects. Compare *checkboxes.*

RAM *(pronounced as a word, not separate letters)*

The part of a computer's memory used for the short-term retention of information (in other words, until the power is turned off). Programs and documents are stored in RAM while you're using them. The name is short for *random-access memory*—although, actually, just about all kinds of memory are accessed randomly. Also see *memory, parameter RAM, contiguous RAM* and *ROM.*

RAM cache *(cash)*

Another name for a *disk cache.*

RAM disk

A portion of *memory* that's set aside to act as a temporary disk, greatly speeding up work you do with programs and files stored on it. Unlike a *disk cache,* you—not the computer—decide what gets stored on a RAM disk.

rdev *(AHR-dev)*

The term used in System 6 for a utility program that displays an icon in the Chooser. Printer drivers are an example. *Rdev* is short for Chooser device (the *c* was already taken—see *cdev*). Called *Chooser extensions* under System 7.

remote

Said of a computer (or network) to which you're connected by modem.

repeaters

Devices that boost the signals along cabling, commonly used in networks and SCSI chains.

read-only

Said of something you can look at and print but not change. Locked files or disks are read-only, and so are some optical disks, like CD ROMs.

read-only memory

See *ROM*.

read/write head

The part of a disk drive mechanism that actually deposits information on *(writes)* and extracts information from *(reads)* the disk.

reboot

To boot again (that was easy). Same as *restart*.

record

In a database program, a collection of related *fields*. For example, in a mailing list, a record might consist of the name, address, city, state, zip code and phone number of one particular person or company.

redraw *(or* refresh*) rate*

How often the image on the screen is re-

drawn. (It looks solid, but actually it's being recreated many times a second.)

relational database

A database program that's capable of relating information in one file to that in another.

release version

The version of a program that's actually shipped to purchasers and stores. Theoretically, all the major *bugs* are out of it by that point. Compare *beta version*.

RenderMan

A scene-description language analogous to PostScript, used for three-dimensional images.

reset button

One of the two buttons on the programmer's switch. It restarts the Mac. Compare *interrupt button.*

resident font

An *outline font* that's stored in a printer's ROM, so it's always available for printing.

resolution

The number of dots (or *pixels)* per square inch (or in any given area). The more there are, the higher the resolution.

resource

A font, sound or keyboard layout that appears in a *suitcase file* or in the System file. Resources aren't considered files in and of themselves.

restart

To cause a computer to reload its *operating system* from disk, as if you just turned it on, but without actually turning off the power. When you restart, you lose all work that you haven't saved.

RISC *(pronounced as a word, not separate letters)*

Reduced instruction set computing—a type of processor chip in which the number of commands has been reduced for faster operation.

ROM (rahm)

The part of a computer's memory used to store programs that are seldom or never changed (on the Mac, they store parts of the *system software)*. The name is short for *read-only memory*, because you can read information from it but can't write information to it the way you can with *RAM*. A *ROM chip* is often called simply a *ROM*. Also see *memory*.

root directory (or root level)

The disk window—the window that contains all the folders and files on a disk. (So called because if you imagine the organization of folders and files on a disk as branches on a tree, this would be the root.)

router

A device that connects separate *networks*. It's smarter than a *bridge* but dumber than a *gateway*.

routine

A group of programming instructions that's intended to accomplish one particular task. A routine is less complex and less ambitious than a *program* (programs are mostly made up of routines).

RTF

Rich text format—a format for transferring files between applications while retaining text and formatting information. Compare *ASCII*.

sample

1. An audio snapshot of a sound wave, taken during digital recording.

2. A digitally recorded sound.

sampling

The process of recording sound digitally. The computer takes *samples* (audio snapshots) of a sound wave at regular intervals and translates them into numbers that can be stored on disk.

sans serif

Said of a font that has no serifs (*sans* being French for *without)*. Optima is a sans serif font.

saving

Transferring information—usually a document—from memory to a disk.

scalable font

Another name for an *outline* font.

scanner

A device that converts images into digital form so that they can be stored and manipulated by computers.

screen

Another name for a *monitor*.

screen blanker

Another name for a *screen saver*.

screen dump

Another name for a *screen shot*.

screen font

The *bit-mapped* version of a *printer font*, used to represent the font on the computer's screen.

screenful

The amount of text (or other data) displayed at any one time on the screen. Used when talking about scrolling—e.g. *clicking here scrolls you up one screenful*. Also called a *windowful* (as in: *it's a windowful, it's a marvelous, that you should care for me*).

screen saver

A program designed to prevent the phosphor on a computer screen from getting exhausted from too much use. Screen savers keep track of how long it's been since you hit a key or the mouse button and automatically black out the screen (or put a moving pattern on it) after a certain amount of time has passed. Hitting any key or the mouse button brings back the image that was on the screen before. Also called a *screen blanker*.

screen shot

A picture of what's currently on the screen (or on some portion of it), sent directly to a printer or saved to disk.

script

What a program or routine you write in HyperCard is called. Some other programs, like FileMaker and MicroPhone, also use the term.

scroll arrow

The arrow at either end of the scroll bar. Clicking on a scroll arrow moves the window's view up or down one line. Clicking on a scroll arrow and holding the mouse button down results in relatively smooth and continuous scrolling.

scroll bar

A rectangular bar that appears on the right and/or bottom edges of a window when there's more in it than what's displayed. Clicking in the gray area of the scroll bar moves the window's view up or down one screenful. Also see *scroll arrow* and *scroll box*.

scroll box

The white box in a scroll bar that indicates how what's displayed in a window relates to the total contents. So, for example, if the box is at the halfway point of the scroll bar, you're looking at the middle of the document. Dragging the scroll box allows you to scroll large distances.

scrolling

Moving through the contents of a window or a list box in order to see things not currently displayed (normally done with the *scroll bar, scroll arrow* and *scroll box).* In word processing programs and *list boxes,* scrolling is usually vertical, but in many other places, horizontal scrolling is equally likely.

SCSI

An industry-standard *interface* for hard disks and other devices that allows for very fast transfer of information. It's short for *small computer system interface* and is pronounced *scuzzy* by virtually everyone. *[Officially, you're supposed to pronounce the individual letters, but I think I'd faint if I ever heard anyone do that).—AN]* SCSI ports have been standard on all Macs since the Plus.

SCSI chain

A group of SCSI devices connected to each other and attached to a Mac's SCSI port.

SCSI ID

The number assigned to a SCSI device to distinguish it from other SCSI devices and so the Mac knows what order to access it in.

scuzzy

See *SCSI.*

selecting

Telling the Mac what you want to be affected by the next command or action. If what you're selecting is in the form of discrete objects, you normally select them by clicking on them. If it's in the form of a continuum, you normally select part of it by dragging across it. To deselect something, you normally click anywhere else (although if you click on another object, you may select it in the process).

The two most important concepts for understanding the Mac are:

- Selecting—in and of itself—never alters anything.
- You always have to select something before you can do anything to it.

(the) selection

Whatever is *selected* (and thus will be affected by the next command or action). The *insertion point* is also a kind of selection, because it indicates where the next event will take place (unless you move it).

selection rectangle

On the *desktop* and in many applications, a dotted box that appears when you click on an empty spot and drag. When you release the mouse button, the box disappears (or becomes a *marquee)* and everything that fell within it is selected. (In some programs, objects must fall entirely within the selection rectangle to be selected; in others, any object touched by the selection rectangle, however slightly, is selected.)

serial device

A modem, printer or other device that connects to the Mac through one of its *serial ports*.

serial port

Either of the jacks on the back of a Mac into which you can plug printers, modems, etc. *(Serial refers to the fact that data is transmitted through these ports serially—one bit after another—rather than in parallel—several bits side by side.)*

serif

A little hook, line or blob added to the basic form of a character to make a font more readable (or for decoration). Serif is also used as an adjective to describe a font that has serifs; the font you're reading (Bookman) is a serif font. Compare *sans serif*.

server

See *file server*.

service bureau

A business that takes material produced on your personal computer and prints it out on an imagesetter or laser printer. Most service bureaus also rent out time on computers, send faxes, do photocopying, do data conversion, and the like.

shared item

In *file sharing*, a file or folder on one user's Mac that has been made accessible to others on the same network.

shareware

Software that's distributed on the honor system, usually through bulletin boards, user groups, information services, etc. You're allowed to try it out and give copies to others, and you only pay the (usually nominal) registration fee if you decide you want to continue using it. Compare *commercial* and *public-domain*.

shift-clicking

Holding down the Shift key while clicking the mouse button. Shift-clicking allows you to select multiple objects or large amounts of text, depending on the application.

SIG *(pronounced as a word, not separate letters)*

A *special interest group* that's part of a larger organization like a *user group*.

SIMM *(pronounced as a word, not separate letters)*

A *single in-line memory module*—a package for memory chips used in many models of the Mac.

single-sided disk

An obsolete kind of Macintosh *floppy disk* that only stores data on one side and holds 400K of information. Compare *double-sided disks*.

68000 *(sixty-eight thousand)*

A *CPU chip* used in the original 128K

Mac, the 512K Mac, the Mac Plus, the SE, the Portable, the original Classic, the PowerBook 100, the original LaserWriter, the LaserWriter Plus, II SC and II NT and the Personal LaserWriters SC and NT.

68020 *(sixty-eight oh twenty, or sometimes simply oh two oh)*
A faster and more powerful *CPU chip* than the 68000, used in the Mac II, the original LC and the LaserWriter II NTX.

68030 *(sixty-eight oh thirty, or sometimes simply oh three oh)*
A faster and more powerful *CPU chip* than the 68020, it incorporates the functions of the PMMU chip. Used in many Macs and some LaserWriters.

68040 *(sixty-eight oh forty, or sometimes simply oh four oh)*
A faster and more powerful *CPU chip* than the 68030, it incorporates the functions of the 68881 and 68882 chips described below. Used in the Centrises and Quadras.

68851 *(sixty-eight eight fifty-one)*
See *PMMU.*

68881 *(sixty-eight eight eighty-one)*
The math *coprocessor* chip used in the Mac II.

68882 *(sixty-eight eight eighty-two)*
The math coprocessor chip used in most Macs that have math *coprocessors.*

size box
An icon consisting of two overlapping boxes, found in the bottom right corner of most windows, that allows you to change the window's size and shape. Compare *close box* and *zoom box.*

slot
See *expansion slot.*

software
The instructions that tell a computer what to do. Also called *programs* or, redundantly, *software programs.* Compare *hardware.*

Usage note: Software is a *stuff* word (like *butter* or *money)*, not a *things* word (like *stick* or *coin*). It's no more correct to say *a software* than it is say *a stuff.*

software piracy
Copying *commercial software* without permission and without paying for it.

sound input port
The jack on the back panel of many Macs for attaching an external microphone.

sound output port
The jack on the Mac's back panel for attaching headphones or speakers.

source
What you call the file, folder or disk from which a file gets copied, moved, installed or received over a *modem.* Compare *destination.*

special interest group
See *SIG.*

spooler

See *print spooler*.

spread

Two facing pages. (Technically, this is a two-page spread, and three-page spreads and more are possible. But these don't come into play much on the Mac.)

stack

A file created by HyperCard.

staircasing

See *jaggies*.

star

A type of *network configuration* in which peripheral *nodes* are connected to a central box like spokes on a wheel. Compare *backbone* and *daisy chain*.

startup disk

The disk that contains the System file and the Finder the Mac is currently using. You can change it, so it doesn't necessarily have to be the disk you actually started up the Mac with.

stationery

A feature of many programs that lets you create various default documents, with different margins, fonts, included text, etc. Unlike a regular document, which opens with the name you've given it, stationery opens as an untitled document (or makes you choose a name for the new document before it will open). In other words, stationery is a kind of template.

In System 7, you can make most documents into stationery (regardless of what application created them) by clicking the Stationery box in their Get Info windows.

storage

The long-term retention of information magnetically (on disks or tapes) or optically (on optical disks or CD ROMs). It persists after you turn your computer off. Compare *memory*. (For more on the distinction, see the first entry in Chapter 4.)

string

Any specified sequence of characters—a word, a phrase, a number, whatever. The term is usually used in the context of searching and replacing; for example: *type in the string you want to find, hit the tab key, then type in the string you want to replace it with.*

strobe

Another name for *flicker*.

style

A variation on a font—like bold, italic, outline or shadow. In this sense, it's also called a *type style*. Compare *Style*.

Style

In Word and other programs, a *Style* is a grouping of *formats*. In this book, we capitalize this meaning of the word, to avoid confusion (as much as possible) with *style* (see the previous definition).

StyleWriter

An *inkjet* printer made by Apple. See also *LaserWriter* and *ImageWriter*.

submenu

A *menu* whose title is an item on another menu, and which appears to the right of that menu when you choose its title (or to the left, if there's not enough room on the right).

subscribe

See *publish and subscribe*.

suitcase file *(or simply* **suitcase)**

A file that stores fonts, sounds or desk accessories, and is identified in the Finder by its suitcase-shaped icon. In System 7, suit-cases operate like folders, and their contents are like files; in System 6, you move fonts, sounds and desk accessories into and out of a suitcase file with Font/DA Mover. You can open (activate) suitcase files (so their contents will appear on menus) with font/DA management programs like Suitcase or MasterJuggler.

support

1. Help with computer problems (either hardware or software), usually in the form of verbal advice. Support can be provided either by the vendor that sells you the product or by its manu-facturer or publisher.

2. To say that a piece of hardware or software supports something

means that it works with it, or enables it to work. For example, System 7 supports TrueType fonts, while System 6 doesn't (usually).

surge protector *(or* **surge suppressor)**

A device that protects computer equipment from sudden variations in electrical current. Every Mac should be plugged into one.

SYLK

Microsoft's *symbolic link* format for data transfer (especially between spreadsheets and databases).

sysop *(SISS-ahp)*

The person who runs a *bulletin board* (short for *system operator)*.

system bomb

See *bomb*.

system crash

See *crash*.

system disk

Any disk containing the system software the Mac needs to begin operation (i.e. the System file and either the Finder or a Finder sub-stitute). If it contains the system software you're using to run your Mac at the moment, it's the *startup disk*.

system extension

See *extension*.

System file (or simply the System)

The basic program the Mac uses to start itself and to provide certain basic information to all applications. The System file can't be launched like a regular application; instead, it launches itself when you start up the Mac and insert a disk that contains it. Together with the Finder, the System file comprises what—on other computers—is called the *operating system*.

System Folder

A standard folder on Mac disks that contains the System file, the Finder and other system software.

system hang

See *hang.*

System 7

The more recent of the two versions of the Mac's *system software* still in widespread use—it's been included with every Mac shipped since the summer of 1991.

System 6

One of the two versions of the Mac's *system software* that's still in widespread use—although it's being replaced by the newer version, System 7.

system software

A catchall term for the basic programs that help computers work; it includes *operating systems, programming languages*, certain *utili-*

ties and so on. Some examples of *system software* on the Mac are the Finder, the System, the Chooser, the control panels and printer drivers.

tab-delimited

Said of database programs and files that follow the Mac standard of using Tab to separate fields.

tear-off menu

A menu you can remove from the menu bar and move around the screen like a window. It stays fully extended when detached, so you don't have to pop it down every time you want to use it. Tear-off menus always remain in front of open document windows. Compare *pop-down menu, pop-up menu* and *submenu.*

telecommunicating

Transferring information between computers over telephone lines.

template (TEM-plit, not -plate)

A document with a special format that you use repeatedly. You modify it to the present use and save it with a different name. One common type of Mac template is called *stationery.*

terminator

A small piece of hardware that keeps signals from echoing back and forth along SCSI or PhoneNet cables.

text box (or text field)

An area, usually in a *dialog box,* where you insert text.

text file

An *ASCII* file—just characters, no *formatting*.

text-only

A term sometimes used to describe *text* files.

(the) text tool

Another name for the *I-beam pointer*.

third-party

Said of hardware or software that doesn't come from the maker of what you're using it with, and that you didn't develop yourself. A couple of examples are a non-Apple hard disk you attach to your Mac, or a spelling checker not published by the publisher of the word processing program you're using it with.

32-bit addressing

A feature of System 7 that enables the Mac to use more than eight *megabytes* of *RAM*.

TIFF *(pronounced as a word, not separate letters)*

A standard graphics format for high-resolution (greater than 72-dpi) *bit-mapped* images, like those generated by most scanners. The name is an abbreviation of *tagged image file format*. Compare *EPS*, *paint*, *PICT* and *PICS*.

title bar

The horizontal strip at the top of a window that contains its name. When the window is active, it's filled with six horizontal stripes and has a *close box*. To move a window, you drag it by the title bar.

toggle

Something which turns off and on each successive time you access it. For example, the common type styles (bold, italic, etc.) are toggles, because the first time you choose them from the menu (or with a command), they turn on, and the next time they turn off. Other kinds of toggles are checkboxes and menu commands that switch names (e.g. *Show Ruler*, *Hide Ruler*).

transparent

Said of programs that work so smoothly and intuitively that you forget they're there. Transparency lets you concentrate on your work, rather than having to hassle with the software.

Trash

An icon into which you put files to be deleted (which happens when you choose *Empty Trash* from the Finder's Special menu). You can also eject a floppy disk by dragging its icon to the Trash. The Trash appears on the bottom right of the Mac desktop (unless you move it).

Trojan Horse program

A program that conceals and transports a virus.

TrueType

An outline font developed by Apple and supported by System 7. Unlike

PostScript fonts, a single TrueType font file works for both the screen and any printer.

Tune-Ups

Utilities from Apple that come out periodically to fix bugs in—and/or enhance features of—the Mac's system software.

Turing test

A method devised by the brilliant British mathematician and logician Alan M. Turing (1912–54) to decide, without prejudice, whether what a computer does can be called thinking. You type questions and statements into a computer that's connected to a computer in another room, and try to determine, by means of the remote computer's replies, whether it's being handled by another person or by a program.

If you think you're talking to a human when you're actually talking to a program, then (Turing's argument goes) the remote computer must be considered capable of thinking, since what it's doing is indistinguishable from what we call thinking when people do it. All computers so far would fail the Turing test (as would most newscasters)—except in certain areas like playing chess, where computers (but not newscasters) are among the best in the world.

24-bit color

Said of images where each *pixel* has 24 *bits* of memory assigned to it. 24-bit color can produce a palette of 16.7 million colors (or shades of gray). Compare *eight-bit color.*

Type 1 font

A PostScript font format, developed by Adobe Systems, that incorporates *hinting*, a way of making the characters of an *outline font* look as good as possible when printed at low resolutions Compare *Type 3 font.*

Type 3 font

A PostScript font format that's well-suited for complex, graphic-oriented fonts (characters that contain shades of gray, for example). Compare *Type 1 font.*

Unix

An *operating system* developed by Bell Labs for minicomputers but now also used on microcomputers like the Mac. Apple's implementation of Unix for the Mac is called *A/UX.*

uploading

Sending a file to a computer that's distant from your own. Opposite of *downloading.*

user

Someone who simply uses programs, as opposed to a programmer, who writes them. It's like the difference between an automobile mechanic and a driver. Just as you don't need to know how a carburetor works to be an expert driver, you don't need to know anything about programming to be an expert Macintosh user.

user (or users) group

A club made up of people who are interested in computers in general, a particular kind of computer, a particular kind of software, or even an individual program. They're typically nonprofit and independent of any computer manufacturer or publisher. Also see *SIG*.

user interface

The way a computer (or a computer program) communicates with people; what it's like to use.

utilities

Programs that perform tasks that are either relatively simple (like searching for specific files on disk) and/or that are support tasks for applications (like checking the spelling in a document).

vaporware

Software that was announced a while ago but still hasn't shipped.

version

A number or name that indicates the...well...version of a piece of software. If the first number changes, it's a major version (for example, System 6 to System 7). If the third number changes, it's a minor version (for example, System 7.0 to System 7.0.1). If the second number changes, it falls somewhere in between (for example, System 7.0 to System 7.1).

video card

A *card* you plug into your Mac to control an external monitor.

virtual memory

A technique that lets a computer treat part of a hard disk as if it were *RAM*.

virus

A program that functions on your computer without your consent. A *benign* virus may do nothing more than duplicate itself, but some are meant to destroy data.

VLF

Very low frequency radiation (between 10KHz and 30KHz) which is generated by computer monitors (as well as other devices that generate electric and magnetic fields). Compare *ELF*.

volume

A general term for a storage device—usually a hard disk, floppy or CD-ROM.

VRAM

Video RAM that's dedicated to handling the image displayed on a monitor. VRAM is built into some Macs (like the LCs and the Quadras), and it also comes on video cards.

window

An enclosed area on the Mac's screen that has a *title bar* (which you can use to drag the window around). Disks and folders open into windows, and documents appear in windows when you're working on them. Compare *box*.

windowful

The amount of text (or other data) displayed at any one time in a window. Used when talking about *scrolling* (e.g. *clicking here scrolls you up one windowful*). Also called a *screenful*.

WYSIWYG *(WIZ-ee-wig)*

What you see is what you get—which means that the image on the computer screen is what will print on paper.

word wrap

The feature, found in virtually all computer programs that generate text, that automatically moves you down to the next line when the line you're on is full, without your having to type [Return].

worksheet

A common name for a spreadsheet document or template.

wristwatch

The form the *pointer* normally takes (and should take) when you have to wait for the Mac to do something. (Unfortunately, some poorly written programs don't always implement

this feature, or do so less often than they need to.)

writing

Transferring information from the computer's *memory* to a storage device, like a hard disk.

x-height

The height of lowercase letters in a font (not counting *ascenders* and *descenders*). In a font with a high x-height, lowercase letters like *x* are closer to the height of the caps than they are in a font with a low x-height. Helvetica, Bookman and Benguiat have relatively high x-heights; Times and Zapf Chancery have relatively low x-heights.

zone

A subdivision of a *network*.

zoom box

A small box on the right side of the *title bar* of most *windows*. Clicking on the zoom box expands the window to fill the screen; clicking again returns it to its original size and shape. (In many Microsoft products, you can do the same thing by simply double-clicking on the title bar.) Compare *close box* and *size box*.

Index

More from Peachpit Press. . .

The Macintosh Bible Guide to MacDraw Pro
Deke McClelland

This is the first book to cover all aspects of MacDraw, the best-selling design program on the Mac. (It supports both current versions—MacDraw Pro and Mac-Draw II.) A special  color insert provides samples of Mac-Draw's colors, patterns and gradient fills. The author is a contributing editor at *Macworld* and *PC World* magazines and has written nearly 30 books; his vast experience informs every page of this comprehensive guide. *(400 pages)*

The Macintosh Bible Guide to Excel 4
Tim Toyoshima

This quick reference guide teaches new Excel 4 users the skills they'll need every time they launch the pro-gram. It also intro-duces some of Excel's advanced features that  can help you speed up, simplify, man-age or add presentation power to your work. The author is a technical writer who has written about Excel exten-sively. *(200 pages)*

The Macintosh Bible Guide to FileMaker Pro, 2nd Edition
Charles Rubin

Claris' own product manager declares this book a "must for every FileMaker Pro user." Best-selling author Charles Rubin offers fast relief for FileMaker  users of all levels, pro-viding clear and understandable solu-tions for scores of the most common problems. *(464 pages)*

The Macintosh Bible Guide to ClarisWorks
Charles Rubin

ClarisWorks is the most popular inte-grated program for the Macintosh. This book comprehensively explains how to use each separate module,  including word pro-cessing, spreadsheet, database, charting, graphics and communica-tions. It then goes on to describe how to integrate these capabilities, and includes plenty of time-saving short-cuts and troubleshooting techniques. *(472 pages)*

More hot Macintosh Bible titles on the next page. . .

The Macintosh Bible
4th Edition
Arthur Naiman, Nancy E. Dunn,
Susan McAllister, John Kadyk,
and a cast of thousands

It's more than just a
book—it's a phenome-
non. Even Apple's own
customer support staff
uses it. Now the Fourth
Edition is here, and its
1,248 pages are
crammed with tips,
tricks and shortcuts to get the most out
of your Mac. And to make sure the book
doesn't get out-of-date, three 30-page
updates are included in the price (we
mail them to you free of charge). Every
Mac owner should have one. *(1,248 pages)*

The Macintosh Bible "What Do I Do Now?" Book, 2nd Edition
Charles Rubin

Completely updated
through System 7, this
bestseller (more than
100,000 copies in print)
covers just about every
sort of basic problem a
Mac user can encounter.
Geared for beginners
and experienced users alike, it shows the
error message exactly as it appears on
screen, explains the problem (or problems) that can produce the message, and
discusses what to do. *(352 pages)*

The Macintosh Bible Software Disks, 4th Edition
Dave Mark

Why pay a fortune for
great software? This
three-disk companion to
The Macintosh Bible
gives you more than
three megabytes of the
best freeware and share-
ware utilities, modem
software, sounds, games, and fonts.

The Macintosh Bible Book/Disk Combo

The Macintosh Bible and the *Software
Disks* for $11 off the combined list
prices.

The Macintosh Bible Super Combo

The Macintosh Bible, the *Software Disks*
and *The "What Do I Do Now?" Book* for
$14 off the combined list prices.

The Dead Mac Scrolls
Larry Pina

Now any Mac owner—
from the novice to the
expert—can keep
repair costs down. In
this unique, encyclo-
pedic guide, Macintosh
repair guru Larry Pina
diagnoses hundreds of
hardware problems, shows the sim-
plest and cheapest way to fix them,
and reveals how much the repairs
should cost. The book covers all types
of Macs and many peripherals too. Of
particular value is the directory of
companies that sell parts or provide
service. *(484 pages)*

The Macintosh Bible Guide to System 7.1
Charles Rubin

System 7 represents
the most dramatic
change ever made to
the Mac's basic system
software, and sets the
stage for all future sys-
tem improvements.
This guide describes
all of its features thoroughly yet con-
cisely. Rated a "Best Buy" by CompuServe, it's an invaluable resource
both for people considering whether to
move to System 7 and for those who
have already decided to switch and
want to make the transition as
smooth as possible. *(256 pages)*

Order Form

To order, call:

800 283 9444 or 510 548 4393 (M–F) • fax: 510 548 5991

#	Title	Price	Total
	This Is The Mac: It's *Supposed* To Be Fun!	$15	
	The Macintosh Bible, 4th Edition	32	
	The Macintosh Bible "What Do I Do Now?" Book	15	
	The Macintosh Bible Software Disks, 4th Edition	25	
	The Macintosh Bible Book/Disk Combo, 4th Edition	46	
	The Super Combo (Mac Bible, disks, What Do I Do Now)	58	
	The Dead Mac Scrolls (a Macintosh Bible Guide)	32	
	The Macintosh Bible Guide to System 7.1	15	
	The Macintosh Bible Guide to MacDraw Pro	22	
	The Macintosh Bible Guide to Excel 4	15	
	The Macintosh Bible Guide to FileMaker Pro, 2nd Edition	22	
	The Macintosh Bible Guide to ClarisWorks	22	

SHIPPING:	First Item	Each Additional			
			Subtotal		
UPS Ground	$4	$1	8.25% Tax (CA only)		
UPS Blue	$7	$2			
Canada	$6	$4	Shipping		
Overseas	$14	$14	**TOTAL**		

If mailing or faxing, please fill out—and include—other side.

Peachpit Press, Inc. • 2414 Sixth Street • Berkeley CA 94710
Your satisfaction is guaranteed or your money will be cheerfully refunded!

MAY 1994

SEP 1994

Order information:

How soon will I get my books?

UPS Ground orders arrive within 10 days on the West Coast and within three weeks on the East Coast. UPS Blue orders arrive within two working days anywhere in the U.S., provided we receive a fax or phone call by 11 a.m. Pacific Time.

What about backorders?

Any book that is not available yet will be shipped separately when it is printed. Requesting such books will not hold up your regular order.

What if I don't like it?

Since we're asking you to buy our books sight unseen, we back them with an *unconditional money-back guarantee.* Whether you're a first time or a repeat customer, we want you to be completely satisfied in all your dealings with Peachpit Press.

What about shipping to Canada and overseas?

Shipping to Canada and overseas is via air mail. Orders must be prepaid in U.S. dollars.

Ship To

Please write as neatly as possible

Name	
Company	
Street	
City	
State	**Zip**
Country	

Payment Method

Visa/MC/AmEx		**Exp. Date**		**Check Enclosed**
Card #				
Phone (day)				
Signature				
Bill me		**P.O. #**		

Don't forget to include the order form on other side!